PREPARATORY COURSE FOR THE ASWB BACHELORS LEVEL EXAM

Orientation and Strategies

**Association for Advanced Training
in the Behavioral Sciences**
212 W. Ironwood Drive, Suite D #168 Coeur d'Alene, ID 83814
(800) 472-1931

© Association for Advanced Training in the Behavioral Sciences. All rights reserved. No part of these materials may be reproduced in any form, or by any means, mechanical or electronic, including photocopying, without the written permission of the publisher. To reproduce or adapt, in whole or in part, any portion of these materials is not only a violation of copyright law, but is unethical and unprofessional. As a condition of your acceptance of these materials, you agree not to reproduce or adapt them in any manner or license others to do so. The unauthorized resale of these materials is prohibited. The Association for Advanced Training in the Behavioral Sciences accepts the responsibility of protecting not only its own interests, but to protect the interests of its authors and to maintain and vigorously enforce all copyrights on its material. Your cooperation in complying with the copyright law is appreciated.

BACHELORS LEVEL

ORIENTATION TO THE EXAM AND STUDY AND TEST-TAKING STRATEGIES: ASWB BACHELORS EXAM

Table of Contents

ASWB Exam Preparation Quick-Start Guide™ 2

I. Description of the ASWB Examination 4
    A. The Purpose of Licensing Examinations 4
    B. The Development of the Examination 4
    C. The Format of the Examination 5

II. Resources Offered by the Association for Advanced Training 7

III. Introduction to the Study and Test-Taking Process 10
    A. Attitudes, Cognitions, and Emotions 11
    B. Effective Study and Test-Taking Strategies 12
    C. Getting Started 13

IV. Types of Questions on the ASWB Exam 14

V. Prepare a Study Schedule 16
    A. The Sequence of Study 16
    B. Time Management 17
    C. The Study Schedule 19

VI. Manage Your Test Anxiety 21
    A. Recognizing the Symptoms of Test Anxiety 21
    B. Reducing Test Anxiety and its Effects 21

VII. Use Effective Study Strategies 25
    A. General Study Guidelines 25
    B. Improve Your Memory 26
    C. Read Actively: PQ3R Method 27
    D. Take and Review Practice Exams 28

VIII. Use Effective Test-Taking Strategies 30
    A. Taking the ASWB Exam: General Guidelines 30
    B. The Five-Step Process: A Systematic Approach for Answering Questions 31
    C. Test-Taking Strategies for Difficult Questions 33
    D. Additional Test-Taking Strategies for Case Study Questions 34

Appendix: Tips for the Days Before, During, and After the Exam 36

ORIENTATION TO THE EXAM AND STUDY AND TEST-TAKING STRATEGIES: ASWB BACHELORS EXAM

The Association for Advanced Training in the Behavioral Sciences (AATBS) has been preparing social workers for their licensing examinations since the 1970s. This means that we have many years of experience with the licensure process, and we use this experience to ensure that you receive the best possible preparation for your exam. This chapter reflects our experience. This chapter includes the following:

- our Quick-Start Guide;
- a description of the Association of Social Work Boards (ASWB) examination, with a focus on the Bachelors level;
- a description of the resources we have developed to help you prepare;
- a summary of key strategies for making the most productive use of your time and effort as you study for and take the exam;
- information on the types of questions you'll encounter on the exam;
- suggestions for preparing a study schedule; and
- detailed information about the three tasks you'll want to address to prepare for the exam – i.e., managing your anxiety, using effective study strategies, and using effective test-taking strategies.

We recommend that you read this chapter before you begin reading the study volumes or using any of our other study tools.

ASWB Exam Preparation Quick-Start Guide™

1. **Read this chapter in full.** Take the online **Assessment Exam** to identify your current areas of strength and weakness.

2. **Create a study plan – think 50/50.** Plan to spend about 50% of your time reading and reviewing the content area chapters in the study volumes and 50% taking and reviewing practice exams. Each of these study tools contains additional information not contained in the other.

3. Using the 50/50 plan will help you gradually build a deeper understanding of the information you must master to pass the ASWB exam and become proficient at using your knowledge and test-taking skill to identify the correct answer to questions like those you'll encounter on the exam.

4. Abilities and learning preferences differ, so you'll want to develop a personalized study plan that's right for you. Information on preparing a personalized plan is provided in this chapter.

5. A suggested 50/50 plan:

   a. **Read the content area chapters in the study volumes.** Begin your studies by starting to read one of the content area chapters. We recommend that you start with the chapter on Human Development, Diversity, and Behavior in the Environment.

   b. While reading the content area chapters, highlight the text, take notes, or use other active study strategies. You can find descriptions of active study strategies in this chapter.

   c. **Start practice exams early in your preparation.** Once you've finished reading *at least* one content area chapter, begin taking practice exams using the test-taking strategies described in this chapter. Take the first round in Study Mode and later rounds in Test Mode.

   d. Be sure to read the rationales for practice questions, especially those for questions you answered incorrectly. The rationales will add to and reinforce your knowledge of the topics addressed by the questions.

   e. Regularly taking and reviewing practice exams will allow you to practice applying content knowledge and effective test-taking strategies to exam-like questions and provide opportunities to monitor and evaluate your progress as you study.

   f. Continuously review the chapters using your notes, flashcards, and other active study strategies.

   g. During the week before your exam date, take your last practice exam in Test Mode. Use a timer and simulate the exam conditions – that is, take the exam while seated at a desk or table in an environment that has minimal distractions and adhere to the time limit.

6. Pass the ASWB exam. ☺

Consider incorporating our other exam preparation resources into your study plan. Our Online Workshop and Memory Aids are valuable tools that can be integrated into the 50/50 plan. Please give us a call if you need assistance in determining how best to adapt our study resources to your specific needs.

I. Description of the ASWB Examination

The Association of Social Work Boards (ASWB) examination is used to license social workers in most states in the U.S., the District of Columbia, and the Virgin Islands.

A. The Purpose of Licensing Examinations

All 50 states have regulations designed to ensure that individuals who practice as professional social workers have the knowledge and skills they need to provide a safe level of practice and these regulations usually include a licensing requirement. Thus, your ability to pass the ASWB exam is a significant criterion the board will use to determine if you have met the minimum standards required to practice safely. So while you might not relish the prospect of taking the exam, you probably realize that licensure is important for both protecting and advancing the social work field.

B. The Development of the Examination

The ASWB exams are developed and maintained by the ASWB and its Examination Committee.

1. Selecting the Exam Questions

In order to establish the exam's content validity – i.e., to determine what questions should appear on the exam and their usefulness for measuring your competency – the ASWB uses a process known as a job analysis. This entails asking social workers in different practice settings across the U.S. to review a list of tasks they commonly perform and to rate each one along three dimensions: how often they perform the task, how important the task is, and whether individuals must be able to perform the task in order to function competently at an entry level. This analysis is repeated every few years and results in an up-to-date "portrait" of social work practice, which is used to determine the types of questions that should appear on the licensing exam.

Note that a job analysis is conducted for each ASWB exam level (Associate, Bachelors, Masters, Advanced Generalist, or Clinical). This is consistent with the ASWB's goal in providing the exam, which is to measure a candidate's entry-level competence. The questions on your test – the Bachelors exam – will reflect your level of schooling and experience.

2. Identifying the Exam Knowledge Areas

After a job analysis is complete (that is, after the most important social work tasks have been defined), content experts examine the results to identify what knowledge is needed to perform the tasks. This information is then used to determine what knowledge areas should be evaluated by the exam so that the exam can serve as an objective measure of your ability to perform the most important social work tasks. The concept underlying this process is relatively simple and can be applied to just about any type of task we perform, from cooking a meal to driving a car. In other words, just about any activity – including social work tasks – can be broken down into discrete parts that describe the knowledge components needed to perform the activity at a minimum level of competency.

3. The Examination Domains

Based on the identified tasks and a content analysis, the examination subjects are divided into domains. These domains correspond to broad areas of social work practice and serve as a general guideline for determining what questions should appear on the exam. Each time the exam is updated, test constructors make sure that a specific percentage of test questions is drawn from each of these areas.

The current Bachelors exam domains are:

    I. Human Development, Diversity, and Behavior in the Environment (25%)

    II. Assessment (29%)

    III. Interventions with Clients/Client Systems (26%)

    IV. Professional Relationships, Values, and Ethics (20%)

The content area chapters in our study volumes cover each of these domains in depth, with a focus on items listed in the ASWB's **Knowledge, Skills, and Abilities Statements (KSAs)** for the current exam. The ASWB defines KSAs as statements describing discrete knowledge components that may be tested in each part of the exam. KSAs are the basis for individual exam questions.

C. The Format of the Examination

1. Questions

The exam will include 170 multiple-choice questions, and you will be given four hours to complete the exam. This is plenty of time to finish. In fact this time-frame gives you approximately 85 seconds to work on each question, and 85 seconds is more than enough time to both carefully read and respond to a typical exam question. You can then use the time you have left over to review your exam.

Of the 170 questions on the exam, 20 are "pretest items" which will not be counted in your score. Instead, these 20 items will be analyzed by psychometric experts to determine whether they can be used as scored items on future versions of the exam. Because you won't be able to differentiate pretest items from questions that count in your score, however, you should consider all 170 questions on your exam to be of equal importance.

The exam will contain a mix of three-and-four-answer options. Exam questions with fewer options will offer test-takers a better experience by reducing time pressure and ensuring a focus on a test-taker's social work knowledge. Only one choice will be scored as correct. Because you are not penalized for guessing, we recommend that you record an answer for every question, even if you think your selected answer may be wrong. Questions that are left unanswered are always scored as incorrect.

Finally, at each level, the ASWB may administer the exam in more than one form. Thus, the exam you and a colleague take on the same day may contain at least a few dissimilar items.

Keep in mind, however, that all versions follow the same "blueprint" (content outline), so that all forms are equally valid.

2. Electronic Format

The exam is administered electronically, which means you will be taking the test on a personal computer. The ASWB emphasizes that even people with no computer experience can take an electronic examination with ease. When using the computer, you will be able to do all the things you would do when taking a paper-and-pencil exam. Before the exam begins, you will be offered a tutorial that teaches you how to operate the testing equipment including how to record your responses, how to change answers, how to flag questions for later review, and how to move forward and backward through the test. The time you spend on this tutorial will not take time away from the four hours you have for the exam: Your four hours begin when you start the exam itself.

II. Resources Offered by the Association for Advanced Training

The three primary resources we offer to help you prepare for your exam are the study volumes (content area chapters), our Online Exam Program, and our toll-free telephone lines, which you may use to get individualized help. Other resources we have available to further improve your studies include Color-Coded Flashcards, Online Flashcards, an Online Workshop Series, and Memory Aids (content summaries).

1. The Study Volumes

Our study volumes contain this Orientation and Strategies chapter, a comprehensive glossary, and four content area chapters covering the exam domains.

Orientation and Strategies Chapter: To improve the effectiveness of your preparation, we recommend that you read this chapter in full before beginning to study the rest of materials. This chapter covers such topics as your attitude toward the exam, methods for reducing test-related anxiety, and important study and test-taking skills and strategies.

Content Area Chapters: The four content area chapters are (1) Human Development, Diversity, and Behavior in the Environment, (2) Assessment, (3) Interventions with Clients/Client Systems, and (4) Professional Relationships, Values, and Ethics. Each chapter corresponds to a domain tested on the ASWB Bachelors exam. As reported earlier, these chapters have been prepared with careful attention to the ASWB's Knowledge, Skills, and Abilities Statements for the current version of the exam. The volume you are currently reading also contains the comprehensive glossary. The glossary provides a quick way of learning terminology, reviewing chapters, and clarifying terms and concepts that are troublesome for you. A thorough and active reading of every content area chapter will help you achieve the knowledge and understanding necessary to answer exam questions correctly.

2. Online Exam Program

The main components of our Online Exam Program are the Assessment Exam and the TestMASTER exams (practice exams). These components are accessed on the AATBS Website.

Assessment Exam: The Assessment Exam consists of 170 multiple-choice questions that evaluate your knowledge of topics from the content domains covered by the ASWB exam. Your content domain scores on this exam will help you identify your areas of strength and weakness so that you can develop a personalized study plan and provide a baseline for evaluating your progress during your preparation. Taking and reviewing the Assessment Exam should be an initial step in your preparation.

TestMASTER Exams: The Online Exam Program includes our TestMASTER exams, which are practice exams. The TestMASTER exams will greatly assist you throughout your preparation:

    a. Each TestMASTER exam has 170 multiple-choice questions that represent the kinds of questions that may appear on the Bachelors level of the ASWB exam. Thus, using TestMASTER allows you to practice the knowledge and abilities needed for the exam.

b. Each question in TestMASTER is accompanied by a detailed rationale that explains the underlying concepts. Thus, using TestMASTER helps you learn and understand content tested by the exam and develop test-taking skills needed for the exam.

c. The questions in TestMASTER can be used in two different ways: You may use the **Study Mode**, which shows the correct answer and presents the rationale right after you answer a question; or the **Test Mode**, which presents the questions as a "mock exam" – i.e., you must complete the full exam before you see any answer key or rationale.

d. Because the ASWB exam is administered on a computer, TestMASTER simulates the test conditions for you. This allows you to become comfortable with the format and desensitized to the testing conditions. While TestMASTER is not identical to the computer system at a test center, TestMASTER models many of the same key features.

3. Coaching

Individualized assistance from our educational coaches *may* be included in your package. All of our coaches have extensive experience in helping candidates prepare for the ASWB exams and can clarify information presented in the study materials, help you construct a personalized study plan, develop an anxiety management program, and identify effective study strategies.

4. Other AATBS Resources

As noted, other resources we have available to help you prepare for your exam include our Color-Coded Flashcards, Online Flashcards, Online Workshop Series, and Memory Aids (content summaries).

Color-Coded Flashcards: This set of over 700 flashcards is color-coded for your convenience and covers 11 content areas divided into color groups that correspond to major domains tested on the ASWB exam. These flashcards provide a portable study tool that can be used during unexpected free time; and, because the cards can be arranged in terms of content domain, they're useful for customizing your review of key concepts.

Online Flashcards: The Online Flashcards (accessed from the AATBS Website) are an alternative to the Color-Coded Flashcards. Advantages of the Online Flashcards are that you can review them whenever you have access to the Internet and they can be used in three modes – Study Mode (view terms and definitions side by side to learn the meaning of the term); Quiz Mode (view by term or definition before the answer is shown); and Test Mode (test your knowledge of terms using multiple-choice cards).

Online Workshop Series: Our 4-Session Online Workshop Series is an interactive program that provides additional content review, exam strategies, and practice with sample questions.

Memory Aids: Our Memory Aids consist of 11 double-sided letter-size sheets, with both text and graphics, that provide a summary of key terms and concepts from every domain tested on the ASWB exams, plus two bonus sheets offering test-taking strategies and mnemonics. They provide a quick and effective way of systematically reviewing key information from the chapters in our study volumes.

You can find additional information about these resources (and others that we offer) by checking our Website (www.aatbs.com) or calling us using our toll-free number (424-415-7730).

III. Introduction to the Study and Test-Taking Process

Your ability to pass the ASWB exam depends on several factors – i.e., mastering the material, maintaining constructive attitudes, cognitions, and emotions, and using effective test-taking strategies.

Mastering the Material: Mastery of the material that you need to be familiar with for the ASWB exam requires that you have adequate content *and* application knowledge. *Content knowledge* refers to familiarity with the terms, concepts, theories, and skills covered by the exam. Deficiencies in content knowledge are usually due to insufficient studying and/or ineffective study strategies. *Application knowledge* is the ability to apply what you know to exam questions. Some candidates are familiar with the topics that are asked about on the exam but don't thoroughly understand them or can't apply what they know to exam questions. Deficiencies in application knowledge are usually due to a lack of practice with the practice exams and/or reliance on inadequate study and test-taking strategies.

Mastery also requires maintaining an appropriate focus when studying. Some candidates don't do as well as they could on the ASWB exam because their focus was either too narrow or too broad: An *overly narrow focus* is illustrated by the candidate who can define a term but can't see the connection between that term and related terms or concepts or doesn't recognize the term when he or she encounters it in a new context presented by an exam question. An *overly broad focus* is illustrated by the candidate who can talk about an abstract theory for hours but doesn't have adequate knowledge of the details and, consequently, is unable to distinguish between two answers to a question that use similar language. By emphasizing key concepts and providing numerous opportunities to apply those concepts to exam-like questions, our study resources help you achieve an appropriate focus as well as acquire the content and application knowledge you'll need to pass the exam.

Maintaining Constructive Attitudes, Cognitions, and Emotions: A lack of success on the exam can be the result of counterproductive attitudes, cognitions, and emotions. For instance, a self-defeating attitude – e.g., "I'll never be able to pass this exam no matter how much I study" – can sabotage your ability to study for the exam; and a high level of anxiety during the exam can interfere with your ability to understand a question or recall the information needed to answer it. This chapter will offer you many suggestions for developing and maintaining constructive attitudes, cognitions, and emotions and for reducing the anxiety that can interfere with your ability to study and identify correct answers to exam questions. In addition, our educational coaches are available by phone and e-mail to suggest strategies for improving your attitude and lessening your anxiety.

Using Effective Test-Taking Strategies: Many of the questions on the ASWB exam can be answered correctly on the basis of familiarity with the relevant term, concept, theory, or skill alone. However, there will also be questions that require content knowledge *plus* good test-taking skills – and even a few questions that can be answered correctly just by applying the right strategies. Consequently, acquiring and using appropriate test-taking strategies is important and can determine whether you pass or fail the exam. Effective test-taking strategies are described later in this chapter. We recommend that you become familiar with these strategies and use them consistently on practice exams and then on the ASWB exam.

A. Attitudes, Cognitions, and Emotions

Your ability to successfully study for and take the ASWB exam depends not only on your knowledge of exam content, but also on your attitudes, cognitions, and emotions, which can either obstruct or enhance your exam preparation and performance. Methods for maintaining constructive attitudes, cognitions, and emotions are introduced below and described in more detail later in this chapter.

1. Maintain a Positive Attitude

Maintaining a positive attitude will help you stick to your study plan as well as allow you to learn and understand material more easily while preparing for the exam and identifying the correct answer to questions when taking the exam. To maintain a positive attitude during your preparation, we recommend that you adopt the following perspectives:

"I Will Pass!": Approach the exam with the attitude that you're going to pass it *this time*. Don't sabotage your ability to study by viewing the exam as "practice" for the next time or by convincing yourself that there is no way that you'll be able to pass. As you prepare for the exam, focus your time and intellectual, emotional, and physical resources toward your goal of passing the exam.

"The Examination is Good": Rather than viewing the exam as "the enemy," try to see it in a favorable light. For example, you might want to try viewing the ASWB exam as a challenge or as an opportunity to extend and refine your knowledge of social work.

2. Avoid Negative Cognitions and Behaviors

Maintaining a positive attitude also requires that you avoid *negative* cognitions and behaviors. Counterproductive cognitions and behaviors that can interfere with your ability to successfully study for and take the exam include the following.

Denial: Taking the ASWB exam *is* a significant life event, and denying its importance or the anxiety it causes is not beneficial. Instead, it's crucial that you acknowledge the importance of the exam, recognize your test anxiety, and learn ways for dealing effectively with it.

Reliance on "Superstition": High levels of anxiety can open the door to "superstitious theorizing" about the exam's content. For example, it's not uncommon to hear a candidate say something like, "I just know the exam will emphasize whatever area I didn't study enough." While preparing for the exam, you'll want to avoid superstitious theorizing since it will only distract you from your task – which is to study, study, and study some more.

Procrastination: Procrastination can be the result of several factors including low motivation, fatigue, perfectionism, lack of self-discipline, or fear of failure. However, to prepare adequately for the ASWB exam, you must quickly identify when you're procrastinating and immediately take action to overcome it. Having a realistic study plan with clear goals for each study session is one way to reduce procrastination.

3. Reduce Test Anxiety

While some anxiety can help sustain your attention and stimulate your concentration when studying for and taking the exam, high levels of anxiety are likely to be a substantial hindrance. Therefore, it's essential that you acquire and practice anxiety management techniques that help you reduce any anxiety or tension that interferes with your ability to prepare for the exam. Later in this chapter, we present a variety of strategies for reducing test anxiety, including methods for controlling negative cognitions that contribute to anxiety and several relaxation techniques that you can use when studying and while taking the exam.

B. Effective Study and Test-Taking Strategies

Effective study and test-taking strategies are important contributors to success on the ASWB exam – and fortunately, studying and test-taking are skills that can be improved. Several study and test-taking strategies are introduced below, and many additional strategies will be described in detail later in this chapter. Although some of the suggestions may seem obvious to you, keep in mind that the pressure of preparing for and taking the exam can interfere with your consistent use of even simple strategies.

1. Study Strategies

To pass the ASWB exam, you must invest considerable time and energy. To optimize the benefits of your study time, we recommend that you incorporate the following strategies, as well as those presented later in this chapter, into your preparation for the exam.

Use Distributed Practice: Distributed practice is more effective than massed practice. In other words, when studying, you're more likely to retain information if you review it in three separate two-hour study sessions than in a single six-hour study session

Use Active Practice: Most people learn best by doing – that is, when learning is *active* rather than passive. Active learning techniques include underlining or highlighting when reading, taking notes, constructing outlines and diagrams, and taking practice exams.

Overlearn: Overlearning refers to studying material past the point of mastery. Overlearning leads to automaticity, which means that it will be easier to rapidly and efficiently retrieve relevant information from long-term memory while taking the exam.

Use Elaborative Rehearsal: Elaborative rehearsal is a type of active learning that involves making new material personally meaningful by relating it to what you already know. For example, if you're having trouble remembering the differences between techniques based on operant and classical conditioning, you might use elaborative rehearsal by relating each technique to an example from your daily life.

2. Test-Taking Strategies

As previously mentioned, passing the ASWB exam relies, to some degree, on your ability to apply effective test-taking strategies to exam questions. Consequently, it's very important that you consistently practice the strategies presented below and later in this chapter when taking practice exams so that you're proficient in applying them to questions by the time you take the exam.

"Divide and Conquer": Rather than viewing a practice exam or the ASWB exam as a single 170-item test, divide it into four "subtests" and pace yourself so that you complete 45 to 50 questions per hour for the first three hours. This will give you time during the last hour to complete the exam (e.g., the remaining 20 to 35 questions) and go back to any questions you flagged for review. This will also ensure that you don't have a large number of questions to answer in the last hour when you're most tired.

Use a Systematic Strategy: Using a systematic strategy for all exam questions is the *best* way to improve your test-taking skill. The five-step process is a systematic strategy that is well-suited to the ASWB exam and is described later in this chapter.

Don't Skip Around: "Skipping around" through the exam wastes valuable time because it requires you to re-read questions; and, if you skipped the most difficult questions, it leaves these items until the end of the exam when you're most tired. Instead, answer the questions in sequence, from the first to the last one. If you're truly baffled by a question, record the answer you believe to be correct, flag the item, and reconsider it later if you have time.

Don't Dwell on Questions: Don't spend too much time on any one question. If you're unable to decide on an answer after reading a question three times, mark your "best guess" as the answer and flag the question so that you can review it at the end of the exam. Then, move on to the next question.

C. Getting Started

So far, this chapter has presented an overview of the ASWB exam, AATBS's study resources, and techniques for enhancing your study and test-taking skills. Now it's time to get started. We recommend that you complete the following activities during the first week of your preparation for the exam:

Read the Rest of This Chapter: In addition to describing numerous study and test-taking strategies, the remaining sections of this chapter present information on developing and sticking to an effective study plan as well as methods for reducing test anxiety and procrastination.

Set up a Location for Studying: It will be much easier to study for the exam if you have a quiet, comfortable place to study that is free from distractions and allows you to organize your study materials so that they're readily accessible.

Determine Your Areas of Strength and Weakness: Complete and score the Assessment Exam exams to determine which content areas you are most and least familiar with.

Prepare Your Study Plan: You'll maximize your chance for success on the exam if you develop and adhere to a realistic study plan. Instructions for developing a personalized plan are provided later in this chapter.

Skim the Study Volumes: Obtain an overview of what you'll be studying by scanning the contents of the study volumes. Pay particular attention to each chapter's table of contents, section and subsection headings, and other boldface words.

IV. Types of Questions on the ASWB Exam

Social workers rely on certain cognitive skills to do their job well – i.e., they *recall* previously acquired information and *apply* that information to a specific situation so that they can reach an accurate conclusion or make an informed decision. Questions on the ASWB exam require the same skills: Some questions will assess your ability to retrieve information from long-term memory, and others will be application questions that evaluate your ability to apply information to a concrete problem or hypothetical situation.

1. Recall Questions

Recall questions require you to retrieve specific information from memory. These questions address a broad range of information including facts, concepts, theories, and ethical responsibilities, and the primary skill required to answer them correctly is the ability to retrieve stored information. When studying the chapters in our materials, your first objective is to learn the information at the recall level, which means that you'll want to use memorization strategies (e.g., reviewing notes, using acronyms and other memory devices, and using flashcards) that will help you remember key definitions, concepts, theories, etc. Here's an example of a recall question:

The technique known as _____ is based on the assumption that sexual dysfunction is often due to performance anxiety.

  A. role-reversal
  B. sensate focus
  C. differential reinforcement

To identify answer "B" as the correct response, you need to recall that sensate focus was developed by Masters and Johnson as a method for reducing performance anxiety. Alternatively, you could use the process of elimination if you cannot remember what sensate focus is but know that the other three techniques are not treatment strategies for sexual dysfunction.

2. Application Questions

Other questions on the Bachelors exam will be application questions that require you to use your knowledge to recognize an example of a term or concept or to make a judgment or decision. To prepare for these questions, you want to want to use strategies that help you apply your knowledge such as writing your own questions, describing a practice theory, ethical standard, or other topic in your own words, and relating new information to a professional experience.

Application questions often take the form of brief case studies, which describe a direct or indirect practice situation and ask you to answer a question about that situation. The actual question (e.g., "What should the social worker do?," "What should the social worker do first?," "What is the social worker's best action?") appears at the end the stem (the "stem" is the question's body). While some application questions will require you to identify the correct answer, others will require you to identify the best answer. Questions seeking the best answer often contain a word such as "first," "primary," or "best" in the stem. Some of these questions will seem to have two or more answers that are correct, but one will be better than the others, while others will seem to have no "good" answers and you'll have to choose the best of the "bad" answers.

Here's an example of an application question:

Which of the following is NOT an example of a paradoxical intervention?

    A. A social worker encourages a rebellious adolescent client to rebel against his parents' rules.

    B. When treating a pessimistic client, a social worker defines the situation as even more dismal than the client does.

    C. A social worker tells a nagging mother to stop nagging her daughter because the girl never listens.

To identify answer "C" as the correct response, you need to do more than recall the definition of paradoxical intervention: You also need to understand paradoxical intervention well enough so you can recognize an example of it. Good test-taking skills would also help: You would have to notice and then remember while reading the answers that the question is asking for the answer that is NOT an example of a paradoxical intervention.

Here's another example:

During the first interview with a social worker, an elderly client referred by his pastor appears moderately depressed and repeats himself several times. In light of these symptoms, what should the social worker do FIRST?

    A. Mobilize the client's social support system.

    B. Take a medical history.

    C. Ask the client to make a list of what he's depressed about.

    D. Explore the client's feelings of loss related to aging.

This question is difficult because even the incorrect answers describe useful interventions in this case. To identify "B" as the correct response, you need to remember that the question asks what the social worker should do "first." With this in mind, you then need to recognize two things: First, the social worker has to gather more data before formulating the problem (e.g., deciding that the client is, in fact, depressed) or planning treatment. Therefore, it's a good idea to look for an answer that describes an assessment ("B" or "D"). Second, it would be important to begin by exploring the possibility that an undiagnosed medical condition is affecting the client's mood and cognitive functioning (and, moreover, because the client is elderly, what appears to be depression could actually be the onset of major neurocognitive disorder). Answer "B" is the only response that meets both of these criteria – the social worker is continuing to assess the problem, and by taking a medical history, the social worker will find out whether the client is currently under a physician's care and when the client had his most recent medical check-up.

V. Prepare a Study Schedule

As with any important event in your life, preparation for the ASWB exam will be most effective if you have a system that keeps you focused on your ultimate goal – which, in this case, is *to pass the exam*. Also, like most important tests, the ASWB exam does not lend itself to "cramming": Candidates who cram do not attain an adequate understanding of the material and often quickly forget what they have studied. Therefore, we recommend that you develop a detailed study schedule that helps ensure that you devote sufficient time to your preparation, study consistently and efficiently, and take needed time off from studying. Characteristics of an effective study schedule include the following:

An effective study schedule is **realistic**. Your schedule should be consistent with your abilities and time constraints. For example, most people find it difficult to study productively for more than three or four hours at a time. If you're one of these people, it would be unrealistic to schedule eight-hour study sessions. You don't want to set yourself up for failure by not being able to stick to your plan.

An effective study schedule has **clearly defined goals and tasks** and indicates exactly what is to be accomplished during each study session. A study log is a useful way for recording goals and tasks for each study session and for monitoring their accomplishment. (The use of a study log is described below.)

An effective study schedule includes **reinforcing activities**. You'll be better able to maintain adequate motivation to study if you schedule rewarding activities and clearly link those activities to the accomplishment of your study goals and tasks. For example, you might take a walk or watch a favorite TV show after you've read and made notes on three sections of a content area chapter.

An effective study schedule includes **contingencies** that describe what you'll do if something prevents you from adhering to your original schedule.

An effective study schedule is **modified when necessary**. We recommend that you take practice exams regularly and use your content area scores to determine if you need to modify your schedule and/or study strategies. For example, if you obtain a score of 60% or less on a content area, you'll want to increase the time you spend reviewing that area and incorporate more active study strategies into your preparation.

A. The Sequence of Study

The entire exam process can be divided into the following four phases:

Phase 1 – Getting Started: The first phase of your preparation begins before you start studying the materials and includes the following tasks:

Set up your study station.

Read this chapter in full.

Complete and score the Assessment Exam (which is part of our Online Exam Program) to identify your current areas of strength and weakness.

Prepare your study schedule.

Skim the content area chapters to get an overview of what you'll be studying.

Phase 2 – Studying and Skills Acquisition: During this phase, you will:

Read and review the content area chapters using the study strategies described in this chapter.

Take and review practice exams using the guidelines and test-taking strategies presented in this chapter.

Modify your study schedule as needed.

Monitor your anxiety and, if necessary, use strategies to maintain it at an optimal level.

Phase 3 – The Countdown: The third phase encompasses the week or two prior to the exam. During this period, plan to:

Conduct a final review of the content area chapters.

Take and review your last practice exam using the strategies described in this chapter.

Monitor your anxiety and, if necessary, use strategies to maintain it at an optimal level.

Phase 4 – The Denouement: Rather than experiencing a sense of relief after the exam, some candidates feel anxious, confused, or dazed. You can avoid "post-exam dysphoria" by having specific plans for the period immediately following the exam. If possible, take a few days off and relax. You earned it! (Specific tips for the days before, during, and after the exam are presented in the Appendix.)

B. Time Management

Preparing for the ASWB exam is an ongoing, almost daily task; and you're more likely to be successful on the exam if your studying is well planned rather than haphazard. In this section, we present methods for helping you manage your time so that you can study as much as you need to, despite your many other obligations.

1. Find the Time to Study

To help manage your time effectively, we suggest that you begin developing your study schedule by recording your obligations on a wall calendar. Doing so will give you a "snapshot" of your life so that you can develop a realistic study schedule.

Begin by listing all of the work, family, and other non-exam-related demands on your time.

Prioritize these demands and decide which ones are "mandatory" and which ones can be eliminated, postponed, or delegated to someone else.

Record all of the mandatory demands on your wall calendar and include an estimate of how much time each demand will require.

Determine the amount of time that is available for studying. Notice which days are free for studying and how many hours are available on those days. Does the amount of time you have available seem appropriate for the amount of material you'll need to study? If your schedule does *not* allow adequate time for studying, see if there are additional non-exam-related obligations you can eliminate, postpone, or delegate. Also, try to find additional times that might be available for studying – e.g., while taking the bus or subway to work or while waiting for your car to be tuned-up.

Record the times you will study (your study sessions) on your wall calendar. Highlight these times with a colored marker.

2. Make the Best Use of Your Time

The following guidelines will help you develop a study schedule that makes the best use of the time you have available for studying:

Factor in Extra Time: A good strategy is to plan to complete your preparation one or two weeks *before* your exam date. This time buffer will protect you from unexpected events (e.g., a family or work crisis) that might otherwise prevent you from completing your tasks before that date.

Study When You're at Your Best: You'll benefit most from your study sessions if you pay close attention to your body's "rhythms" and study when you're most alert and best able to concentrate. For example, many people learn best in the morning and, if you're one of these people, you'll want to schedule as many study sessions during the morning hours as possible.

Set Up a "Study Station": Your studying will be most effective if you have a quiet comfortable place to study that is free from interruptions and distractions. Avoid too much comfort, however, as this can diminish your concentration. An ideal study station consists of a desk or table, a firm but comfortable straight-back chair, and good lighting. For some candidates (especially those who live with others), it may be difficult to designate a single location for studying. If this is true for you, take advantage of whatever quiet places are available at different times during the day and/or evening.

Use "Down Time" Productively: Although we recommend that you use a primary location for study at home, we also urge you to study whenever and wherever an opportunity presents itself. No matter how busy you are, you're likely to experience periods of unproductive time (e.g., when waiting in a doctor's office). Rather than wasting this time, use it as an additional opportunity to study. Consider carrying study materials (e.g., notes or flashcards) so that you can take advantage of any unexpected free time.

Enlist Support From Others: Let your family and friends know when you'll be studying, and explain to them the importance of having adequate study time to prepare for the exam. Be prepared for the possibility that family and friends may not be as sympathetic to your situation as you would like, and don't let their apparent lack of understanding increase your anxiety. Instead, take time to explain to them how you feel and be clear when letting them know what kinds of support you need from them. Remind them (and yourself) that this is a temporary situation.

Schedule Leisure Activities: Scheduling social and other leisure activities is important for at least two reasons. First, participating in enjoyable activities – especially after completing a long study session – will help you stay motivated and ensure that you're feeling "fresh" the next time you study. Second, spending time with family members and friends will alleviate feelings of isolation that can have a negative effect on your ability to study.

Don't Abandon Your Study Schedule: It's easy to get discouraged when an unexpected event forces you to miss a study session. If something happens that prevents you from sticking to your schedule, don't abandon it. Instead, add some time to future sessions.

C. The Study Schedule

Your goal of passing the ASWB exam is most likely to be achieved if you have a well-defined study schedule. Because each candidate has different study needs, preferences, and abilities as well as different non-exam-related responsibilities, there's no universally "correct" schedule: The amount of time *you* can and need to spend studying is not necessarily the same amount of time another candidate can or needs to spend. Consequently, the suggestions we offer in this section for developing a schedule are *guidelines* rather than rules; and, as you apply these guidelines, you'll want to personalize your schedule so that its priorities and structure match your needs as closely as possible.

1. Determining How Much to Study

Important factors to consider when determining how much time to spend studying are your initial level of knowledge and the relative amount of time you'll want to spend studying the content area chapters versus taking and reviewing practice exams.

Initial Level of Knowledge: Your initial level of knowledge will affect the total amount of time you spend preparing for the exam as well as the proportion of time you'll spend studying each content area. With regard to total study time, the lower your total score on the Assessment Exam or the first practice exam, the more important it will be to determine if your low score was due a lack of knowledge, test anxiety, and/or poor test-taking strategies. With regard to time spent studying each content area, keep in mind that, while you may think you're proficient in a particular content area, some exam questions from that area may target material that differs from the information you're familiar with, and your area scores on the Assessment Exam and performance on practice exams will help you determine if this is the case.

Content Area Chapters vs. Practice Exams: We recommend that you divide your study time so that you spend about half of your time reading and reviewing the chapters and the other half taking and reviewing practice exams.

Some of you may also want to consider the emphasis on each domain on the exam (i.e., the percentage of questions about each domain), but three of the four domains of the Bachelors exam receive similar emphasis and no domain will be represented by fewer than 32 questions. Therefore, we recommend that you weigh this factor only if your study time is very limited. For example, if you know you won't have time to both read and repeatedly review all four chapters, you might devote less review time to the Professional Relationships, Values, and Ethics chapter because this domain receives less emphasis on the exam than the others.

Because every correct answer on the exam increases your chances of passing, however, we urge you to try your best to study every content area chapter as thoroughly as you can.

2. Developing a Study Schedule

Developing an effective study schedule is a two-step process. The first step is identifying your study goals and the time you will devote to accomplishing each goal. Study goals are similar for all candidates, but the amount of time you allot to each goal will depend on your initial familiarity with the topics covered by the exam, your learning rate (the amount of time you need to acquire new information), and the amount of time you have to study. The second step is to identify the specific tasks needed to achieve your goals. These tasks are also similar for most candidates but vary somewhat depending on several factors including your resources (e.g., the preparation tools you purchased from AATBS) and your learning style and preferences.

We've found a study log to be the most effective way to record a detailed study schedule. The study log indicates (1) the date and time of each study session, (2) the goal for each session, and (3) the tasks required to achieve each goal. For example, a goal for one study session will be to "study Assessment" and the task might be to "read Sections I and II of the Assessment chapter"; while the goal for another session will be "take practice exam #2" and the task might be "take questions 1-50 in practice exam #2 in Study Mode and review the rationales." We suggest you use your study log as both an agenda and a checklist: Follow it closely and, at the end of each study session, check off the task(s) you've completed. If you didn't complete a task, add it to a future study session; and, when necessary, modify your study log so it continues to meet your learning needs during your entire exam preparation. Using your study log in this way will help ensure that you complete all of your study goals and tasks.

VI. Manage Your Test Anxiety

It is, of course, normal to be anxious about preparing for and taking an important exam. In fact, candidates who don't worry at all about the ASWB exam typically don't do as well as those who worry a little. This is because a *low* level of test anxiety is actually beneficial: It sharpens your mind, keeps you alert, and helps you stay motivated and focused on your goal. In contrast, a *high* level of anxiety can interfere with your ability to understand and retain information while studying and to concentrate and recall information while taking the exam. Consequently, one of your tasks while preparing for the exam is keeping your anxiety at an optimal level.

A. Recognizing the Symptoms of Test Anxiety

It's important to determine if anxiety is having an adverse effect on your ability to prepare for the exam; and you can do this by monitoring your physical, cognitive, and emotional states while reading the study materials and taking practice exams: Does anxiety interfere with your ability to concentrate or understand or retain what you've just read? Does it cause you to procrastinate or work too slowly or too quickly? Or does anxiety impede your ability to accurately read practice exam questions or recall the information you need to choose the correct answer? This information will help you identify the most appropriate strategies for managing your anxiety. For example, if you find that you start engaging in negative self-talk whenever you're about to begin a study session, you'll want to use techniques that will help you replace negative self-talk with more positive thoughts. Or, if anxiety is most intense when you take practice exams and interferes with your ability to focus your attention, you'll want to use deep breathing or a tension-reduction technique to reduce the physical effects of anxiety while answering exam questions.

B. Reducing Test Anxiety and its Effects

When identifying strategies to use to reduce test anxiety, consider the anxiety-reduction techniques that have worked for you in the past and then use those techniques while preparing for the ASWB exam. For example, you may have found exercise or meditation to be beneficial. If your test anxiety is moderate to severe (or if you've not identified effective techniques in the past), you may want to use some of the following techniques and/or seek consultation to identify additional ways to manage it.

1. Adopt a Positive Attitude

An effective way to overcome pessimistic attitudes that are contributing to your anxiety is to adopt the following perspectives:

> **"I Will Pass!":** Approach the exam with the attitude that you're going to pass this time. Don't sabotage your ability to study by viewing the exam as "practice" for the next time or by convincing yourself that there's no way you'll be able to pass. You might compare

yourself to an athlete who is preparing for an event: Like an athlete, you must focus your time and intellectual, emotional, and physical resources on one goal – WINNING. You should avoid starting a new business, buying a house, or getting engaged during the months before the exam. Your focus must be on the goal of passing the ASWB exam.

"The Exam is Good": Rather than viewing the exam as "the enemy," try to see it in a favorable light. Some candidates find it useful to view the ASWB exam as a challenge: Keep in mind that, to reach this point in your career, you've already overcome difficult challenges and, therefore, should feel confident about your ability to succeed on the exam. Other candidates find it helpful to think of the exam as an opportunity to extend and refine their expertise. As you study, try to identify ways in which the information you're acquiring might be useful in your professional practice.

"I'm in Control": Though it's normal to sometimes feel discouraged or overwhelmed while studying, you must find ways to overcome these feelings so that you can continue working toward your goal of passing the exam. Having a realistic study schedule will greatly contribute to your sense of control. Also, you'll feel more in charge of your preparation if you place occasional disappointments in proper perspective. For instance, if you obtain a low score on a practice exam, view it as a source of feedback that will help you decide what changes you need to make in your study schedule and/or study and test-taking strategies.

2. Overcome Procrastination

A high level of anxiety can lead to a cycle of procrastination and avoidance that consists of the following stages:

An initial increase in your level of anxiety reduces your ability to think clearly and direct energy toward the goal of passing the exam.

Persistent anxiety fosters thoughts that increase feelings of isolation ("Nobody can understand what I'm going through") and lower self-esteem ("I just can't pass the exam"). Such thoughts distract you from your real task – studying.

Feelings of self-worth become increasingly tied to anticipated poor performance on the exam ("If I don't pass, that will prove that I'm no good"). You become immersed in self-doubt and self-recrimination rather than in preparing for the exam.

Continued loss of ability to think clearly leads to the (sometimes unconscious) conclusion that "If I don't expose myself (if I don't try), I can't be found lacking by others." This justifies your continued avoidance of the task.

You become aware that you've spent valuable time worrying about possible failure rather than studying. This realization increases your anxiety – and the cycle begins again on an even more intense level.

Becoming immersed in the procrastination-avoidance cycle is not unusual, and it's important that you learn to recognize when you've fallen into the cycle and have techniques for pulling and keeping yourself out of it. Monitoring your thoughts and ability to stick to your study schedule are ways for determining if you're in the cycle. Techniques for keeping yourself out of it include (1) having a realistic study schedule that consists of specific goals and manageable tasks; (2) maintaining a positive attitude and recognizing and reducing negative thoughts; (3) using methods for relieving anxiety and stress and increasing motivation; (4)

finding a study partner who can help you stay on track; and (5) planning to do something you enjoy after completing the day's or week's tasks.

3. Gain Control of Negative Thoughts

Cognitive theories of anxiety link it to negative or dysfunctional thoughts. Although it's unrealistic to attempt to completely eliminate negative thoughts about the exam, use of the following strategies will help you manage them so that their potential to trigger anxiety and hinder your ability to study is minimized.

Use Thought Stopping: Thought stopping is a useful technique for reducing or eliminating counterproductive thoughts. It involves silently yelling "stop!" or snapping a rubber band that you wear on your wrist whenever you become aware that you're having negative thoughts about the exam.

Make Positive Self-Statements: You'll find that thought stopping is most effective for reducing anxiety and increasing motivation when you replace negative thoughts with positive self-statements. If you find yourself saying, "I'm never going to pass the exam," stop and then tell yourself, "I know I can master this material" or "I know I have the ability to prepare for this exam."

Challenge Negative Beliefs: A useful method for challenging negative beliefs is to write them on a piece of paper that you've divided into two columns. In the first column, list your worries and fears. For each one, consider what evidence you have to support it. For instance, if you fear you're going to fail the exam no matter what you do, consider whether this belief is realistic: Is it true that you *never* pass exams no matter how much you study; or do you actually do well on exams when you take the time to study? If your worry or fear is *not* supported by the evidence, write an alternative thought in the second column – e.g., "I've passed important tests in the past, so there's no reason why I can't pass this one." However, if there's some basis in reality for your concern, identify specific actions you can take to address it and write those actions in the second column. For instance, if your concern is that you won't have enough time to study, you'll want to prioritize your obligations so that you have sufficient time to prepare for the exam and increase the efficiency of your studying by using the strategies described in this chapter.

4. Use Relaxation Techniques

If your test anxiety is not sufficiently alleviated by the techniques described above, you may want to try one of the following direct approaches to relaxation.

Deep Breathing: Anxiety is often accompanied by shallow breathing, and one way to reduce anxiety is to breathe more deeply. To do so, slowly take a deep breath from your diaphragm and hold it for several seconds. Then slowly exhale and feel the tension being released from your body. Silently say "calm" or "relax" as you exhale to reinforce the experience. Repeat the process until you feel relaxed. Eventually, the word will become a cue for relaxation that you can use in any setting. You may want to combine deep breathing with thought-stopping by silently saying "stop" to yourself whenever you notice that you're having anxiety-arousing thoughts and then shifting your attention to your breathing.

Visualization: When using this technique, take a few minutes to imagine you're at the beach or other pleasant location when you first notice signs of anxiety. Close your eyes and make sure that the visual image is clear, and then embellish it with the sounds, smells, and feelings that you'd encounter in that location. Add supportive self-statements such as "I feel comfortable and relaxed" and "I can feel the tension flowing from my body." As you get closer to your exam date, focus your visualization on the test itself – i.e., imagine yourself arriving at the test center on-time and relaxed; applying effective test-taking strategies while taking the exam; feeling confident while answering exam questions; and finishing the exam with time to spare. Also imagine being informed that you've passed the exam.

5. Use Tension-Reducing Techniques

Tension-reduction techniques are useful for reducing the muscle tension that often accompanies anxiety. We recommend that you practice using one or more of the following techniques while preparing for the exam and then when you notice your anxiety level increasing while taking the exam.

Head Rolls: Take a deep breath and slowly exhale while dropping your head forward toward your chest and slowly moving it in a circular motion to the right. After completing one or two rotations, stop and take another deep breath and rotate your head to the left. Repeat this several times.

Shoulder Rolls: Let your arms hang loosely for a few seconds and then rotate both shoulders forward very slowly. Breathe deeply and exhale fully while doing this exercise. After several rotations, stop for a few seconds and then reverse the direction of the rotation and repeat.

Arm Shakes: Let your arms hang loosely at your sides. Lightly shake your hands and then gradually let the movement include your lower arms, elbows, and upper arms. Shake your arms more vigorously. After a few moments, stop and let your arms hang loosely at your sides.

VII. Use Effective Study Strategies

Because some ways of studying are more efficient and effective than others, your success on the ASWB exam has less to do with how much time you study than with how you study. Our study materials provide you with the content information you'll need to prepare successfully for the exam, but your ability to master this information will improve substantially if you use study strategies that are tailored to the exam and your own learning needs.

A. General Study Guidelines

Using the following general guidelines will maximize the likelihood that you'll achieve your goal of passing the ASWB exam.

1. Acquire Content and Application Knowledge

Mastery of the material requires adequate content knowledge *and* application knowledge. *Content knowledge* allows you to recall the facts, theories, principles, etc. addressed by exam questions. Deficiencies in content knowledge are often due to insufficient studying and/or reliance on ineffective study strategies (e.g., rote memorization, insufficient review). *Application knowledge* refers to the ability to understand content well enough to think about it critically and apply it to concrete examples and unfamiliar problems, including those described in case study questions. Deficiencies in application knowledge are usually due to reliance on passive study strategies, a tendency to memorize rather than truly understand information, and/or insufficient practice answering exam-like questions.

2. Take Advantage of Your Learning Style

You're probably aware of your predominant learning style, and you should capitalize on this as you prepare for the exam. If you learn information best when you see it, you're a *visual learner* and should emphasize strategies that use this modality – e.g., highlight or underline while reading, color code your notes, and make tables and diagrams to organize information. In contrast, if you learn best by hearing information, you're an *auditory learner* and should incorporate strategies such as reading the study materials aloud and recording your notes so that you can listen to (rather than read) them during review sessions. Finally, if you learn best by doing, you're a *kinesthetic learner* and should emphasize interacting as much as possible with the material by, for example, highlighting and making margin notes as you read and copying and condensing your original notes when reviewing them. Note, however, that you'll actually learn *best* if you use strategies for all three styles. In other words, while it's a good tactic to emphasize your predominant learning style, you'll also want to incorporate some strategies that are most effective for the other two styles.

3. Emphasize Active Learning

Active learning is associated with a number of benefits including enhanced motivation, heightened concentration, and better comprehension and retention. Consequently, we strongly recommend that you read and review the materials *actively* – i.e., that you have specific study tasks for each study session and use a variety of active study strategies to accomplish them. Active study strategies include highlighting when reading, taking notes, creating tables and concepts maps, describing terms and theories in your own words, and writing and answering questions.

4. Review Frequently

You're more likely to recall information that you've seen and heard frequently over time, so be sure to schedule ample time for review. A good strategy is to take 10 to 15 minutes at the end of each study session to review what you've just studied and review that information again at the beginning of your next study session. You'll also want to schedule a lengthier review of the materials at regular intervals.

B. Improve Your Memory

The following strategies will enhance your ability to acquire, store, and retrieve the information you'll be studying for the exam.

1. Improve Your Concentration

Sustained concentration is essential for the acquisition of information. If you have trouble maintaining concentration during study sessions, try using some of the following techniques:

- Take advantage of your natural biorhythms by scheduling study sessions for times that you're most alert.

- Study in a location that is as free from distractions as possible. Also, make sure that all of the study materials and tools you'll need are available *before* you begin studying so that you don't have to stop to look for them.

- Schedule brief study sessions (30 to 60 minutes) initially. Over time, you'll be able to focus for longer periods and gradually extend the length of your study sessions.

- Train yourself to focus on the material by reminding yourself that it's important to concentrate at the beginning of each study session and, during the session, by saying "concentrate" whenever your mind begins to wander.

- Visualize your concentration as a space that surrounds you and imagine pushing all distractions – internal and external – out of that space.

- Set an alarm to signal a study break. This will help you focus more on the material in front of you and less on "watching the clock."

- If you find that you cannot concentrate sufficiently to comprehend what you're reading, switch to an active study strategy such as formulating questions or making flashcards.

- There might be times when it's more productive to stop studying and deal with whatever is distracting you (e.g., a phone call you forgot to make, a bill you forgot to pay). Immediately after finishing that task, resume your work so that you adhere as closely as possible to your study schedule.

2. Organize the Material

Many models of long-term memory depict it as consisting of networks of interrelated information. An implication of these models is that it's useful to study in ways that support the construction of networks by organizing information in meaningful ways. One way to enhance the organization of material in memory is to keep concepts from different content areas separate by studying only one content area during a single study session. (If you've scheduled a long study session and think you'll have trouble focusing on the same content area for the entire time, study one area for half the session, take a break, and then study a different area.) Another strategy for organizing information is to use an active study strategy that makes the relationships among terms and concepts explicit – e.g., prepare an outline, draw a diagram, or construct a table or concept map.

3. Make the Material Meaningful

Elaborative rehearsal involves making information meaningful and improves retention and retrieval. Elaborative rehearsal can take a variety of forms: defining terms or describing concepts in your own words; formulating personal or hypothetical examples; creating visual images; formulating and answering questions; and relating new information to previously acquired knowledge (e.g., comparing an unfamiliar practice theory to one you're already familiar with).

4. Use Flashcards

Because flashcards can be arranged in terms of content area, level of difficulty, and/or degree of mastery, they are especially useful for reviewing material. We suggest that you prepare flashcards for information that you're having difficulty understanding or recalling and for new information you encounter in practice questions that has not yet been added to the chapters or the purchased flashcards.

5. Take and Review Practice Exams

Regularly taking and reviewing practice exams will not only provide you with opportunities to practice retrieving information from memory and applying information to new problems and situations but will also ensure that you're familiar with the content and format of ASWB exam questions, give you opportunities to practice using effective test-taking strategies, and provide the feedback you'll need to determine if you should modify your study schedule and/or study strategies. Consequently, it's essential that you allot sufficient time in your study schedule to take and review all of your practice exams. Additional information on taking and reviewing practice exams is provided in Part D, below.

C. Read Actively: PQ3R Method

The PQ3R reading method described below consists of five components (preview, question, read, recall, and review) and incorporates active strategies that will increase your ability to understand, retain, and recall information.

> **Preview:** At the beginning of a study session, take a few minutes to skim the chapter or section(s) of the chapter you are about to study. Look at the table of contents, section headings, and boldface words. Get a sense of what is already familiar to you and what is new, and mark sections or paragraphs that address unfamiliar material with an asterisk or arrow to remind yourself to pay particular attention to them when you read the text.

Question: Before reading a section of a chapter, turn the headings and other boldface words into questions. For example, the Interventions with Clients/Client Systems chapter section on Communication Skills and Techniques has the words "empathic communication" and "types of empathic responding" in boldface. Questions for this section might be "What is empathic communication?" and "What are the different types of empathic responding and how do they differ?" Because your study time is limited, you may want to formulate questions only for information you are unfamiliar with.

Read: Read the text that follows the heading or other boldface words that you used to frame your question and find the answer. Reading with a purpose (to find the answer) will add an active element to your studying, which will help you acquire and retain the information. Once you've found the answer to your question, restate it in your own words; but, if you're unable to do so, re-read the text. As you read, you may have to adjust your speed: If you're already familiar with the information, skimming the text is probably adequate; however, if the information is unfamiliar, you'll need to read more slowly and may need to read the text more than once. Use as many of the following active study strategies as you can while reading, especially when the information is very difficult or complex:

> **Highlight:** Highlighting as you read will enhance your concentration, encourage you to think about what you're reading, and make it easier to find topics you want to take notes on or review later. Be careful to highlight only the most important information – e.g., a key concept and its definition, the major assumptions or predictions of a theory. Don't highlight complete sentences, and try to limit your highlighting to no more than one-third of the text.
>
> **Annotate:** While reading, circle or put a question mark next to things you don't understand and want to review later. Also, make brief notes in the margins, construct an acronym for a list of stages or steps, or write a phrase that summarizes a paragraph.
>
> **Summarize:** At the end of a section or subsection, summarize the most important points in a few sentences. For difficult or complex material, you may also want to write multiple-choice, matching, or fill-in-the-blank questions about the key information. Write your summary and/or questions in the margin of the text or on a separate piece of paper.
>
> **Take Notes:** After you finish reading a section of a chapter, go back and take notes on the information that you've highlighted or annotated.

Recall: Use glossaries and/or flashcards to evaluate your learning and practice retrieving information from long-term memory.

Review: Review your notes and flashcards at the end of each study session, at the beginning of the next study session, and during scheduled reviews.

D. Take and Review Practice Exams

Practice exams are an essential part of your preparation for the ASWB exam: They allow you to practice applying content knowledge and effective test-taking strategies to exam-like questions and provide opportunities to monitor and evaluate your progress as you study.

Also, because practice exams include questions that address new information that hasn't yet been incorporated into the chapters, they serve as an additional source of content information. Be sure that you schedule sufficient time to take and review *all* of the TestMASTER exams.

1. Taking TestMASTER Exams

TestMASTER exams can be taken in either Test or Study Mode:

In **Test Mode**, you take the entire exam in a single session or take part of an exam in one session and complete another part in one or more subsequent sessions. You then review the rationale for each question once you've finished the entire exam.

In **Study Mode** you can also take an exam in one or more sessions but each question's rationale is presented immediately after answering the question.

We recommend that you take the TestMASTER exams in the following way:

1. Begin using TestMASTER early, during the first or second week of your preparation for the exam.

2. Take, at least, the first round of TestMASTER exams in Study Mode and later rounds in Test Mode. Be sure to take *at least* one practice exam using Test Mode in a way that simulates the actual exam (e.g., set the goal of completing the practice exam within four hours).

When you take a TestMASTER exam in exam-like conditions, notice how you respond: Do certain kinds of questions elicit more anxiety than others? Do you find yourself getting more anxious over time or are you most anxious in the beginning of the exam? Do you get more fatigued as time passes or do you experience a "burst" of energy in the last 30 or 60 minutes? This information will help you identify methods for maximizing your performance on the exam. (NOTE: Many candidates ask what they should score on TestMASTER exams to ensure they pass the ASWB exam. This question is difficult to answer since there's not a perfect correlation between TestMASTER exam and ASWB exam scores. Steady improvement on TestMASTER exams, rather than a specific score, is a better predictor of success on the ASWB exam. Although we would recommend 75% or higher on at least 3 consecutive TestMASTER exams to feel more prepared).

2. Reviewing TestMASTER Exams

After completing a TestMASTER exam, you should review the questions you answered incorrectly during the same or a subsequent study session by re-reading the questions and their rationales. Try to determine why you missed these questions: Was it due to a lack of content knowledge or to ineffective test-taking strategies? If you missed a question due to a lack of knowledge or understanding, study the rationale and, if necessary, go back to the chapter or your notes to review the relevant information. For topics addressed by TestMASTER questions that are not covered in the content area chapters, read the rationale and add the information to your notes. If you missed a question due to ineffective test-taking strategies, be sure to practice more effective strategies on future practice questions.

VIII. Use Effective Test-Taking Strategies

Some candidates have adequate content knowledge by the time they take the ASWB exam but do not pass because they have difficulty applying their knowledge to exam questions. Fortunately, like studying, test-taking is a skill that *can* be improved. In this section, we describe test-taking strategies that will enhance your test performance. Consistently using these strategies on practice exams during your preparation will ensure that you're proficient in applying them to questions by the time you take the ASWB exam.

A. Taking the ASWB Exam: General Guidelines

Keep the following general guidelines in mind when taking practice exams and then when taking the ASWB exam.

1. Do Your Best: Your goal when taking practice exams and the ASWB exam should be to *do your best*. Don't assume that you should or will know the answer to every question. Remember that you don't have to get all of the questions correct to pass the ASWB exam!

2. Divide and Conquer: Rather than viewing the ASWB exam as a single 170-item test, divide it into four "subtests" and pace yourself so that you complete 45 to 50 questions per hour for the first three hours. This will give you time during the last hour to complete the exam (e.g., the remaining 20 to 35 questions) and go back to any questions you flagged for review. Be careful not to allow time concerns to distract you however. Check the time at reasonable intervals to make sure you're answering questions at the right pace, but avoid "watching the clock." Practice using this strategy when you take a practice exam in exam-like conditions with a four-hour time limit.

3. Don't Skip Around: "Skipping around" through the exam is *not* a good strategy. It wastes valuable time because it requires you to re-read questions; and, if you skipped the most difficult questions, it leaves them until the end of the exam when you're most tired. Instead, answer the questions in sequence, from the first to the last one. If you're truly baffled by a question, select the answer you believe to be correct (your "best guess"), flag the question, and reconsider it later if you have time. Try to keep the questions you flag to a minimum – we recommend no more than 20 of the questions.

4. Use a Systematic Strategy: Using a systematic strategy for reading and answering exam questions is the *best* way to improve your test-taking skill; and we recommend using the five-step strategy described below. Practice using this strategy on practice questions so that you're using it automatically by your exam date.

5. Be Careful When Changing Answers: When taking practice exams, check to see if the first answer you choose after carefully considering the question stem and answer options is usually the correct one. If you're like most people, you'll find that your first choice will be the correct answer. If this is true for you, don't "second guess" yourself once you've selected a response. Instead, change an answer only when you've recalled additional information relevant to the question; you realize that you initially misread or misinterpreted the stem or answer options; or you accidentally selected the wrong answer on the computer.

6. Don't Dwell on a Question: Don't spend too much time on any one question because doing so will reduce the time you have to answer other questions and may increase your anxiety. If you're unable to decide on an answer to a question after reading the stem and answer options three times, select your "best guess" as the answer and flag the question so that you can review it at the end of the exam. Then, move on to the next question.

7. Take Breaks: You can take breaks in your seat at any time during the exam and away from your seat with permission of the test proctor. When taking a break in your seat, use deep breathing or one of the tension-reduction techniques described in this chapter. Doing so will "clear your head" and reduce any tension that has developed while answering questions. You might be concerned that taking breaks will prevent you from completing the exam. However, you have four hours to answer 170 questions (over one minute per question), which is more than enough time to complete and review the entire exam.

B. The Five-Step Process: A Systematic Approach for Answering Questions

An important aspect of becoming "test-wise" (becoming a better test taker) is consistently using a systematic approach when answering exam questions, and the five-step process described below is an effective approach for the ASWB exam. Our experience in helping candidates prepare for the exam has confirmed that many candidates often experience two problems when answering exam questions: They often choose the wrong answer to questions because they misread or misinterpret stems and/or answer options, and they have trouble comparing answer options and eliminating distractors. The five-step process addresses both of these problems.

Step 1 – Read the Entire Stem: It's very important to read the question stem carefully *and* in its entirety before reading the answer options and selecting an answer. As you read the stem, identify key words and phrases and be careful not to leave out important words or substitute words for those that are actually there. Note if the stem includes a qualifier (e.g., "first," "best," "must," "not," "least," "except") since that will affect how you interpret the question.

Here's an example: *Although it's necessary to avoid stereotypes when working with members of ethnic and racial minority groups, some generalizations can be made. For example, when working with Hispanic and Hispanic American clients, it's important to keep in mind all of the following EXCEPT:*

When reading this stem, you'd want to note that it is asking for the *exception*, which means that you'll want to look for the answer that is false about working with Hispanic and Hispanic American clients.

Step 2 – Identify the Content Area and Restate the Question: Many of the questions on the ASWB exam will be straightforward and won't require you to spend time interpreting them. However, some questions will be complex, convoluted, or vague. For instance, some questions might require you to apply a term or concept to an unfamiliar or unexpected situation; others will use unfamiliar language; and still others will include "extra" information that you won't need to determine the answer. Step 2 will help you clarify any ambiguities in the stem by (1) restating the question in your own words in a single sentence and (2) identifying the content area addressed by the question. Restating the question is not always necessary but, when the question is long or convoluted, doing so will help you determine precisely what is being asked. Identifying the content area is important because it can help you retrieve relevant information from memory.

The stem for the above example is a negative stem and is somewhat "wordy." Therefore, restating the question would be helpful. A good restatement is "Which of the following is false about Hispanic and Hispanic American clients?" In terms of content area, this information is related to the topic of human diversity.

Step 3 – Answer the Question in Your Own Words: A good test-taking strategy is to formulate an answer in your own words before reading the answer options. One advantage of this strategy is that it will help "activate" memories relevant to the topic before you read the answers. Another advantage is that it will ensure that, when reading the answer options, you won't be sidetracked by an answer that "sounds good" but isn't the correct response to the question. If you can't come up with a precise answer, try to recall some facts, terms, or other information relevant to the topic addressed by the question. In some cases, the stem will not provide enough information to allow you to come up with an answer or relevant terms. In this case, skim the options to find out what the question is asking about. Then come up with your own answer before carefully re-reading and considering each answer.

It would be impossible to come up with a precise answer for the example question before reading the answers, so you'd want to recall what you know about working with Hispanic and Hispanic American clients. Let's assume that you recall that sex roles are tend to be inflexible in Hispanic families and that level of acculturation is an important consideration when working with clients from racial and ethnic minority groups.

Step 4 – Read and Grade all of the Answers: After coming up with your own answer (or information relevant to the topic), read each answer option carefully to look for a "match." Mentally grade each answer using a plus, minus, or question mark: A plus means the answer seems correct (it matches what you came up with); a minus means that the answer seems incorrect; and a question mark means that it's not clear whether the answer is right or wrong. Keep in mind that it's always important to read all of the answers before choosing one.

Let's continue with our example from above:

Although it's necessary to avoid stereotypes when working with members of ethnic and racial minority groups, some generalizations can be made. For example, when working with Hispanic and Hispanic American clients, it's important to keep in mind all of the following EXCEPT:

   A. different levels of acculturation among Hispanics can influence their perceptions of and responses to therapy.
   B. family therapy is often contraindicated because of the hierarchical nature of the Hispanic family.
   C. behavioral and other active, problem-oriented therapies are usually more acceptable than insight-oriented therapies.
   D. sex-roles tend to be demarcated clearly and are fairly rigid.

Answer "A" is consistent with what you recalled about minority clients – that is, answer "A" is true, so it gets a minus since this question is asking which answer is false. Let's assume that answer "B" doesn't sound correct but you're not sure, so you give it a question mark. Let's also assume that the language of answer "C" acts as a cue and reminds you that Hispanic clients tend to prefer an active, directive approach in therapy. Therefore, answer "C" gets a minus because it is true and this question is asking which answer is false. Finally, answer "D" is also consistent with what you recalled about Hispanic families – so it also gets a minus because it is true rather than false. Answers "A," "C," and "D" all got a minus, which leaves answer "B" as the best answer (and it is, in fact, the correct one).

Step 5 – Carefully Select Your Answer: The final step is to select your answer by pressing the appropriate key on the keyboard and then pressing enter. Be sure the answer you select on the keyboard is the one you identified as the correct one!

C. Test-Taking Strategies for Difficult Questions

The following strategies are useful when a question seems to have multiple correct answers or addresses a topic you're unfamiliar with.

1. Re-Read the Stem and Options: Whenever a question seems to have more than one correct answer (or no correct answer), re-read the stem and the answer options. You may find that you misinterpreted the stem or that there is a single word or phrase in the stem or one of the answers that makes one answer the correct or best one.

Here's an example:

A female client, age 24, has been experiencing auditory hallucinations and persecutory delusions for the past three months. She says she feels like her neighbors are spying on her and are trying to hurt her. During an interview, the client is often incoherent and frequently responds to the social worker's questions by giggling. Although it is a hot day, she is wearing a wool scarf and gloves. Based on this information, the MOST likely diagnosis is:

    A. schizophrenia.
    B. schizophreniform disorder.
    C. delusional disorder.

If you did not read this question carefully (which would be possible if you're anxious!), you may have missed the duration of symptoms in the stem, which would have made it difficult to choose between answers "A" and "B." However, the duration of the client's symptoms (three months) makes answer "B" the correct response.

2. Make an "Educated Guess": There is no penalty for guessing on the ASWB exam, so it's to your advantage to make an educated guess (or just a "guess") when you're truly baffled by a question. You can increase the likelihood that your guess is the correct answer by using the following techniques:

    Use the Process of Elimination: For most questions, you'll be able to find a reason to eliminate at least one or two of the answers because the answer addresses a topic that is not relevant to the question; describes a common misconception about the topic; contains an absolute (e.g., "always" or "never"); or is too general or too narrow in focus. Once you've eliminated one or two of the answers, you'll be selecting an answer from a fewer number of options, which will increase your chance of choosing the correct one. Of course, this will depend on how many answer options are provided (three-or-four options).

Assume the Client Advocacy Position: For questions addressing ethical issues, your best guess is the answer that represents what is best for the client. In other words, if the choice is between actions that benefit the social worker, the field of social work, or the client, the one that benefits the client is usually the right choice.

Use Common Sense: If a question is about something you've never heard of, use your "common sense" to select an answer.

Here's an example:

A social worker who uses solution-focused therapy is working with a family who was referred because they are having problems getting their children to go to school, and the children are often seen running around on the streets during the day. The mother seems bewildered and the father appears to be depressed. The social worker's first intervention is to ask the "miracle question" which involves:

    A. asking when this problem first started.

    B. asking each family member to explain how the problem affects him or her.

    C. asking how things would be if this problem was already solved.

Even if you can't recall what a "miracle question" is, you'd probably be able to identify answer "C" as the correct answer as long as you know that solution-focused therapists focus on solutions to problems rather than their causes and because it's the only answer that sounds like a "miracle" (a desirable event).

3. Keep it Simple: Some candidates have difficulty with questions because they overanalyze the question stem and/or answer options. When a stem seems too simple, these candidates may add information to it. Alternatively, they may choose the answer option that seems most complex and overlook the simpler (and correct) response. When taking the exam, avoid thinking that there must be a "trick" if a question seems too simple (there *will* be some easy questions on the exam). Also, be aware that, if you find yourself thinking something like "but what if…" while reading a question, you're probably overanalyzing it!

D. Additional Test-Taking Strategies for Case Study Questions

These additional strategies are particularly useful for the case study questions on the ASWB exam.

1. Be Alert to Health and Safety Concerns: The examiners will be testing your ability to provide safe as well as effective social work services. Therefore, some case study questions may include information pointing to some form of risk (e.g., suicide, health danger, abuse). Watch out for this. Always consider the client's welfare when selecting a response. Related to this is the need to always consider the client's right to self-determination. An answer that fails to respect a client's right to and need for self-determination is likely to be wrong unless the question describes a valid reason for overriding the client's wishes, such as, for example, a high risk of suicide.

2. Draw From All Areas of Your Knowledge: A case study question may require you to consider a wide range of factors, such as risk evaluation, professional values (e.g., respecting client self-determination), ethical practice, etc., in order to identify the correct answer. That is, just as a competent social worker draws on the full range of their professional knowledge when providing services to clients, you may need to draw on information from more than one exam domain when making a decision about a case study question. Using this strategy is particularly helpful when a case study question seems to have multiple correct answers. For example, the best answer for a case study question about direct practice might be one that incorporates an important ethical consideration that should influence the intervention the social worker chooses.

3. Apply Your Knowledge of Social Work Practice, Not What You Do at Your Agency, Clinic, etc.: There may be instances, especially for exam questions that ask you to select an action or intervention, when you expect to see an answer that's consistent with what you've been trained to do at your place of employment. While much of what you've been trained to do at work is probably consistent with what most social workers do, occasionally there may be small differences that apply only where you work. Obviously this kind of information can't be the subject of an exam question. Instead a more "generic" application of social work practice will be tested by the ASWB exam. Therefore, we give this suggestion to put you in the proper frame of mind for the exam: Think of general social work practice, not the particular policies or practices of your agency, clinic, etc.

Appendix: Tips for the Days Before, During, and After the Exam

During the week before the exam, confirm the time of your exam appointment and verify the location and how to get there. If possible, drive to the exam location so that you know how long the drive will take. Look into alternative routes in case you run into an accident or road construction on exam day; and arrange to have a relative, friend, or neighbor available to drive you in the event of car trouble on the day of the exam. If you're staying in a hotel the night before your exam, confirm your reservation.

1. The Day Before the Exam: On the day before the exam, eat well-balanced meals, schedule something relaxing for the afternoon and evening, and get a good night's sleep. If you're traveling to another city to take the exam, try to travel in the early part of the day or the day before so that you'll have time to relax. If you can't refrain from studying, limit yourself to a few topics (those you've had the most trouble remembering) and to your flashcards or other brief notes. Here's a list of do's and don'ts for the day before the exam:

DON'T try to cram.

DON'T take a practice exam. (No matter how well you do, you may find a reason to be discouraged.)

DO make sure that your transportation is arranged (fill the gas tank, check the tires, etc.)

DO practice the anxiety management techniques that you plan to use while taking the exam.

DO engage in an enjoyable and non-demanding activity (e.g., watch a movie).

DO go to bed early.

2. The Day of the Exam: Wake up early so you don't have to rush (set two alarms so you don't oversleep), and eat a well-balanced meal before arriving at the test center. Exercise or meditate if either of these is a part of your normal morning routine. (Mild exercise can be helpful for relieving anxiety, but you should avoid a heavy workout just before the exam.)

Candidates will be assigned to seats in the exam room. Watches, coats, books, papers, backpacks, briefcases, large purses, lunch bags/boxes, etc., are not allowed in the exam room. If you have brought any of these items with you, you will be asked to leave them in a designated area (usually a locker). You might find it relaxing to talk to the people sitting near you before the exam begins, but avoid conversations that are anxiety-producing.

Here is a list of do's and don'ts for the day of the exam:

DON'T drink a lot of coffee, tea, or soda just prior to the exam. (One cup of coffee or one caffeinated soda may stimulate your thought process, but two may over-stimulate.)

DO wear comfortable clothes and dress in layers since the exam room may be too hot or too cold.

DO bring everything you need – i.e., your Authorization to Test e-mail or letter and two forms of ID (one primary and one secondary). The primary ID must be a non-expired government-issued form of identification that has a photo of you on it (e.g., a driver's license, passport, military ID, permanent resident visa/Green Card). The first and last name on the IDs must match the first and last name on your Authorization to Test.

DO leave for the exam in *plenty* of time. Plan on arriving *at least* 30 minutes before your exam appointment.

DO think positively. By the time you take the exam, you will have acquired the knowledge and skills you need to pass the exam.

DON'T be concerned if you're anxious. Instead, use your anxiety as a source of energy for the exam and remember that you have a previously rehearsed anxiety-reduction strategy that you can use during the exam.

DO ask the proctor for a whiteboard and, if you need them, ear plugs.

DO confirm the procedures for taking the test and for taking breaks.

DO ask to be reseated if you're assigned to a seat in an undesirable location (e.g., next to the bathroom or directly under a heating or cooling vent).

DO read all of the instructions and take the tutorial (even if you think you don't need it!).

DO pace yourself. For example, after completing the first 25 questions, check to see how much time has elapsed.

DON'T become overwhelmed by difficult questions or dwell on any question for too long.

DO use the test-taking strategies you have practiced.

DO read each question carefully.

DO select your answers on the computer screen carefully.

DO review your answers when you've finished the exam to check for careless errors or omitted answers.

3. The Day After the Exam: It's not unusual for candidates to feel exhausted on the day following the exam. Plan to relax that day or engage in an enjoyable activity. Reward yourself for the work you did to prepare for the exam!

Please feel free to call us with any questions or suggestions you may have as you prepare for your exam or after you've taken it. We wish you success!

PREPARATORY COURSE FOR THE ASWB BACHELORS LEVEL EXAM

Glossary

**Association for Advanced Training
in the Behavioral Sciences**
212 W. Ironwood Drive, Suite D #168 Coeur d'Alene, ID 83814
(800) 472-1931

© Association for Advanced Training in the Behavioral Sciences. All rights reserved. No part of these materials may be reproduced in any form, or by any means, mechanical or electronic, including photocopying, without the written permission of the publisher. To reproduce or adapt, in whole or in part, any portion of these materials is not only a violation of copyright law, but is unethical and unprofessional. As a condition of your acceptance of these materials, you agree not to reproduce or adapt them in any manner or license others to do so. The unauthorized resale of these materials is prohibited. The Association for Advanced Training in the Behavioral Sciences accepts the responsibility of protecting not only its own interests, but to protect the interests of its authors and to maintain and vigorously enforce all copyrights on its material. Your cooperation in complying with the copyright law is appreciated.

BACHELORS LEVEL

GLOSSARY

ABSOLUTE POVERTY: The possession of meager income and assets so that the person cannot maintain a subsistence level of income. See also *relative poverty*.

ACCOMMODATION (Piaget): The modification of existing cognitive schemas to incorporate new knowledge.

ACCULTURATION: The cultural modification of an individual, group, or people by adapting to or borrowing traits from another culture. Includes the degree to which a member of a culturally diverse group within a society accepts and adheres to the behaviors, values, attitudes, etc., of his/her own group and the dominant (majority) group. Contemporary models of acculturation view it as an ongoing process and emphasize that individuals can take on the values, attitudes, and behaviors of their new culture without abandoning those of their indigenous culture.

ACTIVE LISTENING: Helping skill that requires social workers to, first, attend to a client's verbal and nonverbal messages and, then, reflect back what they have heard so that the client will know that his/her message has been understood accurately. Active listening skills include using encouragers, clarification, paraphrase, reflection, and summarization, and exploring silences.

ACTIVITIES OF DAILY LIVING: Social workers refer to the ability or inability to perform activities of daily living (ADLs) as a measurement of a person's functional status. ADL criteria are useful for clients with physical disabilities, clients who are elderly, and clients who have chronic diseases or serious mental disorders (e.g., schizophrenia). See also *basic activities of daily living* and *instrumental activities of daily living*.

ACUTE STRESS DISORDER: The diagnosis of acute stress disorder requires the development of at least nine symptoms following exposure to actual or threatened death, severe injury, or sexual violation in at least one of four ways (direct experience of the event; witnessing the event in person as it happened to others; learning that the event occurred to a close family member or friend; repeated or extreme exposure to aversive details of the event). Symptoms can be from any of five categories (intrusion, negative mood, dissociative symptoms, avoidance symptoms, arousal symptoms) and have a duration of three days to one month.

ADAPTATION (Piaget): According to Piaget, cognitive development occurs when a state of disequilibrium brought on by a discrepancy between the person's current understanding of the world and reality is resolved through adaptation, which entails the processes of assimilation and accommodation. "Assimilation" refers to the incorporation of new knowledge into existing cognitive schemas, while "accommodation" is the modification of existing schemas to incorporate new knowledge.

ADDITIVE EMPATHIC RESPONDING: Empathic responses that reach beyond the factual aspects and surface feelings of a client's message to also reflect its implied content and underlying feelings. Because they are interpretive, these responses can increase a client's awareness of his/her feelings and new ways of resolving a problem.

ADJUSTMENT DISORDERS: The adjustment disorders involve the development of emotional or behavioral symptoms in response to one or more identifiable psychosocial stressors within three months of the onset of the stressor(s). Symptoms must be clinically significant as evidenced by the presence of marked distress that is not proportional to the severity of the stressor and/or significant impairment in functioning, and they must remit within six months after termination of the stressor or its consequences.

ADMINISTRATIVE SUPERVISION: Supervision function concerned with providing the work structure and agency resources workers need to perform their jobs effectively.

ADULT PROTECTIVE SERVICES (APS): Social, medical, legal, residential, custodial, and other services provided for adults who are unable to provide this care for themselves and have no friends, family, etc., who can provide the care. Individuals who receive these services are typically unable to act for themselves, which places them at risk for being harmed or harming others. Eligibility or need for services is usually determined by the courts.

ADVANCE DIRECTIVE: A legal document through which an individual makes his/her wishes known about health-care decisions in the event that he/she should become incapacitated and unable to communicate these wishes. See also *durable power of attorney for health care* and *living will*.

ADVOCATE: A social worker role that involves working with and on behalf of clients to ensure that they receive the services and benefits to which they are entitled and that the services are delivered in ways that protect their dignity.

AGORAPHOBIA: A diagnosis of agoraphobia requires the presence of marked fear of or anxiety about at least two of five situations (using public transportation, being in open spaces, being in enclosed spaces, standing in line or being part of a crowd, and being outside the home alone). The individual fears or avoids these situations due to a concern that escape might be difficult or help will be unavailable in case he/she develops incapacitating or embarrassing symptoms; and the situations nearly always provoke fear or anxiety and are actively avoided, require the presence of a companion, or are endured with intense fear or anxiety. The fear or anxiety is persistent and is not proportional to the threat posed by the situations. Treatment-of-choice is in vivo exposure with response prevention (flooding).

AIDS DEMENTIA COMPLEX: One of the most common neurological complications of HIV disease. Produces behavioral changes and diminished mental functioning. In the DSM-5, is called neurocognitive disorder due to HIV disease.

ALCOHOL WITHDRAWAL: Alcohol-induced disorder diagnosed in the presence of at least two characteristic symptoms within several hours to a few days following cessation or reduction of alcohol consumption: autonomic hyperactivity; hand tremor; insomnia; nausea or vomiting; transient illusions or hallucinations; anxiety; psychomotor agitation; generalized tonic-clonic seizures.

ALCOHOL WITHDRAWAL DELIRIUM (DELIRIUM TREMENS or DTs): Alcohol-induced disorder diagnosed in the presence of prominent disturbances in attention, awareness, and cognition following cessation or reduction of alcohol consumption that are sufficiently severe to warrant clinical attention. Common associated features include autonomic hyperactivity, vivid hallucinations, delusions, and agitation.

ALPHA (LEVEL OF SIGNIFICANCE): The probability of rejecting the null hypothesis when it is true (i.e., the probability of making a Type I error). The value of alpha is set by an experimenter prior to collecting or analyzing the data. In psychological research, alpha is commonly set at either .01 or .05. (The null hypothesis states there is no relationship between independent and dependent variables and implies that any observed relationship is simply the result of sampling error.)

AMBIVALENCE: Contradictory emotions that occur at the same time within a person. Persistent ambivalence is associated with chronic indecisiveness, mixed feelings, and a sense of being conflicted or stuck.

AMERICANS WITH DISABILITIES ACT (ADA): Legislation that requires companies with 25 or more employees to avoid using procedures that discriminate against people with physical or mental disabilities and, when a disabled person is able to perform the essential functions of a job, to consider the person qualified and to make reasonable accommodations.

AMPHETAMINE OR COCAINE INTOXICATION: Symptoms include euphoria, anxiety, paranoid ideation, tachycardia, dilated pupils, perspiration, confusion, and seizures.

ANACLITIC DEPRESSION: Withdrawal, depression, and developmental delays resulting from the loss of an attachment figure during infancy, especially when the loss occurs during the second half of the first year of life.

ANALOGUE STUDIES: Studies conducted in a "facsimile of reality" (e.g., studies conducted in a laboratory or other artificial setting). A problem with analogue studies is that their results may have limited generalizability.

ANDROGYNY: Having mannerisms, behaviors, appearance, and other characteristics of both genders.

ANHEDONIA: An inability to feel joy or express many pleasurable emotions.

ANOMIE: A social condition that may develop when a society or community experiences unusual stress. Is characterized by a lack societal norms, a lack of social structure, and, among individuals, apathy, isolation, and a loss of personal and social values.

ANOREXIA NERVOSA: The essential features of anorexia nervosa are (a) a restriction of energy intake that leads to a significantly low body weight; (b) an intense fear of gaining weight or becoming fat or behavior that interferes with weight gain; and (c) a disturbance in the way the person experiences his/her body weight or shape or a persistent lack of recognition of the seriousness of his/her low body weight. Onset is typically in adolescence. Treatment includes contingency management, cognitive therapy, and family therapy.

ANTECEDENT: An event or other stimulus that precedes a behavior and is thought to influence it.

ANTEROGRADE AMNESIA: A loss of memory for events and information subsequent to a trauma or other event that precipitated the amnesia. It involves an inability to form new memories.

ANTISOCIAL PERSONALITY DISORDER: Antisocial personality disorder is characterized by a pattern of disregard for and violation of the rights of others that has occurred since age 15 and involves at least three characteristic symptoms (e.g., failure to conform to social norms with respect to lawful behavior, deceitfulness, impulsivity, reckless disregard for the safety of self and others, lack of remorse). The person must be at least 18 years old and have a history of conduct disorder before 15 years of age.

ANXIETY (Freud): For Freud, anxiety is a factor in both normal personality functioning and pathological behavior. He distinguished between three types of anxiety: reality (objective) anxiety, neurotic anxiety, and moral anxiety. All serve to alert the ego to the presence of external or internal threats (e.g., an unresolved conflict between the id and the superego) and involve excitation of the autonomic nervous system.

APHASIA: Impairment in the production and/or comprehension of language. Broca's aphasia involves difficulty producing written or spoken language with little or no trouble understanding language. Wernicke's aphasia is characterized by an inability to comprehend written or spoken language.

APPROPRIATE AFFECT: This is present when a person is in touch with his/her emotions and can express them as he/she feels them in response to specific emotional or situational stimuli (e.g., the person cries when discussing sad material).

APPROPRIATION: The designation of funds to a specific group, agency, or program. These funds are typically allocated by a governmental agency to enable a recipient to meet a specific goal.

ARITHMETIC MEAN: The measure of central tendency that is the arithmetic average of a set of scores. Can be used when scores are measured on an interval or ratio scale.

ASSIMILATION (Piaget): The incorporation of new knowledge into existing cognitive schemas.

ATAXIA: A lack of coordination while performing voluntary movements; there may be a loss of balance, as well.

ATTENTION-DEFICIT/HYPERACTIVITY DISORDER (ADHD): ADHD is the appropriate diagnosis when an individual has at least six symptoms of inattention and/or six symptoms of hyperactivity-impulsivity, and the symptoms had an onset before 12 years of age, are present in at least two settings (e.g., home and school), and interfere with social, academic, or occupational functioning. About 15 percent of children with ADHD continue to meet the full diagnostic criteria for the disorder as young adults and another 60 percent meet the criteria for ADHD in partial remission. In adults, inattention predominates the symptom profile. Treatment usually involves a CNS stimulant (e.g., methylphenidate) and behavioral and cognitive-behavioral techniques.

AUTISM SPECTRUM DISORDER: For a diagnosis of autism spectrum disorder, the individual must exhibit (a) persistent deficits in social communication and interaction across multiple contexts as manifested by deficits in social-emotional reciprocity, nonverbal communication, and the development, maintenance, and understanding of relationships; (b) restricted, repetitive patterns of behavior, interests, and activities as manifested by at least two characteristic symptoms (e.g., stereotyped or repetitive motor movements, use of objects, or speech; inflexible adherence to routines, or ritualized patterns of behavior); (c) the presence of symptoms during the early developmental period; and (d) impaired functioning as the result of symptoms. The best outcomes are associated with an ability to communicate by age 5 or 6, an IQ over 70, and a later onset of symptoms.

AUTONOMIC NERVOUS SYSTEM (ANS): A division of the peripheral nervous system that is involved in the control of visceral functions (e.g., heart rate, blood pressure, respiration, digestion, and sweating). Consists of the sympathetic and parasympathetic branches.

AVERSIVE COUNTERCONDITIONING (AVERSION THERAPY): Behavioral therapy based on counterconditioning that reduces the attractiveness of a stimulus or behavior by repeatedly pairing it with a stimulus that produces an undesirable or unpleasant response. Pairing alcohol consumption with electric shock to reduce alcohol use is an example of aversive counterconditioning. In this situation, the alcohol is the conditioned stimulus (CS) and the electric shock is the unconditioned stimulus (US).

AVOIDANT PERSONALITY DISORDER: Avoidant personality disorder is characterized by a pervasive pattern of social inhibition, feelings of inadequacy, and hypersensitivity to negative evaluation, as indicated by at least four characteristic symptoms (e.g., avoids work activities involving interpersonal contact due to a fear of criticism, rejection, or disapproval; is unwilling to get involved with people unless certain of being liked; is preoccupied with concerns about being criticized or rejected; views self as socially inept, inferior, or unappealing to others).

BASES OF SOCIAL POWER: Methods used to induce compliance in another person. Include coercive, reward, expert, legitimate, referent, and informational.

BASIC ACTIVITIES OF DAILY LIVING: Skills needed in typical daily self-care (e.g., bathing, dressing, feeding, toileting).

BASIC NEEDS: Items considered by social planners to be necessary for maintaining personal well-being. Include adequate food, shelter, clothing, heating fuel, clean water, and security from bodily harm.

BASIC TEMPERAMENT: Tendencies to act in certain predictable ways. Some investigators argue that basic temperament (e.g., activity level, sociability, emotionality) is one of the characteristics that has a strong genetic component.

BECK'S COGNITIVE THERAPY: A form of cognitive-behavioral therapy that views depression and other psychopathology as the product of certain cognitive phenomena including dysfunctional cognitive schemas, automatic thoughts, and cognitive distortions. Is referred to as "collaborative empiricism" because of its emphasis on the collaborative relationship between therapist and client. The therapist uses Socratic dialogue (questioning) in order to help the client reach logical conclusions about a problem and its consequences.

BECK DEPRESSION INVENTORY-II: Measure of the depth of a person's depression (the severity of his/her complaints, symptoms, and concerns). May be used with individuals age 13 and older with at least an 8th-grade reading level.

BEHAVIORAL ADDICTION: A recurring compulsion by an individual to engage in a specific activity (e.g., shopping) despite harmful consequences, as identified by the person, to his/her physical health, psychological or emotional well-being, and/or social functioning.

BEHAVIORAL FAMILY THERAPY: The behavioral approach to family and marital therapy addresses the following goals: (a) increasing the couple's recognition and initiation of pleasurable interactions; (b) decreasing the couple's aversive interactions (negative exchanges); (c) teaching the couple effective problem-solving and communication skills; and (d) teaching the couple to use a contingency contract to resolve persisting problems.

BEHAVIORAL REHEARSAL: Technique used to help a client learn a new behavior so that he/she can better cope with a specific interpersonal situation such as a job interview. Relies on role-playing, modeling, and coaching to provide opportunities to practice the new behavior in a protected environment before trying it out in the real world. As a client practices the behavior, the social worker offers feedback and may demonstrate or model the behavior.

BENZODIAZEPINES: A type of anxiolytic (antianxiety drug). More effective for alleviating anticipatory anxiety than panic symptoms. Side-effects include drowsiness, ataxia, slurred speech, and other signs of CNS depression. Abrupt cessation can cause rebound hyperexcitability.

BETA-BLOCKERS (PROPRANOLOL): Propranolol and other beta-blockers block or diminish the cardiovascular excitatory response to the hormones epinephrine and norepinephrine. They are used to treat cardiovascular disorders, glaucoma, and migraine headache and are also useful for reducing the physical symptoms of anxiety. Common side-effects of propranolol include bradycardia, nausea, diarrhea, dizziness, decreased sexual ability, and trouble sleeping.

BINGE-EATING DISORDER: Binge-eating disorder is diagnosed in the presence of repeated episodes of binge eating that occur, on average, at least once a week for three months and are associated with three or more of the following: eating much more quickly than normal; eating until feeling uncomfortably full; eating large amounts of food when not feeling physically hungry; eating alone due to feeling embarrassed by how much one is eating; feeling disgusted with oneself, depressed, or very guilty after an episode. Binge-eating disorder does not include the recurrent inappropriate compensatory behavior (e.g., purging, excessive exercise) seen in bulimia nervosa.

BIOETHICS: The philosophical study of ethical controversies arising from advances in biology and medicine. The field addresses such issues as debates over the boundaries of life (e.g., abortion, euthanasia), surrogacy, the allocation of scarce health-care resources, experimentation with human subjects, behavioral control (e.g., through the use of psychotropic medications), and the right to turn down medical care for religious or cultural reasons.

BIOPSYCHOSOCIAL APPROACH: Assumes that biophysical, psychological, and social factors all play an important role in human functioning and encourages social workers to consider and integrate a broad of range of influences when evaluating a client's development and behavior at all levels (individual, family, community, etc.) and to examine a client's appraisals of these influences and reactions to them in terms of physiology, emotion, cognition, and behavior.

BIPOLAR I DISORDER: A diagnosis of bipolar I disorder requires at least one manic episode that lasts for at least one week, is present most of the day nearly every day, and includes at least three characteristic symptoms (e.g., inflated self-esteem or grandiosity, decreased need for sleep, flight of ideas). Symptoms must cause marked impairment in social or occupational functioning, require hospitalization to avoid harm to self or others, or include psychotic features. This disorder may include one or more hypomanic episodes or major depressive episodes. Treatment usually includes lithium or an anti-seizure medication and cognitive-behavior therapy or other form of therapy.

BIPOLAR II DISORDER: A diagnosis of bipolar II disorder requires at least one hypomanic episode and at least one major depressive episode. A hypomanic episode lasts for at least four consecutive days and involves at least three symptoms that are also associated with a manic episode but are not severe enough to cause marked impairment in functioning or require hospitalization. A major depressive episode lasts for at least two weeks and involves at least five characteristic symptoms, at least one of which must be a depressed mood or a loss of interest or pleasure.

BLOCK GRANT: System of disbursing funds that permits the recipient to determine how best to distribute the money.

BOARD OF DIRECTORS: A group of people authorized to establish an agency's objectives and policies and oversee the activities of agency personnel who have day-to-day responsibility for implementing those policies. In a private or voluntary social agency, the board of directors has ultimate responsibility for the agency's programmatic and financial operations. In public agencies, a board has less power and takes on more of an advisory or administrative role.

BODY DYSMORPHIC DISORDER: The essential feature of body dysmorphic disorder is a preoccupation with one or more perceived defects or flaws in physical appearance that are not observable or appear minor to others. In addition, at some point, the person has engaged in repetitive behaviors (e.g., mirror checking, excessive grooming, skin picking) or mental acts (e.g., comparing his/her appearance with that of others) in response to these concerns.

BODY IMAGE: How an individual perceives their physical self and the resulting thoughts and feelings. The feelings can be positive, negative or both, and are influenced by both individual and environmental factors.

BORDERLINE PERSONALITY DISORDER: The essential feature of borderline personality disorder is a pervasive pattern of instability in interpersonal relationships, self-image, and affect, and marked impulsivity. At least five characteristic symptoms must be present (e.g., frantic efforts to avoid abandonment; pattern of unstable, intense interpersonal relationships that are marked by fluctuations between idealization and devaluation; an identity disturbance involving a persistent instability in self-image or sense of self; recurrent suicide threats or gestures; transient stress-related paranoid ideation or severe dissociative symptoms).

BOUNDARIES (Structural Family Therapy): The barriers between family members, between subsystems, and between the family and the environment that determine how much contact is permitted. For structural family therapists, family dysfunction is related to boundary problems – i.e., boundaries that are overly rigid (disengaged) or overly permeable (enmeshed).

BRIEF PSYCHOTIC DISORDER: Brief psychotic disorder characterized by the presence of one or more of four characteristic symptoms (delusions, hallucinations, disorganized speech, grossly disorganized or catatonic behavior) with at least one symptom being delusions, hallucinations, or disorganized speech. Symptoms are present for at least one day but less than one month with an eventual return to full premorbid functioning.

BROKER: A social worker role that involves linking clients with the resources they need. To perform this role effectively, workers must be familiar with community resources and their eligibility criteria.

BRONFENBRENNER'S ECOLOGICAL MODEL: Bronfenbrenner described development as involving interactions between the individual and his/her context, or environment, and his ecological model describes the context in terms of five environmental systems or levels: microsystem, mesosystem, exosystem, macrosystem, and chronosystem.

BUFFERING HYPOTHESIS: The hypothesis that lower susceptibility to stress, greater life satisfaction, and other positive outcomes are associated with a perception that one has adequate social support.

BULIMIA NERVOSA: Bulimia nervosa is characterized by (a) recurrent episodes of binge eating that are accompanied by a sense of a lack of control; (b) inappropriate compensatory behavior to prevent weight gain (e.g., self-induced vomiting, excessive exercise); and (c) self-evaluation that is unduly influenced by body shape and weight. Treatment usually includes nutritional counseling, cognitive-behavioral therapy, and in some cases, antidepressants.

BUREAUCRACY: A highly rational, stable, and predictable organizational structure that consists of different units that are hierarchically arranged (delegation of authority), with each unit performing a specialized function according to clearly defined rules (division of labor).

CAMPAIGN (Macro Change): Strategy used to gain support and acceptance for community or organizational change. Is used when the target system needs to be convinced of the importance of the change or to allocate resources but communication is still possible between the action and target systems. Related tactics include education, persuasion, co-optation, lobbying, and mass media appeal. See also *collaboration (macro change)* and *contest*.

CAPITATION: A payment method for health-care services in which a fixed payment is made at regular intervals to a medical provider by a managed care organization for an enrolled patient. Generally, the physician, hospital, or other health-care provider is paid a contracted rate for each member assigned (referred to as "per-member-per-month" rate) regardless of the number or nature of services provided. The contractual rates are usually adjusted for age, gender, illness, and regional differences.

CASE ADVOCACY (CLIENT ADVOCACY): A form of advocacy that involves working with and on behalf of a client to ensure that the client receives the services and benefits to which he/she is entitled and that the services are delivered in a way that protect his/her dignity.

CASE CONFERENCE: Agency and organizational procedure in which professionals working with a client meet to discuss his/her case. Typically involves a discussion of the client's problem, prognosis, and treatment. In addition to professionals working on the case, a case conference may include other professionals who have knowledge or expertise about the client's problem and friends and family members of the client.

CASE FINDING: Outreach approach in which social workers seek and identify individuals or groups who are vulnerable to or are experiencing the problems for which their social agency has responsibility to provide services or other forms of assistance.

CASE MANAGEMENT: A procedure used to identify, plan, access, coordinate, and monitor services from different social agencies and staff on behalf of a client. Clients needing case management services usually have multiple problems that require assistance from multiple providers, several problems that need to be addressed at the same time, and special difficulties in seeking and using help effectively.

CASE STUDIES: A general term used to describe an in-depth investigation of a single individual, family, organization, etc. A shortcoming is that their results might not be generalizable to other cases.

CATASTROPHIC ANALOGY: A way of viewing social systems. Proposes that they change so much and so often that they appear chaotic – there is extreme conflict in the system and a lack of order and predictability, and it can be difficult to determine the system's future direction.

CATCHMENT AREA: The geographic area served by a social agency.

CATECHOLAMINE HYPOTHESIS: Theory that attributes depression to deficient norepinephrine and mania to excessive norepinephrine.

CATEGORICAL ASSISTANCE: State welfare programs for particular groups of people identified in the Social Security Act (e.g., the disabled, needy).

CATEGORICALLY NEEDY: Individuals who are automatically eligible for certain welfare benefits without a means test because they fit certain predetermined criteria.

CATHARSIS: The healthful (therapeutic) release of ideas through "talking out" conscious material, accompanied by an appropriate emotional reaction. Also, the release into awareness of repressed ("forgotten") material from the unconscious.

CAUSE (CLASS) ADVOCACY: Work on behalf of groups of people who lack the resources or ability to advocate for themselves.

CENTRALIZATION: The concentration of the administrative power of a group, organization, or political body.

CENTRALIZED COMMUNICATION NETWORKS: Networks in which all communication must pass through a central person or position within the organization. These networks work best for simple tasks.

CENTRAL NERVOUS SYSTEM (CNS): The nerve cells, fibers, and tissues that make up the spinal cord and brain.

CEREBRAL CORTEX: The outer covering of the cerebral hemispheres of the brain. Involved in higher-order sensory, emotional, motor, and intellectual activities. Divided into two hemispheres (right and left), with each containing four lobes: frontal, parietal, temporal, and occipital.

CHILD PROTECTIVE SERVICES (CPS): Social, residential, medical, legal, and custodial care services given to children whose parent or other caregiver is not meeting their needs. Social workers who work in government agencies often help law enforcement personnel with investigations to find out if children need these services and help children get the services when they need them. The social workers may also provide the services themselves. In most states, the child protective service (CPS) unit of the Department of Social Services, Department of Human Resources, or Department of Public Welfare is the primary agency responsible for decisions related to the prevention, investigation, and treatment of child abuse and neglect. The foremost goal of services provided by CPS units is the protection of abused and neglected children.

CIRCULAR QUESTIONS: Questions designed to help family members identify differences in their perspectives in order to increase their understanding of events or circumstances so they can derive solutions to their own problems.

CLARIFICATION: A helping skill used in response to vague or unclear client messages. Using this skill is appropriate when the social worker doesn't understand a client's message, would like the client to become more explicit, or wishes to check his/her understanding of a client's message.

CLASSICAL CONDITIONING: In classical conditioning, a neutral (conditioned) stimulus is repeatedly paired with an unconditioned stimulus so that the neutral stimulus alone eventually elicits the response that is naturally produced by the unconditioned stimulus. In Pavlov's original studies, the meat powder was the unconditioned stimulus (US) and salivation was the unconditioned response (UR). A tone was the conditioned stimulus (CS). As the result of pairing the tone with the meat powder, the tone eventually elicited salivation – the conditioned response (CR).

CLASSICAL EXTINCTION: The gradual elimination of a classically conditioned response by repeatedly presenting the conditioned stimulus without the unconditioned stimulus. Often, an extinguished response shows spontaneous recovery (i.e., it recurs following extinction).

CLIENT-FOCUSED MEASURES: Techniques developed specifically for a particular client and used to assess the extent of his/her problem, follow his/her progress during treatment, and determine when intervention can be terminated. Include individualized rating scales, goal attainment scales, and client logs.

CLOSED-ENDED QUESTIONS: Interview questions that elicit responses that provide either factual information or a simple "yes" or "no." Used primarily in the latter portion of an interview to obtain missing factual data.

CLOSED GROUP: Therapy group that begins and ends with the same membership, and usually has a pre-set termination date. Impractical for long-term therapy but commonly used in short-term, task-oriented forms of group work.

COALITION (Organizations, Communities): An alliance of organizations or other groups brought together to achieve a common goal. May be "ad hoc" (organized to address a single issue only), semipermanent (organized around longer-range goals), or permanent.

COERCIVE FAMILY INTERACTION MODEL: Proposes that children initially learn aggressive behaviors from their parents who rarely reinforce prosocial behaviors, use harsh discipline, reward their children's aggressiveness with approval and attention and that, over time, aggressive parent-child interactions escalate. Patterson and colleagues developed a parent intervention designed to stop this coercive cycle by teaching parents child-management skills and providing them with therapy to help them cope more effectively with stress.

COERCIVE POWER: A source of power for supervisors and other leaders involving the ability to control tangible punishments (demotion, poor performance rating, etc.) and psychic punishments (criticism, disapproval). See also *bases of social power.*

COGNITIVE DISSONANCE THEORY: Festinger's theory of attitude change that proposes that inconsistencies in cognitions produce discomfort (dissonance), which motivates the individual to reduce the dissonance, often by changing his/her cognitions.

COGNITIVE RESTRUCTURING TECHNIQUES: Techniques used to help clients manage their emotional reactions and behave more effectively through modifying their distorted cognitions or errors in logic, particularly their distorted interpretations of reality. The use of these techniques is based on theory underlying the cognitive therapies which assumes that how people interpret and think about an event or experience (their self-talk) gives rise to an emotional reaction, which, in turn, gives rise to behavior.

COHORT (INTERGENERATIONAL) EFFECTS: The effects of being part of a group (cohort) that was born at a particular time and, as a result, was exposed to unique educational, cultural, and other experiences. Cohort effects can confound the results of a cross-sectional study since any observed differences between age groups might be due to these effects rather than to differences in age only.

COLLABORATION (Administration): In social work administration, an agreement (joint venture) in which two or more agencies agree to work together to set up and operate a new program or service.

COLLABORATION (Direct Practice): Involves two or more other professionals working together to serve a client (individual, family, or group). The professionals may work together as part of a single helping team or work relatively independently of one another while making sure to communicate and coordinate their respective efforts in order to prevent a duplication of services.

COLLABORATION (Macro Change): Strategy used to gain support and acceptance for community or organizational change. Is used when there is a working relationship in which the action and target systems agree that change must occur, and the target system supports the allocation of resources. Related tactics include implementation and capacity building (e.g., empowerment). See also *campaign* and *contest*.

COLLABORATIVE THERAPY: Treatment format in which two or more social workers (or other therapists) each treat a single member of a family and coordinate their efforts.

COLLECTIVE ACTION: An organized effort that includes many people and attempts to effect political, economic, or cultural change.

COLLECTIVISM (Social Policy): In regard to social policy, an ideology that assumes that some individual choice must be limited to better serve the common good.

COLLECTIVISM (Worldview): Assumes that groups connect and mutually obligate individuals – the personal is subordinate to the larger social group or context. A person with this worldview (a) emphasizes family life over personal self-concept; (b) does not connect his/her sense of well-being to a sense of personal control; (c) attributes events or behaviors to situational factors; (d) sees events in terms of what he/she believes the expectations of others might be; (e) prefers indirect, high-context communication; and (f) in conflict situations, prefers an accommodation and negotiation approach.

COMBINED THERAPY: Intervention model in which a client participates concurrently in both individual therapy and group therapy.

COMMITTEES ON INQUIRY: Groups of professional peers and others who look into alleged ethical violations, illegal activities, or other disputes between professionals or between professionals and clients and attempt to determine if any wrong-doing has been committed.

COMMUNICATION THEORY: "A range of concepts to describe how people, groups and organizations exchange information and highlights the complexity of the meaning and messages conveyed and received" (Social Care Institute for Excellence).

COMMUNITY DEVELOPMENT: Community organizing efforts made by professionals and community members to improve social ties among residents of a community, motivate residents for self-help, develop reliable local leadership, and create or restore local institutions. Relies on a grass-roots, nonbureaucratic approach that emphasizes community solidarity. Efforts are purposeful and involve a clear strategy and set of activities. Associated interventions include social action, public education, national and local planning, and community organizing.

COMMUNITY OF IDENTIFICATION AND INTEREST: A nonplace community in which people are united by common interests, values, and commitments or brought together based on their shared ethnicity, race, religion, sexual orientation, social class, ideology, lifestyle, profession, or workplace.

COMMUNITY ORGANIZING: A type of macro (indirect) practice used to help individuals and groups resolve social problems and improve social welfare through organized collective action. Key objectives are to help community members achieve social justice and economic and social development and to develop the capacity of community members to help themselves. The individuals or groups who are helped have common interests or are from the same geographic region. Community organizing models include social planning, social action, and locality or community development.

COMPLEMENTARY COMMUNICATION: Communication occurring between participants who are unequal and that emphasizes their differences (e.g., communication between a dominant and a subordinate participant).

COMPLIANCE: Occurs when a person changes his/her behavior in order to obtain a reward or avoid a punishment. Compliance is public and does not involve a private change in opinions or attitudes. Reward and coercive power tend to produce compliance and a change in behavior, particularly when a person knows he/she is being observed. See also *bases of social power; identification (social influence);* and *internalization*.

COMPULSIONS: Repetitious and deliberate behaviors or mental acts that the individual feels driven to perform either in response to an obsession or according to rules that must be applied rigidly. The goal of compulsive acts is to reduce distress or prevent a dreaded situation from happening, but the acts are either excessive or are not connected in a logical way to this goal. The individual may attempt to resist a compulsion but experiences anxiety and tension as the result of doing so.

CONCRETE OPERATIONAL STAGE: Third stage in Piaget's model of cognitive development (age 7 to 11 years). During this stage, children acquire logical operations and use logic to reason about concrete events or situations. Children at this stage can conserve.

CONCURRENT THERAPY: Treatment format in which a social worker sees different members of a family or client system separately in individual sessions. This intervention model is used most commonly in couples therapy to encourage the clients to reveal thoughts, feelings, and behaviors that they might not feel able to disclose in the presence of their spouses.

CONDITIONED RESPONSE (CR): In classical conditioning, a response that is elicited by a conditioned stimulus (CS) as the result of pairing the CS with an unconditioned stimulus. The conditioned response is similar to, but not identical to, the unconditioned response (it is usually weaker in strength or magnitude).

CONDITIONED STIMULUS (CS): In classical conditioning, the previously neutral stimulus that, as the result of being paired with an unconditioned stimulus, now elicits a conditioned response (CR).

CONDUCT DISORDER: The diagnosis of conduct disorder requires a persistent pattern of behavior that violates the basic rights of others and/or age-appropriate social norms or rules as evidenced by the presence of at least three characteristic symptoms during the past 12 months and at least one symptom in the past six months. Symptoms are divided into four categories: aggression to people and animals; destruction of property; deceitfulness or theft; and serious violation of rules. The disorder cannot be assigned to individuals over age 18 who meet the criteria for antisocial personality disorder.

CONFABULATION: Fabrication of experiences or situations in order to fill in and cover up gaps in memory.

CONFIDENTIALITY: The ethical duty to protect from disclosure any information about a client, research or evaluation subject, supervisee, employee, etc., obtained during the course of a professional relationship. A social worker can disclose confidential information, when appropriate, with valid consent from a client or a person legally authorized to consent on behalf of a client. In addition, the assumption that a social worker will keep information confidential does not apply when the worker needs to disclose certain information to prevent serious, foreseeable, and imminent harm to a client or another identifiable person or when laws or regulations require the worker to disclose certain information without a client's consent. Confidential information includes the identity of the client, content of things said by the client, professional opinions about the client, and material from the client's records.

CONFLICT INDUCTION: Community organizing technique used to compel community members to actively debate issues or value differences and form new coalitions. The social worker brings up issues and differences directly to motivate group members to work on them.

CONFRONTATION (CHALLENGE): Respectful and gentle efforts to help a client recognize that he/she is using distortions, deceptions, denials, avoidance, or manipulations that are getting in the way of desired change. The social worker challenges and invites the client to examine a thought or behavior that is self-defeating or harmful to others and to take action to change it. Efforts to confront a client generally emphasize factors that the social worker believes are contributing to the client's problems and preventing the client from making progress.

CONGRUENT COMMUNICATION: Communication in which two or more messages are sent via different levels (e.g., verbally and nonverbally) but none of the messages seriously contradicts any of the others.

CONJOINT THERAPY: Treatment format in which a social worker (or other therapist) treats a family or couple by meeting with the family members or partners together for regular sessions. Sometimes, conjoint therapy is provided by a team of therapists rather than by only a single therapist.

CONNORS 3: Scales used to evaluate behaviors and other concerns in youth ages 8 to 18. In contrast to its predecessor (Conners' Rating Scales-Revised), offers a more thorough assessment of ADHD and addresses comorbid disorders, such as oppositional defiant disorder and conduct disorder. The Conners 3 includes parent rating scales (Conners 3-P), teacher rating scales (Conners 3-T), and self-report rating scales (Conners 3-SR).

CONSERVATION (Piaget): The ability to recognize that certain properties of an object or substance do not change when its appearance is altered in a superficial way (e.g., when a liquid is poured from a short, fat glass into a tall, thin one, the ability to recognize that the amount of liquid has not changed). The ability to conserve develops gradually during the concrete operational stage and is due to the emergence of decentration and reversibility.

CONSIDERATION (Leadership): A dimension of leadership behavior that refers to the amount of warmth, concern, rapport, and support displayed by the leader. Leaders high in consideration are person-oriented and concerned with the expressive aspects of the job. Leaders who communicate both support (expressive) and high performance expectations (instrumental) are likely to have the most effective work groups. See also *initiating structure*.

CONSULTATION: A process in which a human services professional assists a consultee with a work-related problem within a client system. The goal is to help both the consultee and the client system in some specified way. Several principles guide consultation: First, consultation always has a problem-solving (educational) function. Second, a consultant has no administrative authority over staff members, and a consultee may turn down the consultant's suggestions. The determining factor is the value of the consultant's idea not his/her status as a consultant. Third, consultation relies on the quality of the relationship between the consultant and consultee. Thus, a consultant must be skilled at developing and maintaining relationships with consultees. Consultation is used by most social workers on an as-needed basis.

CONTACT COMFORT: Research by Harlow with rhesus monkeys indicated that a baby's attachment to his/her mother is due, in part, to contact comfort, or the pleasant tactile sensation that is provided by a soft, cuddly parent.

CONTACT HYPOTHESIS: Proposes that prejudice may be reduced through contact between members of the majority and minority groups as long as certain conditions are met (e.g., members of the different groups have equal status and power and are provided with opportunities that disconfirm their negative stereotypes about members of the other group).

CONTEST (Macro Change): Strategy used to gain support and acceptance for community or organizational change. Is used when there is deep disagreement or conflict between the action and target systems. Related tactics are confrontational and include bargaining and negotiation, large group or community action, and class action lawsuits. See also *collaboration (macro change)* and *contest*.

CONTINGENCY CONTRACT: A type of contingency management that involves a formal written agreement between two or more people (e.g., between therapist and client, parent and child, teacher and students) that clearly defines the behaviors that are to be modified and the rewards and punishments that will follow performance of those behaviors. Behavioral change may be required by one or all parties to the contract.

CONTINUOUS SCHEDULE OF REINFORCEMENT: In operant conditioning, providing reinforcement after each emission of the target response. Associated with rapid acquisition of a response and susceptibility to extinction.

CONVENTIONAL MORALITY (Kohlberg): According to Kohlberg, the stage of moral development in which moral judgments are based on adherence to authority. Includes the "good boy/good girl" and "law and order" stages. Is characteristic of most adolescents and adults.

CONVERSION DISORDER: The symptoms of conversion disorder involve disturbances in voluntary motor or sensory functioning and suggest a serious neurological or other medical condition (e.g., paralysis, seizures, blindness, loss of pain sensation) with evidence of an incompatibility between the symptom and recognized neurological or medical conditions.

CO-OPTATION (INFORMAL AND FORMAL): Tactic used to manage opposition to change by absorbing target system members and other opponents into the action system. Once people become part of the action system, they are likely to assume some "ownership" of the change effort. Co-opting individuals is called "informal co-optation"; and co-opting an organized group is called "formal co-optation." Formal co-optation of a number of groups leads to coalition building.

COPAYMENT: Condition of an insurance policy that requires the patient to contribute to the cost of the service he/she receives. Typically, the policy holder must pay a percentage of the service fee, and the insurance company pays the balance.

COPING STRATEGY VS. EGO DEFENSE MECHANISM: A coping strategy is a deliberate and conscious effort to solve a problem or handle personal distress, while an ego defense mechanism is an habitual, unconscious maneuver used to avoid facing a problem.

CORRELATION COEFFICIENT: A numerical index of the relationship (degree of association) between two or more variables. The magnitude of the coefficient indicates the strength of the relationship; its sign indicates the direction (positive or negative).

COST EFFECTIVENESS/COST-BENEFIT ANALYSIS: Budgeting technique that quantitatively evaluates different program alternatives. The cost effective analysis (CEA) component evaluates the costs and benefits of a given program approach. The answer is a "cost-benefit ratio" (the cost over the benefit). A program's cost-benefit ratio is then compared to the cost-benefit ratios of other program alternatives to determine which approach is most cost effective.

COUNTERCONDITIONING: In classical conditioning, the elimination of a response by pairing the response or associated stimuli with a stimulus that naturally elicits an incompatible and more desirable response.

COUNTERTRANSFERENCE: A set of conscious or unconscious emotional reactions to a client experienced by a therapist, usually in a clinical setting. Freud considered countertransference to be detrimental to psychoanalysis and believed that a therapist must always be aware of any countertransference feelings to ensure that they do not interfere with the progress of treatment. Current forms of psychotherapy view countertransference as a helpful tool in gaining understanding of a client's process. Social workers should seek consultation when doing so is necessary to prevent countertransference-related problems, such as a loss of objectivity, from interfering with treatment.

CRITICAL PERIOD VS. SENSITIVE PERIOD: A "critical period" is a time during which an organism is especially susceptible to positive and negative environmental influences. A "sensitive period" is more flexible than a critical period and is not limited to a specific chronological age. Some aspects of human development may depend on critical periods, but, for many human characteristics and behaviors, sensitive periods are probably more applicable.

CROSS-SECTIONAL ANALYSIS: Technique for collecting and displaying data that provides several perspectives on a single population at a specific point in time; it does not reveal changes over time. The data collection may sometimes be "retrospective," which involves asking people to reflect back on their past experiences and attitudes.

CROSS-SECTIONAL STUDIES: Studies conducted to assess the effects of aging and/or developmental changes over time (e.g., to assess the effects of age on IQ). Involves comparing groups of individuals representing different age groups or developmental levels at the same point in time. Cohort effects are a possible confound when conducting these studies.

CROSS-SEQUENTIAL DESIGN: Used to assess the effects of aging and/or developmental changes over time. Combines cross-sectional and longitudinal methodologies by assessing members of two or more age groups at two or more different times.

CULTURAL ENCAPSULATION: Refers to the tendency of therapists and counselors to interpret everyone's reality through their own cultural assumptions and stereotypes.

CULTURAL PARANOIA: Term used to describe appropriate mistrust and suspiciousness of African-Americans toward whites resulting from racism and oppression. In therapy, may be a cause of nondisclosure.

CYCLE OF VIOLENCE (Walker): A three-stage cycle of violence that describes many abusive spousal/partner relationships. Includes tension building, acute battering incident, and loving-contrition ("honeymoon").

CYCLOTHYMIC DISORDER: Cyclothymic disorder involves fluctuating hypomanic symptoms and numerous periods of depressive symptoms that do not meet the criteria for a major depressive episode, with symptoms lasting for at least two years in adults or one year in children and adolescents.

DECENTRALIZATION: The delegation of responsibilities and activities by the leadership level of an organization to lower-level organization members who are closer to the problem or activity.

DECENTRALIZED COMMUNICATION NETWORKS: Networks in which information flows freely between people in an organization without going through a central person. These networks work well for complex tasks.

DECISION SUPPORT SYSTEMS (DSS): In an agency, the use of computers to collect and organize information and make decisions from among specified choices. A computer program uses a predefined set of facts and rules to determine the best decision, and an administrator then either agrees with or rejects the computer's decision.

DEFENSE MECHANISMS: For psychoanalysts, mental strategies that operate unconsciously, deny or distort reality, and are employed by the ego to reduce anxiety arising from the discrepant demands of the id, the superego, and reality. Include, among others, repression, reaction formation, and sublimation.

DEFENSIVENESS (AND DEFENSE MECHANISMS): All people use defense mechanisms to cope with anxiety, stress, and problems of living, but defensiveness can interfere with a person's ability to accurately perceive reality and get along with others. Rigid or excessive use of defenses impedes realistic problem solving, and very high levels of defensiveness and distortions of reality are characteristic of personality disturbances.

DEFENSIVENESS ("FAKING GOOD"): A conscious effort by a client to convince a clinician that he/she is better off than is really the case.

DELIRIUM: A diagnosis of delirium requires (a) a disturbance in attention and awareness that develops over a short period of time, represents a change from baseline functioning, and tends to fluctuate in severity over the course of a day and (b) an additional disturbance in cognition (e.g., impaired memory, disorientation, impaired language, deficits in visuospatial ability, perceptual distortions). Symptoms must not be due to another neurocognitive disorder and must not occur during a severely reduced level of arousal (e.g., during a coma), and there must be evidence that symptoms are the direct physiological consequence of a medical condition, substance intoxication or withdrawal, and/or exposure to a toxin.

DELUSIONAL DISORDER: Delusional disorder involves one or more delusions that last at least one month. Overall psychosocial functioning is not markedly impaired, and any impairment is directly related to the delusions. The DSM-5 distinguishes between the following subtypes: erotomanic, grandiose, jealous, persecutory, somatic, mixed, and unspecified.

DELUSIONS: False beliefs that are firmly held despite what other people believe and/or the existence of clear and indisputable evidence to the contrary.

DEMAND CHARACTERISTICS: Cues in an experimental situation that inform research participants of how they are expected to behave during the course of the study. Demand characteristics threaten a study's internal and external validity.

DENIAL: A defense mechanism in which an individual admits that an anxiety-evoking impulse, thought, etc., exists but denies that it is personally relevant. A relatively primitive defense mechanism related to a child's faith in the magical power of thoughts and words.

DEPENDENT PERSONALITY DISORDER: Dependent personality disorder involves a pervasive and excessive need to be taken care of, which leads to submissive, clinging behavior and a fear of separation as manifested by at least five symptoms (e.g., has difficulty making decisions without advice and reassurance from others, fears disagreeing with others because it might lead to a loss of support, has difficulty initiating projects on his/her own, goes to great lengths to gain nurturance and support from others, is unrealistically preoccupied with fears of being left to care for him/herself).

DEPENDENT VARIABLE: The variable that is observed and measured in a research study and is believed to be affected in some way by the independent variable. In direct practice evaluation, the client's functioning is considered the dependent variable.

DESCRIPTIVE RESEARCH: Research conducted to describe behavior rather than to test hypotheses about behavior. Includes observational techniques, surveys and questionnaires, archival research, and case studies.

DESCRIPTIVE SURVEY DESIGN: May be used to obtain measures on dependent variables at different points in time and to estimate client satisfaction with programs and to conduct needs assessments. In program evaluation, relies on representative sampling and is used to obtain explicit, quantitative data that can be generalized to other populations. Subjects participate in an interview or fill out a questionnaire and then data from these are analyzed using descriptive and correlational statistics.

DETRIANGULATION: A term used to explain the process of Bowen's therapy. Bowen believed that when a two-person relationship becomes too intense or too distant, the opposing members seek to join with the same person against the other, forcing this third party to alternate loyalties between the two. Triangulation stabilizes the system and, therefore, perpetuates the family's pathology. According to Bowen, focusing on this stabilizing process is sometimes more effective for bringing about change than an emphasis on presenting issues.

DIABETES MELLITUS (TYPE 1 AND TYPE 2 DIABETES): A disorder involving a build up of glucose in the blood as the result of hypoinsulinism. Forms of diabetes include type 1, type 2, and gestational (developing during pregnancy). Type 1 diabetes is an autoimmune disorder. Its symptoms develop quickly and may include increased thirst and urination, constant hunger, weight loss, blurred vision, extreme fatigue, apathy, confusion, and mental dullness. Type 1 diabetes occurs most often in children and young adults. In type 2 diabetes, symptoms develop gradually and may include fatigue, nausea, frequent urination, increased thirst, weight loss, blurred vision, frequent infections, slow healing of wounds, and cognitive symptoms similar to those occurring in type 1. Type 2 diabetes is associated with obesity, family history of diabetes, history of gestational diabetes, low levels of physical activity, and older age. Due to increased rates of obesity among young people, however, type 2 diabetes is becoming more common among children, adolescents, and young adults.

DIAGNOSTIC UNCERTAINTY: When using the DSM-5, diagnostic uncertainty about a client's diagnosis is indicated by coding one of the following: Other specified disorder is coded when the clinician wants to indicate the reason why the client's symptoms do not meet the criteria for a specific diagnosis, while unspecified disorder is coded when the clinician does not want to indicate the reason why the client's symptoms do not meet the criteria for a specific diagnosis.

DIALECTICAL BEHAVIOR THERAPY: Linehan's (1987) dialectical behavior therapy (DBT) was designed as a treatment for borderline personality disorder and incorporates three strategies: (a) group skills training to help clients regulate their emotions and improve their social and coping skills; (b) individual outpatient therapy to strengthen clients' motivation and newly-acquired skills; and (c) telephone consultations to provide additional support and between-sessions coaching. Research has confirmed that it reduces premature termination from therapy, psychiatric hospitalizations, and parasuicidal behaviors.

DIATHESIS-STRESS MODEL: A model of certain mental disorders that attributes them to a combination of genetic predisposition and environmental stress factors.

DIFFERENTIAL REINFORCEMENT: Differential reinforcement (e.g., DRA, DRO, and DRI) is an operant technique that combines positive reinforcement and extinction. During a specified period of time, the individual is reinforced when he/she engages in behaviors other than the target behavior. The alternative behaviors are reinforced, while the target behavior is extinguished.

DIFFERENTIATION (of Self): For extended family systems (Bowenian) therapists, the separation of an individual's intellectual and emotional functioning from that of his/her family members. Allows the individual to resist being overwhelmed by the family's emotional states.

DIMINISHED CAPACITY TO PARENT (Wallerstein): The deterioration in the relationships between children and their parents following divorce. Following divorce, mothers and fathers spend less time with their children, are less sensitive to their children, have trouble separating their own needs from the needs of the children, and are often inconsistent, but more restrictive and demanding, in terms of control and punishment.

DIRECT ASSESSMENT OF SUICIDE: Involves questioning a client directly about his/her intent to commit suicide with an emphasis on three indicators that directly suggest an elevated and more imminent risk of a suicide attempt – intent, plan, and means. Risk to life is highest when a client has both a concrete, lethal suicide plan and the means available to carry it out.

DIRECT PRACTICE SYSTEMS (CHANGE AGENT, CLIENT, TARGET, ACTION): In direct practice, four systems are critical to a successful planned change process: (a) The change agent system includes the social worker and, as relevant, his/her agency. (b) The client system is the person (or group) who has requested the social worker's/agency's services and expects to benefit from what they do. (c) The target system is the person, group, or organization that needs to change and is targeted for change so that the client will benefit from the intervention. In direct practice, the client system and the target system are often the same. (d) The action system includes all of the people, groups, and organizations that the social worker (i.e., change agent system) works with or through in order to influence the target system and help the client system to achieve the desired outcome.

DISABILITY BENEFIT: A form of categorical assistance. Involves the provision of cash, products, and/or services to an individual who is unable to perform certain activities due to a mental or physical condition. For example, DI and SSI.

DISABILITY INSURANCE (DI): (A.k.a. Social Security Disability Insurance, SSDI.) Social security program that provides for the economic needs of individuals who can no longer earn an income because of chronic disability or incapacity. The disability must be expected to last for at least a year or to result in death. Others who may qualify for DI include individuals with HIV infection and disabled children. Pays benefits to individuals and certain members of their family if they are insured (individuals are insured if they have worked long enough and paid social security taxes).

DISCIPLINARY STRATEGIES: "Power-assertive" discipline (punishment) includes physical punishment, threat of punishment, and physical efforts to control a child's behavior. It tends to increase children's aggressive tendencies. "Love withdrawal" involves withdrawing love when a child's behavior is considered inappropriate. Children of parents who apply this strategy tend to be excessively anxious and to have difficulty expressing their emotions. "Induction" involves using explanation and rationality to influence a child's behaviors and provides him/her with opportunities to learn how to exercise self-control and develop internal moral standards. Compared to children who are punished, these children tend to be more thoughtful and generous toward others.

DISCRIMINATION VS. PREJUDICE: Discrimination refers to behaviors such as unequal treatment, while prejudice refers to attitudes, which may or may not include behavioral manifestations.

DISENGAGEMENT VS. ENMESHMENT: With disengagement, boundaries are too rigid, not allowing adequate communication between subsystems; and with enmeshment, boundaries are overly diffuse, allowing too much communication with other subsystems. In contrast, healthy boundaries are optimally permeable: They protect the integrity of a subsystem while also allowing interaction between subsystems and can adapt to the changing needs of the family system.

DISINHIBITED SOCIAL ENGAGEMENT DISORDER: Disinhibited social engagement disorder is characterized by a pattern of behavior that involves inappropriate interactions with unfamiliar adults as evidenced by at least two symptoms (e.g., reduced or absence of reticence in approaching or interacting with unfamiliar adults, overly familiar behavior with unfamiliar adults). The child must have a developmental age of at least 9 months and have experienced extreme insufficient care that is believed to be the cause of the disturbed behavior.

DISPLACEMENT: A defense mechanism. Involves the transfer of an instinctual drive from its original target to a less threatening target so that the drive can be more safely expressed.

DISRUPTIVE MOOD DYSREGULATION DISORDER: Disruptive mood dysregulation disorder involves (a) severe recurrent temper outbursts that are displayed verbally and/or behaviorally and occur, on average, three or more times per week; *and* (b) a mood that is persistently irritable or angry between the outbursts. The temper outbursts and mood symptoms have been present for 12 or more months and occur in at least two of three settings (i.e., at home, at school, with peers). The diagnosis cannot be assigned for the first time before age 6 or after age 18, and the symptoms must have an onset before age 10. If criteria for both disruptive mood dysregulation disorder and oppositional defiant disorder are met, only the diagnosis of disruptive mood dysregulation disorder should be given. And, while bipolar I and bipolar II disorder are *episodic* conditions (include discrete periods of mood disturbance that can be differentiated from how the child usually is), disruptive mood dysregulation disorder is not an episodic condition.

DISSOCIATIVE AMNESIA: A diagnosis of dissociative amnesia requires an inability to recall important personal information that cannot be attributed to ordinary forgetfulness and causes clinically significant distress or impaired functioning. It is often related to exposure to one or more traumatic events. The most common forms of amnesia are localized and selective.

DOORKNOB COMMUNICATION: Any client disclosure of important or difficult information just as a session is about to end. Some experts believe this behavior reflects an unconscious effort by the client to prolong an interview or set up the therapist for an accusation of indifference. Schulman believes that it reflects either information important to the client that the client has been uncomfortable discussing earlier in the session or important information that the client did raise earlier in the session but that the social worker overlooked.

DOUBLE-BIND COMMUNICATION: A set of contradictory or logically inconsistent communications from the same person along with an injunction that the receiver of the communications must not comment on their inconsistency. For example, a mother says "I love you" to her child while pushing the child off her lap.

DOWN SYNDROME: Autosomal disorder usually caused by the presence of an extra chromosome 21. The cause of 10 to 30 percent of all cases of mild to moderate intellectual disability. Associated with physical abnormalities including slanted, almond-shaped eyes, heart lesions, cataracts, and respiratory defects.

DUAL DIAGNOSIS: Term traditionally used when a client has both a major psychiatric disorder, such as a psychotic or bipolar disorder, and a substance use disorder.

DUAL PERSPECTIVE: Proposes that the social environment includes two sets of influences: The nurturing environment is composed of individuals with whom a person interacts frequently and sometimes in an intimate way, and the sustaining environment includes individuals a person encounters in the wider community and broader society. Ideally, a person is accepted, respected, and supported in both environments.

DUAL PERSPECTIVE WORKSHEET: Assessment tool used to depict the location of supports and barriers or problems that affect a client's interactions with his/her social environment. Allows you and the client to identify areas of strength that might be resources for change and areas that need to be changed. Also helps you determine whether your intervention should target elements of the client's nurturing environment, sustaining environment, or both.

DUAL RELATIONSHIPS (AND MULTIPLE RELATIONSHIPS): The act of assuming two ("dual") or more ("multiple") roles at the same time or sequentially with a client or former client. Examples include (a) providing therapy to an employee, friend, or relative, (b) going into business with a client, and (c) becoming friends with a former client. When a dual or multiple relationship exists, there is a risk that the client (or former client) will be exploited, primarily because of the power differential that is a basic part of the social worker-client relationship.

DURABLE POWER OF ATTORNEY FOR HEALTH CARE: A type of advance directive used to legally designate another person to have the authority to make one's health-care decisions if one becomes too ill or impaired (physically or cognitively) to make one's own decisions or communicate one's medical preferences.

DUTY TO WARN (DUTY TO PROTECT): Technically refers to the duty to notify the police and to attempt to warn the victim when a client reveals a serious intention to harm a reasonably identifiable individual. The "duty to warn," which is sometimes called the "duty to protect," was first laid out by the Tarasoff decision in California in the 1970s. A subsequent rehearing of Tarasoff established a more flexible "duty of care," which may or may not involve warning the intended victim: That is, to fulfill his/her "duty to warn" an intended victim, a therapist may warn this person, notify the police, *or* take other reasonable steps.

EARNED INCOME TAX CREDIT (EITC): A federal income tax credit for low-income workers. The credit reduces the amount of tax they owe (if any) and is intended to offset some of the increases in living expenses and social security taxes. Eligible persons who owe no taxes, or whose tax liability is smaller than their tax credit, receive all or part of the EITC as a direct payment. Some workers are prepaid their credits through their employers as "negative withholding" from paychecks. EITC is administered by the Internal Revenue Service as part of its responsibility for collection of federal income taxes.

ECLECTICISM: A continuing trend in psychotherapy involving increasing integration of therapeutic techniques drawn from several schools of psychotherapy.

ECOLOGICAL SYSTEMS PERSPECTIVE: Framework combining systems theory and ecological concepts that advocates a transactional view of the person-environment relationship. The transactional view suggests that a person and his/her environment are engaged in constant circular exchanges in which each is reciprocally shaping and influencing the other over time. Transactions between a person's coping patterns and the qualities of his/her environment constitute a person-situation duality. In social work, the objective is to help people find ways of meeting their needs (of achieving an adaptive person-environment fit) by connecting them to needed resources and by improving their capacity to use resources and cope with negative environmental influences.

ECOSYSTEM: Concept pertaining to the physical and biological environment and the interaction of all components. Ecosystems theory is used to describe and analyze people and other living systems and their transactions.

EDUCATIONAL SUPERVISION: Supervision function concerned with providing the training that enables workers to achieve their objectives and the skills that prepare them to perform their jobs effectively and to function more autonomously.

EDUCATION FOR ALL HANDICAPPED CHILDREN ACT (P.L. 94-142): Passed in 1975 and mandates that public school education must accommodate the needs of all children. The law guarantees an appropriate free public education to all children ages 3 to 21 who need special education services, including those with physical disabilities, learning disorders, and other disabilities. An individualized educational program (IEP) must be developed for each student with a qualifying disability. The IEP must be written by a team of school personnel (which may include a school social worker) in collaboration with the student's parents and must provide the least restrictive environment for each student – this environment must be as similar as possible to the regular classroom setting taking into account the nature of the student's disability. Additionally, while reliable, valid, and nondiscriminatory psychological tests can be used, assignment to special education classes cannot be made on the basis of IQ tests only. Over time, P.L. 94-142 has been amended and, in 1990, it was renamed the Individuals with Disabilities Education Act, or IDEA, (P.L. 101-476).

EGO: As defined by Freud, the structure of the psyche that attempts to deal with reality in a practical, rational way (secondary process thinking) and that mediates the conflicting demands of the id, the superego, and reality; the "executive function" of the personality. Operates on the basis of the reality principle.

EGO DYSTONIC: (A.k.a. ego alien.) Descriptive of impulses, behaviors, wishes, etc., that are unacceptable to the ego, or to the person's ideal conception of self.

EGO FUNCTIONS (EGO TASKS): Include self-regulation and self-control; judgment; reality testing capacity; thought processes (cognitive functioning); capacity for interpersonal relationships (object relations); integrative functioning (synthesis); and defensive functioning (ego defense mechanisms). When healthy ego functions are characteristic of a person's long-term and current functioning (i.e., they don't disappear under conditions of stress), they are associated with effective functioning and a subjective sense of personal well-being. Generally, a social worker evaluates a client's ego functioning as it relates to the problem areas he/she has identified.

EGO SYNTONIC: Descriptive of values, feelings, behaviors, ideas, etc., that are consistent with a person's ego or sense of self; they feel real and acceptable to the consciousness.

ELDER ABUSE: Physical battering, neglect, psychological or emotional harm, and/or exploitation (e.g., financial) of older adults. Most often inflicted by those responsible for their care (e.g., their adult children, legal custodians, etc.). Two common causes of elder abuse are caregiver stress (a caregiver becomes overwhelmed by the demands of caring for a dependent older person and is then physically abusive in a moment of anger or begins to neglect the older person's needs) and caregiver impairment (the caregiver's mental illness or substance abuse).

EMOTIONAL MALTREATMENT (Children): (A.k.a. emotional abuse or neglect, psychological maltreatment.) The failure to provide for the appropriate emotional development of a child resulting in psychological damage to the child. May consist of acts of commission or acts of omission. May include verbal or emotional assault; isolation or close confinement; attempted physical assault; exploiting or corrupting the child; withholding necessities from the child as a form of punishment; and withholding emotional responsiveness from the child. Generally the most difficult form of child abuse to identify.

EMOTION-FOCUSED COPING VS. PROBLEM-FOCUSED COPING: Emotion-focused coping is used to reduce one's emotional response to stress, while problem-focused coping is used to deal directly with the source of stress. Usually a person must deal with his/her emotional reactions before moving on to problem-solving, but emotion-focused and task-focused coping often occur simultaneously.

EMPATHIC COMMUNICATION (EMPATHIC RESPONDING): A helping skill that involves first, empathic recognition of the client's feelings, and then, demonstrating through accurate reflection of those feelings one's understanding of the client's inner experiencing. See also *additive empathic responding* and *reciprocal empathic responding*.

EMPATHY: The ability to perceive, understand, and experience the emotional state of another person (Barker, 1987). Empathic responding is used throughout the helping process to develop rapport, maintain a working relationship, and enable social workers to move toward confronting a client's problematic issues. Fundamental to empathic responding is reflecting an understanding and acceptance of not only the client's overtly expressed feelings but also his/her underlying emotions. Can be conveyed through verbal and nonverbal communication.

EMPIRICALLY BASED PRACTICE: Social work intervention that uses research for practice and problem-solving. The social worker collects data to monitor interventions, makes note of problems, methods, and outcomes in terms that can be measured, and assesses the effectiveness of the interventions used. Methods for empirically assessing interventions are integrated into the social worker's practice and the results are used to guide his/her interventions. Whereas traditional social work applies existing theory to practice, empirically-based social work generates theories through conclusions that are based on observed empirical relationships.

EMPIRICALLY SUPPORTED TREATMENTS (ESTS): Specific psychological treatments that have been shown to be efficacious in controlled clinical trials. The research indicates that ESTs, in general, have the following characteristics: (a) Most ESTs include homework as a component; (b) ESTs generally focus on skill building, not insight or catharsis; (c) ESTs are problem-focused; (d) ESTs incorporate continuous assessment of client progress; and (e) ESTs involve brief treatment contact, requiring 20 or fewer sessions.

EMPOWERMENT: The process of helping individuals, families, groups, and communities increase their personal, interpersonal, socioeconomic, and political strength and develop influence toward changes their circumstances.

EMPOWERMENT APPROACH: A way of working with clients to help them acquire the personal, interpersonal, and political power they need to take control of their lives and bring about changes in policies, organizations, and public attitudes that are impacting their lives and the lives of their families in negative ways. Before choosing an empowerment strategy, the social worker must make sure that the client has, or is able to learn, the competencies needed to bring about changes in his/her environment and that the client's difficulties are caused primarily by social or political barriers and a lack of resources.

EMPTY CHAIR TECHNIQUE: (A.k.a. double-chair technique.) A technique used to help clients understand their feelings about themselves or a significant other. Is useful for clarifying issues involved in an interpersonal conflict so that clients can view the conflict in a different light and gain insight into the reasons underlying their own behavior. Using the technique involves placing an empty chair opposite the client, asking the client to explain to the chair (which represents the other person or the situation) his/her perceptions and/or feelings, and then asking the client to sit on the chair (to assume the role of the other person or the situation) and respond to what was just said. The social worker uses interviewing skills to explore the dialogue as it develops.

ENACTMENT: Technique used to create a situation in which you can observe clients' interactions directly. Generally entails asking clients to recreate a past conflict in your presence but can also involve having clients role-play contrived situations to find out how they interact when engaged in common activities such as planning, parenting, and decision-making.

ENCOURAGERS (PROMPTS OR FURTHERING RESPONSES): Single words, short phrases, or nonverbal gestures that encourage a client to continue talking. They convey an interest in and attention to what the client is saying. Examples include verbal encouragers ("minimal prompts") such as "I see" or "Please go on"; nonverbal encouragers, which include hand gestures, facial expressions, and nodding one's head; and accent responses, which entail repeating in a questioning or emphatic way a phrase or word the client has used.

ENMESHMENT: See *disengagement vs. enmeshment*.

ENURESIS: Enuresis involves repeated voiding of urine into the bed or clothes at least twice a week for three or more consecutive months. Urination is usually involuntary but can be intentional and is not due to substance use or a medical condition. Enuresis is diagnosed only when the individual is at least 5 years old or the equivalent developmental level. The bell-and-pad (urine alarm) is the most common treatment.

EQUIFINALITY: A term associated with family systems therapy that states that no matter where one enters the system, the patterning will be the same. According to this concept, different causes can produce the same results; therefore, a therapist studies patterns of behavior and interaction rather than individual topics.

EQUILIBRATION: According to Piaget, the tendency toward biological and psychological balance. Equilibration underlies cognitive development.

EQUIPOTENTIALITY: The concept in general systems theory that one cause may produce different results.

EQUITY THEORY: A theory of motivation that predicts that motivation (e.g., motivation to remain in a relationship) is affected by the comparison of input/outcome ratios.

ETHNOCENTRISM: Belief that one's own culture, ethnic or racial group, or nation is superior to others.

EVIDENCE-BASED PRACTICE: Combines the results of research with clinical experience, professional ethics, and client's needs and preferences, helping to guide the social worker in developing effective interventions. This helps to improve the services a social worker performs in focusing on the most effective approaches. Using a multi-step process, practitioners identify the questions for which they require answers, seek empirical evidence to answer those questions, and then apply selected approaches and evaluate the outcomes (Jenson & Howard, 2008).

EXCEPTIONAL ELIGIBILITY: Social service delivery policy in which benefits and services are developed for individuals in a special group (such as war veterans) due to sympathy for the group or political pressure. Eligibility is not necessarily based on need or circumstances.

EXISTENTIAL THERAPY: The existential therapies are derived from existential philosophy and share an emphasis on the human conditions of depersonalization, loneliness, and isolation and the assumption that people are not static but, instead, are in a constant state of "becoming."

EXPERT POWER: A source of power for supervisors and other leaders that exists when the leader has special knowledge and skills that his/her subordinates need. See also *bases of social power*.

EXPERT WITNESS: An individual who testifies before a lawmaking body or in a court of law because of his/her exceptional knowledge in a specific area. Information given by the witness is used to enlighten the court in assessing evidence.

EX-POST FACTO RESEARCH: "After the fact" research in which the experimental treatment (independent variable) has been applied prior to the onset of the study. Because ex-post facto studies do not allow the experimenter to control the assignment of subjects to treatment groups, they are considered a type of quasi-experimental research.

EXTENDED FAMILY SYSTEMS THERAPY (Bowen): School of family therapy that extends general systems theory beyond the nuclear family. The emphasis is on intellectual and emotional differentiation of individual family members; and key terms include differentiation of self, undifferentiated family ego mass, emotional triangles, and multigenerational transmission process. Therapy often begins with the construction of a genogram. The therapist often sees two members of the family (spouses) and forms a therapeutic triangle in which the therapist comes into emotional contact with the family members but avoids becoming emotionally triangled.

EXTERNAL VALIDITY: The degree to which a study's results can be generalized to other people, settings, conditions, etc.

EXTINCTION: See *classical extinction* and *operant extinction and extinction bursts*.

FACILITATIVE CONDITIONS (Rogers): For person-centered therapists, the three core conditions – empathy, genuineness (congruence), and unconditional positive regard – that must be provided to a client in therapy so that he/she can be steered back onto the path toward growth and self-actualization.

FACTIONAL ANALOGY: A way of viewing social systems. Assumes that conflict is fundamental and instability and change are ongoing: A social system is seen as made up of competing subunits that are disposed to conflict; and conflict is seen as so basic that change is likely to be disorderly and unstable. Rather than assuming that order can be restored, social workers using this analogy face conflict head-on.

FACTITIOUS DISORDER: Individuals with factitious disorder imposed on self falsify physical or psychological symptoms that are associated with their deception, present themselves to others as being ill or impaired, and engage in the deceptive behavior even in the absence of an obvious external reward for doing so. Individuals with factitious disorder imposed on another falsify physical or psychological symptoms in another person, present that person to others as being ill or impaired, and engage in the deceptive behavior even in the absence of an external reward. For both types of factitious disorder, falsification of symptoms can involve feigning, exaggeration, simulation, or induction (e.g., by ingestion of a substance or self-injury).

FADING: Fading refers to (a) the gradual withdrawal of prompts when teaching a new response and (b) a procedure used to eliminate an inappropriate stimulus-response connection by gradually replacing the inappropriate stimulus with appropriate stimuli so that the response becomes associated with the latter.

FAILURE TO THRIVE: Occurs when a baby's weight falls below the 5th percentile for his/her age. In "organic failure to thrive," there is an underlying medical condition that causes the slowed rate of growth. In "nonorganic failure to thrive," no medical cause can be found. Risk factors for nonorganic failure to thrive include maternal childhood deprivation, the infant's temperament (i.e., he/she is difficult to feed), and certain family characteristics such as high levels of stress, parents who don't understand the baby's nutritional needs, and poverty.

FAMILY LIFE-CYCLE THEORY: Proposes that families pass through expected stages that are demarcated by entrances and exits of family members and the shifts in role function that these changes in membership require. These stages include between families (unattached young adult), joining families through marriage (newly married couple), the family with young children, the family with adolescents, launching children and moving on, and the family in later life. Factors such as traumatic events and a rigid, dysfunctional family structure can make it difficult for a family to accomplish its developmental tasks and increase the likelihood that normal developmental change will be experienced as a crisis.

FAMILY MAP: Associated with structural family therapy; a symbolic representation of the family structure created from the therapist's observations of a family. Differs from a genogram in that it reflects the arrangement of the family members around issues of concern. Through a series of connected and interrelated frameworks, the map attempts to illustrate coalitions and boundaries and helps with planning the course of therapy. It allows the therapist to keep in mind both the individual's relationship to the family system and the family system's relationship to the individual.

FAMILY MYTHS: Beliefs shared by all family members with regard to each other and their relative positions in the family. Myths go unchallenged and maintain family homeostasis.

FAMILY RITUALS: Regular, predictable behaviors of the family that have a sense of rightness about them. The whole collection of observable behaviors that add up to rules. May be conscious or unconscious and may increase family cohesiveness or be seen as burdensome.

FAMILY RULES: Family rules – either overt or unconscious – illustrate a family's values and determine the behavior of the members. For example, a family rule may be "nobody challenges father." In this case, the implied rule prevents any members of the family from disagreeing or arguing with father. Thus, the "rule" directs and controls the family's behavior. Therapists often help a family modify rules that are no longer appropriate and causing difficulties in the family.

FEDERAL EDUCATIONAL RIGHTS AND PRIVACY ACT (BUCKLEY AMENDMENT): Federal law that grants parents (and students over the age of 18) the right to inspect their children's (their own) educational records.

FEEDBACK LOOP: In systems theory and cybernetics, the flow of information back into the system. Negative feedback loops minimize change and maintain the system's status quo (equilibrium), while positive feedback loops alter or disrupt the system's normal functioning.

FEMINIST THERAPY: Form of therapy that has its origins in the women's movement and that is based on the premise that "the personal is political." Focuses on empowerment and social change and acknowledges and minimizes the power differential inherent in the client-therapist relationship. Feminist therapy must be distinguished from nonsexist therapy, which focuses more on personal causes of behavior and personal change.

FETAL ALCOHOL SYNDROME (FAS): Caused by exposure to alcohol during prenatal development and may produce a variety of physical, behavioral, and cognitive symptoms depending on the amount consumed by the pregnant woman. Symptoms of FAS are largely irreversible and include facial deformities, retarded physical growth, heart defects, intellectual disability, hyperactivity, and irritability. Risk for FAS is highest, and symptoms are most severe, when the mother drinks heavily every day or, in the early stages of pregnancy, engages in binge drinking.

FIELD THEORY: Lewin's theory of human behavior that describes it as a product of interdependent factors in the person and his/her physical and social environment.

FIRST-GENERATION (TRADITIONAL) ANTIPSYCHOTICS: The first-generation antipsychotic drugs (e.g., phenothiazines) are used for the management of schizophrenia and other psychoses. They are most effective for positive symptoms (delusions, hallucinations, agitation, thought disorders). Side-effects include anticholinergic effects, extrapyramidal effects (e.g., tardive dyskinesia), and neuroleptic malignant syndrome. These drugs exert their beneficial effects primarily by blocking dopamine receptors, and their effectiveness provides support for the dopamine hypothesis which attributes schizophrenia to overactivity at dopamine receptors.

FIRST ORDER CHANGE: Changes in a system that are superficial and leave unaltered the fundamental organization of the system. Changes may look dramatic, but the system itself remains the same in terms of process and dynamics. In therapy, a family can be said to undergo first order change whenever it adapts but does not cease its symptomatic functioning. The family may previously have been symptomatic in "that" way but now it is symptomatic in "this" way.

FIXATION: In psychoanalysis, the notion that psychosexual development can be arrested at a particular stage such that the personality becomes structured around the unresolved conflict of that stage.

FIXED INTERVAL (FI) SCHEDULE: In operant conditioning, an intermittent reinforcement schedule in which the subject is reinforced for each predetermined interval of time in which he/she makes at least one response. Associated with a "scallop" on the cumulative recording of the subject's responses.

FIXED RATIO (FR) SCHEDULE: In operant conditioning, an intermittent reinforcement schedule in which the subject is reinforced following a predetermined number of responses (e.g., after each 10th response). The cumulative record exhibits "post-reinforcement pauses," especially as the number of responses required for reinforcement increases.

FLAT AFFECT (EMOTIONAL BLUNTING): A muted or apathetic response to stimuli that would normally evoke a stronger response (e.g., the client discusses a traumatic life event in a detached, matter-of-fact way). May indicate a mental disorder (e.g., depression or schizophrenia), substance use, or a medication side-effect.

FLAT-RATE FEE: A fixed, pre-established fee charged by a professional for a particular service. The fee for a given service is the same for every client, and the amount charged is related to the service itself rather than the client's ability to pay.

FLIGHT OF IDEAS: A verbal presentation in which the client's responses seem to "take off" based on a particular word or thought, unrelated to any logical progression or the original point of the communication.

FLOODING: A classical extinction technique that involves exposing the individual in vivo or in imagination to high anxiety-arousing stimuli. The key is exposing a client for long enough that he/she comes to see that none of the consequences he/she fears actually take place. When done in vivo, it is also known as in vivo exposure with response prevention.

FOCUSING RESPONSES: Social work interview technique used to keep the conversation from wandering or jumping from one subject to another.

FOOD ASSISTANCE PROGRAMS: For example, the Food Stamp, WIC, and school lunch programs. Social welfare benefits for qualified individuals to ensure that their nutritional needs are met.

FOOD STAMP PROGRAM: Social security program designed to improve the diets of poor and low-income families by enhancing their ability to buy food. The program issues monthly allotments of coupons that are redeemable at retail food stores or provides benefits through electronic benefit transfer (EBT). The EBT system allows food stamp customers, using a plastic card similar to a bank card, to buy groceries by transferring funds directly from a food stamp benefit account to a retailer's account. Households cannot use food stamps to buy alcoholic beverages or tobacco, lunch counter items or foods to be eaten in the store, vitamins or medicines, pet foods, or nonfood items (other than seeds and plants).

FORCE FIELD ANALYSIS (FFA): Technique used to identify and assess significant factors that promote or inhibit change in a community or organization. Involves analyzing social forces supporting an intended program or policy change (driving forces) and those opposing it (restraining forces): This includes rating each force's strength (power, consistency, openness to outside influence) and identifying and rating entities who might successfully oppose a driving or restraining force and, thereby, change its strength. These assessments are used to guide intervention planning.

FORMAL OPERATIONAL STAGE: Final stage in Piaget's model of cognitive development; begins around age 11 or 12. People at this stage are aware of their own thought processes and can think more systematically about abstract and hypothetical concepts and ideas.

FORMAL POWER: Power that stems from the position a person holds and the authority delegated to that position. Formal power is acquired automatically when a person assumes a position of leadership.

FORMATIVE EVALUATION (Direct Practice Evaluation): Evaluation used to guide ongoing practice decisions. A tool for monitoring an intervention and identifying when one needs to modify a planned intervention.

FORMATIVE EVALUATION (Program Evaluation): Describes the research goal when a program is in the process of being developed: The goal is to determine what modifications are needed so that the program achieves its goal and objectives. Formative evaluation is most useful when observational methods are used. Compared to summative evaluation, formative evaluation tends to be less threatening to program personnel because its results are used to modify a program rather than to make decisions about whether or not it should continue. Results of formative evaluation are not usually generalizable to other programs.

FREUDIAN PSYCHOANALYSIS: The goal of psychoanalytic psychotherapy is to reduce or eliminate pathological symptoms by bringing the unconscious into conscious awareness and integrating previously repressed material into the personality. During psychoanalysis, the analysis of free associations, dreams, resistances, and transferences consists of a combination of confrontation, clarification, interpretation, and working through.

FUNCTIONAL ANALYSIS: In behavioral assessments, an assessment of the environmental variables (i.e., antecedents and consequences) that control a behavior.

FUNCTIONAL BUDGETING AND PROGRAM BUDGETING: Relatively sophisticated budgeting techniques that are based on program planning and budgeting systems (PPBS). These approaches produce cost and expenditure data in relation to programs rather than in relation to the entire agency; and produce data such as total program costs, cost per unit of service, cost per output (client completion of program or service), and cost per outcome (the cost of producing measurable change in a client's quality of life).

FUNCTIONAL COMMUNITY: A community defined in terms of a purpose, function, or problem that needs to be addressed. Social workers, for example, belong to the welfare or human services functional community.

FUNCTIONAL POWER: Power that depends on the person holding the leadership position. Functional power must be earned.

FUSION: Associated with Bowen; the blurring of intellectual and emotional boundaries between the self and others arising out of an overly strong emotional attachment. Fusion is the opposite of differentiation of self.

GANTT CHART: Scheduling technique that graphically represents all of an organization's or program's activities, the people responsible for performing the activities, and a time-line for completing each activity. Horizontal bars on a calendar show the time allotted to each activity. The chart does not indicate the relationships among activities and, therefore, is less detailed than a PERT chart.

GEMEINSCHAFT AND GESELLSCHAFT: "Gemeinschaft" refers to community. It focuses on intimacy and relationship and emphasizes the mutual, common, and intimate bonds that bring people together in local units. The group is valued whether or not its members are creating a product or achieving a goal. Examples include the domestic unit, neighborhood, and groups of friends. "Gesellschaft" refers to society or association (e.g., the city or state). It represents formalized, task-oriented relationships in which people organize to achieve a purpose, goal, or task. People may benefit personally from these relationships, but their purpose is to create a product, achieve a goal, or complete a task.

GENDER DYSPHORIA (in Adolescents and Adults): The essential feature of gender dysphoria in adolescents or adults is a marked incongruence between assigned gender and experienced or expressed gender that is manifested by at least two symptoms (e.g., marked incongruence between one's primary and/or secondary sex characteristics and one's experienced or expressed gender, strong desire for the primary and/or secondary sex characteristics of the opposite gender, strong desire to be of the opposite gender, strong conviction that one has the feelings and reactions that are characteristic of the opposite gender). Symptoms must have a duration of at least six months and cause clinically significant distress or impaired functioning.

GENDER DYSPHORIA (in Children): For gender dysphoria in children, the diagnostic criteria are a marked incongruence between assigned gender at birth and experienced or expressed gender as evidenced by a strong desire to be the opposite sex and at least five symptoms (e.g., strong preference for wearing clothes of the other gender, strong preference for cross-gender roles during play, strong preference for toys and activities typically used or engaged in by the other gender, strong preference for playmates of the opposite gender, strong desire for primary and/or secondary sex characteristics of one's experienced gender). Symptoms must have a duration of at least six months and cause clinically significant distress or impaired functioning.

GENDER IDENTITY: An individual's sense of self as a male, female, a blend of both, or neither. This may be similar or different than the assigned sex at birth.

GENDER ROLE DEVELOPMENT: According to Kohlberg's cognitive-developmental theory, gender-role development involves a sequence of stages that parallels cognitive development: By age 2 or 3, children acquire a gender identity (i.e., they recognize that they are either male or female). Soon thereafter, children realize that gender identity is stable over time (gender stability). By age 6 or 7, children understand that gender is constant over situations and know that people cannot change gender by superficially altering their external appearance or behavior (gender constancy).

GENERAL ADAPTATION SYNDROME: According to Selye, the human response to stress is mediated by adrenal-pituitary secretions (e.g., cortisol) and involves three stages: alarm reaction, resistance, and exhaustion. The model predicts that prolonged stress can result in illness or death.

GENERAL ASSISTANCE (GA): (A.k.a. General relief, general public assistance.) Aid provided by state and local governments to needy individuals or families who do not qualify for major assistance programs and to individuals whose benefits from other assistance programs are insufficient to meet basic needs. General assistance is often the only resource for individuals who cannot qualify for unemployment insurance or whose benefits are inadequate or exhausted. Help may either be in cash or in-kind, including such assistance as groceries and rent. The eligibility requirements and payment levels for general assistance vary from state to state and often within a state. Payments are usually at lower levels and of shorter duration than those provided by federally financed programs. General assistance is administered and financed by state and local governments under their own guidelines.

GENERALIZED ANXIETY DISORDER (GAD): GAD involves excessive anxiety and worry about multiple events or activities, which are relatively constant for at least six months, the person finds difficult to control, and cause clinically significant distress or impaired functioning. Anxiety and worry must include at least three characteristic symptoms (or at least one symptom for children) – restlessness or feeling keyed up or on edge; being easily fatigued; difficulty concentrating; irritability; muscle tension; sleep disturbance. Treatment usually involves cognitive-behavioral therapy or a combination of cognitive-behavioral therapy and pharmacotherapy.

GENERAL SYSTEMS THEORY: The theory that the "whole" can be understood only in terms of the organization and interactions of its components; the theoretical framework underlying family therapy. Systems can be either "open" or "closed": Open systems receive input from and discharge output to the environment; closed systems have no exchange with the environment. Families are primarily open systems.

GENOGRAM: An assessment tool used to obtain and record information about a client's family patterns and history. Provides a schematic diagram of the family system describing at least three generations of family relationships, geographical locations, and significant life events.

GENOTYPE VS. PHENOTYPE: "Genotype" refers to a person's genetic make-up; "phenotype" refers to observable characteristics, which are due to a combination of genetic and environmental factors.

GESTALT THERAPY: A humanistic therapeutic technique based on the concepts of Gestalt psychology ("the whole is greater than the sum of its parts"). Gestalt therapy adopts a here-and-now approach, views "awareness" as the primary goal of treatment, and defines neurosis as a "growth disorder" reflecting certain "boundary disturbances" (e.g., introjection) and involving an abandonment of the self for the self image.

GLOBALIZATION: The "growing interconnectedness and integration of economies across national borders"; also involves "the diffusion of social, cultural and political ideas" (Gabel and Healy, 2012).

GOALS AND OBJECTIVES (Direct Practice): A goal is an outcome sought by the social worker and client and is generally phrased as a broad statement that describes the desired outcome. Objectives (behavioral objectives) are discrete steps that will be taken to achieve the desired outcome. They define a series of behavioral changes that must take place in order to reach a goal. Objectives are more specific than goals and are always written in a manner that facilitates measurement and evaluation.

GOODNESS-OF-FIT MODEL (Thomas and Chess): Proposes that behavioral and adjustment outcomes are best for children when parents' caregiving behaviors match the child's temperament.

GRANT: A transfer of money or other assets from a government, organization, or person to another organization or person so that the latter can achieve a particular function or purpose (typically, to educate or otherwise improve the well-being of people and cultural institutions).

GRASS-ROOTS ORGANIZING: Community social work method directed toward helping community members develop shared goals, strengthen their relationships, and organize in a way that will help them achieve their goals. The emphasis is on organizing all people who will be affected by a change rather than just the community's leaders. It differs from a more bureaucratic means to social change, or one involving decisions that come from power centers in the community.

GROUP COHESION: The feeling of solidarity among group members. Cohesiveness is high in smaller groups; when initiation or entry into the group is difficult; when members are relatively homogeneous; and when there is an external threat.

GROUP POLARIZATION AND RISKY SHIFT PHENOMENON: The tendency of groups to make more extreme decisions (either more conservative or more risky) than individual members would have made alone. The tendency to make decisions in the risky direction only is referred to as the "risky shift phenomenon."

GROUPTHINK: Mode of group thinking in which group members' desires for unanimity and cohesiveness override their ability to realistically appraise or determine alternative courses of action. Can be alleviated by encouraging dissent, having someone play devil's advocate, and refraining from reaching a decision or solution too quickly.

GROUP TREATMENT APPROACH (REMEDIAL MODEL): Type of small group work in which the group is seen as a therapeutic environment that has the potential to influence members to change their behavior. Treatment groups help members cope with serious problems or correct dysfunctional behavior, and the social worker assumes the role of a therapist, expert, and group leader. The primary focus is on the members as individuals and on the problems they are having outside the group, but a member's behavior during group meetings may be used as a way of assessing and illustrating his/her attitudes and behavioral patterns.

GROWTH/DEVELOPMENT AND TRAINING GROUPS: Social work groups used to promote members' normal growth and development and teach ordinary skills for living. Groups used to teach and train are goal oriented, and the social worker assumes the roles of leader, teacher, and planner and arranger of group activities and relies heavily on programming. Some of these groups emphasize member interaction, building trust, and developing a sense of belonging to the group and others do not. Examples of topics addressed in these groups include parent training, learning communications skills, learning job skills, learning about a medical condition, etc.

GUARDIAN (LEGAL GUARDIAN): An individual who is legally responsible for the management and care of another individual. Usually, this other individual is a child or is an adult who has been determined by a court to be incapable of acting on his/her own behalf.

GUARDIAN AD LITEM: A person (usually an attorney) appointed by the court to represent the child(ren) in a legal dispute concerning their custody or welfare. This person is empowered to investigate the background, living conditions, family relationships, and any other relevant matter in order to make a recommendation to the court as to what would be in the best interests of the child(ren) in terms of placement, visitation, and other matters ruled on by the court. The guardian usually makes a report to the court recommending an outcome. The judge, however, makes the final determination on the disposition of the child(ren).

HAART (HIGHLY ACTIVE ANTIRETROVIRAL THERAPY): Term used to describe a medication regimen taken by patients with HIV/AIDS that includes combination of anti-HIV drugs from at least two of the main classes. This combination helps combat new resistant strains of the virus that emerge as HIV makes copies of itself and also decreases the rate of opportunistic infections.

HALLUCINATIONS: Sensory perceptions occurring without external stimulation of the associated sensory organ.

HAWTHORNE EFFECT: Refers to a change in performance resulting from participation in a research study (the novelty of the situation, increased attention, etc.).

HAZARDOUS EVENT (Crisis): An initial shock that disrupts a person's equilibrium and initiates a series of reactions that may culminate in a crisis. The hazardous event may be anticipated (e.g., marriage, retirement) or unanticipated (e.g., the unexpected death of a family member).

HELPING SOCIAL NETWORKS: Networks that allow individuals in a community to give and receive reciprocal help for specific problems and that exist whether a person uses them or not. They differ from close-knit networks because their concerns are specialized (i.e., they are problem-anchored), their membership is heterogeneous, and their members may lack other common values.

HETERONOMOUS VS. AUTONOMOUS MORALITY: Piaget distinguished between two stages of moral development. The stage of "heteronomous morality" (morality of constraint) extends from about age 7 through age 10. During this stage, children believe that rules are set by authority figures and are unalterable. When judging whether an act is "right" or "wrong," they consider whether a rule has been violated and what the consequences of the act are. Beginning at about age 11, children enter the stage of "autonomous morality" (morality of cooperation). Children in this stage view rules as being arbitrary and alterable when the people who are governed by them agree to change them. When judging an act, they focus more on the intention of the actor than on the act's consequences.

HIGH-CONTEXT VS. LOW-CONTEXT COMMUNICATION: Refers to different communication styles exhibited by different cultural groups. Members of many culturally diverse groups in America exhibit high-context communication, which relies on shared cultural understanding and nonverbal cues. In contrast, Anglos are more likely to exhibit low-context communication, which relies primarily on the verbal message.

HISTRIONIC PERSONALITY DISORDER: Histrionic personality disorder is characterized by a pervasive pattern of emotionality and attention-seeking as manifested by at least five characteristic symptoms (e.g., discomfort when not the center of attention, inappropriately sexually seductive or provocative, rapidly shifting and shallow emotions, consistent use of physical appearance to gain attention, considers relationships to be more intimate than they are).

HIV/AIDS (ACQUIRED IMMUNE DEFICIENCY SYNDROME): A.k.a. HIV disease. A viral disease caused by the human immunodeficiency virus (HIV), which may be transmitted by sexual contact, blood-to-blood contact, and from a pregnant woman to her unborn child. HIV suppresses the body's immune system and, therefore, results in a vulnerability to a range of opportunistic infections including Kaposi's sarcoma (a form of cancer) and a rare form of pneumonia. These diseases are known as opportunistic infections because they take advantage of a compromised immune system that is no longer able to fight them off.

HOARDING DISORDER: Hoarding disorder involves a persistent difficulty discarding or parting with possessions regardless of their actual value. The difficulty results in the accumulation of items that block and clutter living areas and significantly interferes with their intended use and stems from a perceived need to save the items and distress associated with discarding them. If living areas are uncluttered, it's only because of intervention by third parties.

HOLDER OF THE PRIVILEGE: The person who decides what confidential information is to be released, particularly in the context of legal proceedings. Generally, laws related to privilege make the client the holder of the privilege.

HOMEOSTASIS: The self-maintenance of a system (e.g., a family) in a state of equilibrium or status quo. Homeostasis is facilitated by negative feedback loops, which provide the system with the information it needs to make appropriate adjustments in its functioning.

HORIZONTAL COMMUNITY: Consists of linkages between and among organizations and neighborhoods that are located within the same geographic region and, usually, serve the community.

HOSPICE CARE: An interdisciplinary approach to caring for individuals with terminal illness when recovery is unlikely (most hospices accept patients who have a life expectancy of six months or less and are referred by their personal physician). Care may be provided in the individual's home, a nursing home, or a hospice unit in a hospital or community agency. Hospice care integrates medical, psychological, and social approaches. It emphasizes quality of life; holistic approaches to pain control (psychological and spiritual pain); palliative care (specialized care when curative treatments are no longer available); and the involvement of family and others in caring for the patient. Hospice programs also support caregivers by offering convalescent and respite care.

HOSPITALISM: A term used by Spitz to describe the syndrome found in infants who have been separated from their mothers or other primary caregiver. Symptoms include listlessness, unresponsiveness, indifference, and retarded growth.

HOUSING ASSISTANCE: In most communities, there are three kinds of housing assistance available: (a) Public housing, in which low-income housing is operated by the housing authority; (b) Section 8 housing, in which the housing authority gives tenants a certificate or voucher that says the government will subsidize their rent payments, and tenants find their own housing; and (c) privately owned subsidized housing, in which the government provides subsidies directly to the owner who then applies those subsidies to the rents he/she charges low-income tenants.

HUMAN PLASTICITY: The concept that variations in the environment can affect a person's personality, cognitive and social functioning, and physical and mental health, independent of his/her genetic endowment. Describes one way that the environment can influence development over the lifespan.

HUMAN RELATIONS: Management theory that developed as an alternative to scientific management and places greater emphasis on worker needs, motives, and relationships.

HUMAN RESOURCE PLANNING: The process used by an agency to predict personnel needs to implement its mission. Human resource plans include job analysis (which is used to develop job descriptions); a recruitment and selection strategy; plans for staff orientation, supervision, training, and development; a performance-appraisal system based on the job analysis; and policies and procedures for termination.

HUNTINGTON'S DISEASE: Inherited disorder characterized by cognitive decline, chorea (involuntary tremors, twitching), and athetosis (slow writhing movements).

HYPERTENSION: "Primary (essential) hypertension" is diagnosed when high blood pressure is not due to a known physiological cause, while "secondary hypertension" is diagnosed when elevated blood pressure is related to a known disease. Primary hypertension accounts for about 85 to 90 percent of all cases of high blood pressure; untreated, it can lead to cardiovascular disease, and it is a major cause of heart failure, kidney failure, and stroke. High risk is associated with gender (males), obesity, cigarette smoking, excessive use of salt, and genetics (e.g., African-American heritage).

HYPERTHYROIDISM: A condition caused by hypersecretion of thyroxine by the thyroid gland and characterized by a speeded-up metabolism, elevated body temperature, accelerated heart rate, increased appetite with weight loss, nervousness, and insomnia.

HYPOGLYCEMIA: Low blood glucose. A condition caused by excessive secretion of insulin by the pancreas and characterized by hunger, dizziness, headaches, blurred vision, palpitations, anxiety, depression, and confusion.

HYPOMANIC EPISODE: A distinct period of abnormally and persistently elevated, expansive, or irritable mood that lasts for at least four days and is accompanied by at least three of the symptoms associated with a manic episode. The episode represents a clear change in mood and functioning but (in contrast to a manic episode) is not sufficiently severe to cause marked impairment in functioning or to require hospitalization, and there is an absence of psychotic symptoms.

HYPOTHYROIDISM: A condition caused by hyposecretion of thyroxine and characterized by a slowed metabolism, slowed heart rate, lethargy, lowered body temperature, impaired concentration and memory, and depression.

ID: According to Freud, the aspect of the psyche that is present at birth, contains the libido and other instincts, and seeks immediate gratification of its impulses. Operates on the basis of the pleasure principle and relies on primary process thinking.

IDENTIFICATION (Freud): The internalization of the characteristics of the same-sex parent into one's superego; represents the successful resolution of the Oedipus conflict.

IDENTIFICATION (Social Influence): Occurs when a person changes his/her behavior because he/she wants to be liked by or identified with another person. The behavior change reflects a private change in opinion or attitude, but the change is maintained only as long as the person continues to like or admire the influencing agent. Referent power is likely to produce identification. See also *bases of social power; compliance;* and *internalization*.

IDENTIFIED PATIENT: The family member who is identified by the family as bearing the symptom. The IP has typically been labeled by the family as "crazy" or "sick."

IDENTITY STATUSES (Marcia): Marcia proposes that the achievement of an identity (including values, beliefs, and goals) involves four stages that take place primarily during adolescence and young adulthood: diffusion, foreclosure, moratorium, and achievement.

INCOME MAINTENANCE PROGRAMS: Social welfare programs that provide individuals with sufficient goods and services or financial aid to maintain a certain standard of living.

INDEPENDENT VARIABLE: The variable that is manipulated in a research study for the purpose of determining its effects on the dependent variable. Also known as the experimental variable. In direct practice evaluation, the intervention is the independent variable.

INDIAN CHILD WELFARE ACT: Gives tribes in the U.S. control over the adoption of Native American children. Adoptions involving Native American children require a release from the birth parents and the tribe, and the tribe may veto the adoption of a Native American baby by a non-Native American family (even if the birth family has agreed to the adoption) and place the child with a Native American family

INDIRECT PRACTICE: Social work activities undertaken to provide services more effectively and efficiently and to bring about changes in policies, programs, or budgets. Indirect practice activities do not involve personal contact with clients and usually are undertaken with a committee, coalition, or other group.

INDIVIDUALISM (Social Policy): In regard to social policy, an ideology that attempts to place few restrictions on personal freedom and individual will.

INDIVIDUALISM (Worldview): Individualism centers on the personal rather than on the social group or social context in which a person lives. A person with this worldview (a) emphasizes personal self-concept over family life; (b) relates his/her sense of well-being to a sense of personal control; (c) attributes events or behaviors to dispositional factors; (d) sees events in terms of personal preferences; (e) prefers goal-oriented, direct, low-context communication; and (f) in conflict situations, prefers a confrontational and attributional approach.

INDIVIDUALS WITH DISABILITIES EDUCATION ACT, OR IDEA, (P.L. 101-476): See *Education For All Handicapped Children Act*.

INFORMATION AND REFERRAL SERVICE (I&R): Agency (or office within an agency) that notifies individuals about existing programs, resources (including referrals to other services), and benefits and how to obtain and use them.

INFORMATION PROCESSING THEORY: Views cognitive development as a function of both continued development of the brain and nervous system and learning experiences and practice that allow a child to progressively improve his/her mental abilities and strategies. Focuses on specific processes – how children acquire information (perception), remember information and retrieve it (memory), and use information to solve problems. Infant measures of information processing may be effective for identifying children at risk for future learning problems.

INFORMED CONSENT: The giving of permission by a client to a social worker and agency to use a specific intervention, including diagnosis, treatment, follow-up, and research. The practice is designed to protect individuals by guaranteeing their safety, privacy, and freedom. Generally, true informed consent can be obtained only when the individual is competent, free from pressure and coercion, and knowledgeable about the treatment to be provided including alternative treatments.

INITIATING STRUCTURE (Leadership): A dimension of leadership behavior that refers to the extent to which a leader defines, directs, and structures his/her own role and the roles of subordinates. Leaders high in initiating structure are task-oriented and concerned with the instrumental aspects of the job. Leaders who communicate both high performance expectations (instrumental) and support (expressive) are likely to have the most effective work groups. See also *consideration*.

INPUT, THROUGHPUT, AND OUTPUT: Systems (e.g., organizations) are made up collections of parts that receive inputs, operate on these inputs via throughput, and produce outputs. In social agencies, "inputs" include resources, clients, the types and severity of clients' problems, and the values, expectations, and opinions about the agency held by community members, funding sources, regulatory bodies, and other parts of the environment. "Throughputs" are the services provided by the agency and the way the agency is structured to apply its technology to the inputs it receives. "Output" is the completion of a service to a client – the key aspect of service output is outcome, which is a measure of quality-of-life change for the client.

IN-SERVICE TRAINING: Planned, formal training provided to a group of agency personnel with the same job classification or the same job responsibilities and designed to meet their general educational needs. The generic content is useful for all the members of the group but is specifically relevant to none of them.

INSIGHT LEARNING (Kohler): (A.k.a. the "aha" experience.) Refers to the apparent sudden understanding of the relationship between elements in a problem-solving situation.

INSOMNIA DISORDER: Insomnia disorder is characterized by dissatisfaction with sleep quality or quantity that is associated with at least one characteristic symptom – difficulty initiating sleep; difficulty maintaining sleep; early-morning awakening with an inability to return to sleep. The sleep disturbance occurs at least three nights each week, has been present for at least three months, occurs despite sufficient opportunities for sleep, and causes significant distress or impaired functioning.

INSTITUTIONAL RACISM: The denial or restriction of material conditions (e.g., access to health care) and access to power to members of minority groups.

INSTITUTIONAL SOCIAL SERVICES: Social services provided by major public service systems that administer benefits such as financial assistance, housing programs, health care, or education.

INSTRUMENTAL ACTIVITIES OF DAILY LIVING: Skills beyond basic self-care that evaluate how individuals function in their homes, workplaces, and social environments.

INTAKE PROCEDURES: Procedures used by social agencies to make initial contacts with clients productive and helpful. The social worker emphasizes obtaining preliminary information from the client in order to determine whether he/she can work with the client or should refer the client to a more suitable agency or professional.

INTEGRATED COMMUNITIES: A "well-integrated" community is associated with a low rate of mental disorders. Indicators of high integration include strong community associations and groups, able and adequate leadership, diverse recreational and leisure opportunities, cohesive informal social networks, high income level and stable incomes, acknowledgment and resolution of differences between cultures, and an emphasis on religious and spiritual values.

INTELLECTUAL DISABILITY: Intellectual disability is diagnosed in the presence of (a) deficits in intellectual functions (e.g., reasoning, problem solving, abstract thinking); (b) deficits in adaptive functioning that result in a failure to meet community standards of personal independence and social responsibility and impair functioning across multiple environments in one or more activities of daily life; and (c) an onset of intellectual and adaptive functioning deficits during the developmental period. Four degrees of severity (mild, moderate, severe, and profound) are based on adaptive functioning in conceptual, social, and practical domains.

INTERDISCIPLINARY TEAMING: (A.k.a. interprofessional teaming, multidisciplinary teaming.) A form of intervention in which the members of different professions or disciplines (e.g., social work, medical, psychiatric) work together on behalf of a client. For team practice to be effective, team members from different professions must be able to reach an agreement regarding approaches to care and willing to move beyond their own expertise to address the needs of the "whole" client.

INTERMITTENT (PARTIAL) REINFORCEMENT SCHEDULE: In operant conditioning, any pattern of reinforcement that is not continuous. Includes fixed interval, fixed ratio, variable interval, and variable ratio schedules. Associated with greater resistance to extinction than a continuous schedule.

INTERNALIZATION: Occurs when a person changes his/her behavior because he/she actually (privately) accepts the beliefs, attitudes, or behaviors of another person. Expert, legitimate, and informational power are most likely to result in internalization. See also *bases of social power; compliance;* and *identification (social influence)*.

INTERNAL VALIDITY: The degree to which a research study allows an investigator to conclude that observed variability in a dependent variable is due to the independent variable rather than to other factors.

INTERPERSONAL THERAPY: Interpersonal therapy (IPT) was originally developed as a treatment for depression but has since been applied to other conditions as well. Although IPT recognizes the contributions of early experience, biological predisposition, and personality to depression, its focus is on one of four areas of interpersonal functioning – grief, interpersonal role disputes, role transitions, and interpersonal deficits.

INTERPRETATION (INTERPRETIVE RESPONSE): An explanatory statement that responds to something about a client's thinking or behavior that the client is not aware of with the goal of increasing the client's self-understanding and understanding of the problem, fostering his/her insight, and/or helping him/her make new connections. This helps the client view a problem from a different perspective, which can open the door to new solutions. An interpretive response includes not only what a client has verbalized but also an inference the social worker has drawn from implicit parts of the client's message.

INTERVAL SCALE: The scale of measurement that has equal intervals between successive points on the measurement scale. Most standardized educational and psychological tests provide scores that represent an interval scale. With an interval scale, the property of equal intervals allows you to perform the mathematical operations of addition and subtraction with the data.

INTROJECTION: A defense mechanism. Involves ascribing the thoughts and behaviors of others to oneself to better control one's affective responses to those thoughts and behaviors. Typically operative at a very early age.

IN VIVO EXPOSURE WITH RESPONSE PREVENTION (FLOODING): See *flooding*.

ISOLATION OF AFFECT: A defense mechanism. Involves severing the conscious psychological connection between an unacceptable impulse or behavior and its original memory source; the person remembers the experience but separates it from the affect associated with it.

I-STATEMENTS (I-MESSAGES): Statements used to send clear and direct messages, thereby reducing the likelihood that the person receiving the message will be put on the defensive. An I-statement consists of a brief, clear description of a behavior by the other person that one is bothered by, the feeling one experienced as a result of that behavior, and description of the tangible impact the behavior has had on oneself or others. During intervention, I-statements made by a social worker are useful for managing situations of confrontation or conflict with a client and turning them into opportunities for the client to grow. The I-statement can also be taught to clients as a method for helping them deal with interpersonal conflict.

JOINING: In structural family therapy, the therapist's linking (blending) with the family as a group and with each family member by showing that he/she understands their unique experiences. Includes adopting a family's behaviors, affective style, and communication patterns.

KOHLBERG'S LEVELS OF MORAL DEVELOPMENT: According to Kohlberg's cognitive-developmental theory, moral development coincides with changes in logical reasoning and social perspective-taking and involves three levels that each include two stages: preconventional (punishment and obedience; instrumental hedonism); conventional (good boy/good girl; law and order); and postconventional (morality of contract, individual rights, and democratically-accepted laws; morality of individual principles of conscious).

KORSAKOFF SYNDROME: Alcohol-induced disorder characterized by anterograde and retrograde amnesia and confabulation. Has been linked to a thiamine deficiency. (In the DSM-5, this condition is called alcohol-induced major neurocognitive disorder, amnestic-confabulatory type.)

KUBLER-ROSS: Kubler-Ross developed a five-stage model of adjustment to the idea of one's own death: denial, anger, bargaining, depression, and acceptance.

LATENT LEARNING (Tolman): Proposes that learning can occur without reinforcement and without being manifested in actual performance improvement. Tolman's research showed that rats formed "cognitive maps" of mazes even without being reinforced for doing so.

LAW OF EFFECT (Thorndike): Thorndike's law of effect proposes that, when behaviors are followed by "satisfying consequences," they are more likely to increase or occur again.

LEADERSHIP STYLES: (a) "Autocratic leaders" make decisions alone and instruct subordinates what to do on the basis of those decisions. (b) "Democratic leaders" involve subordinates in the decision-making process. (c) "Laissez-faire leaders" leave it up to their subordinates to make decisions with little guidance or help.

LEARNED HELPLESSNESS MODEL: Seligman's learned helplessness model proposes that depression is due to exposure to uncontrollable negative events and internal, stable, and global attributions for those events. A reformulation of the theory by Abramson, Metalsky, and Alloy emphasizes the role of hopelessness.

LEGITIMATE/POSITIONAL POWER: A source of power that automatically stems from the authority associated with a leadership position (such as supervisor) and does not depend on the person holding the position. See also *bases of social power*.

LIBERALISM: Ideology that embraces the values of egalitarianism and social responsibility as means of achieving social and economic change and the belief that, as societies become more complex and its members less self-sufficient, government should take action to address the problems of individuals who are less able to cope.

LIBIDO: According to Freud, the psychic energy that is generated by the instinctual drives of the id.

LIFE CYCLE MATRIX: Assessment tool used to graphically depict the developmental stage of all individuals in a household.

LIFE HISTORY GRID: Assessment tool used to graphically depict significant events in a client's life and the development of significant problems over time. Allows you to organize and depict data related to various periods in a client's life.

LINE-ITEM BUDGETING: Simple budgeting technique that involves identifying expenditure categories and estimating the number of dollars that would be needed to cover all expenses in each category for one year. Categories typically include personnel and operating expenses such as rent, utilities, supplies, and travel, etc.

LINKAGE: Bringing together the resources of various agencies, personnel, etc., and coordinating their efforts on behalf of a client or social objective.

LITHIUM: Drug used to alleviate mania and mood swings in bipolar disorder. Lithium can be toxic and blood levels need to be monitored. Retention of lithium is affected by the body's sodium levels and users must make sure their salt levels do not fluctuate. Early signs of toxicity include diarrhea, nausea, vomiting, sedation, slurred speech, coordination problems, and confusion.

LIVE SUPERVISION: Supervision procedure in which a supervisor observes an interview in real time and is able to give the worker immediate feedback. The supervisor may sit in on the interview or watch it through a one-way mirror or video camera pickup. Traditional live supervision formats include "knock-on-the-door" supervision and "bug-in-the-ear" supervision. More current formats, including "bug-in-the-eye" (BITE) supervision, rely more on computer technology.

LIVING WILL: A type of advance directive in which a person documents in advance the kind of care he/she wants to receive and not receive at the end stage of life in the event that he/she is no longer able to communicate these preferences at that time.

LOCALITY (COMMUNITY) DEVELOPMENT MODEL: Community organizing model that focuses on promoting economic and social development for the whole community and helping the community help itself. The client system includes all groups within a geographic-spatial community, and community power centers are viewed as potential collaborators in an action. Emphases include voluntary cooperation, self-help, development of local leadership, education, and democratic processes.

LOCUS OF CONTROL: A construct developed by Rotter to describe the extent to which an individual believes that life events are under his/her own control ("internal locus of control") or under the control of external forces ("external locus of control"). The research suggests that "high internals" attribute their success to intrinsic factors and are more achievement-oriented, self-confident, and willing to work hard to achieve personal goals; are less anxious, suspicious, and dogmatic; and tend to be better adjusted than "high externals."

LONGITUDINAL STUDIES: Studies in which a group of subjects are followed and evaluated over an extended period of time in order to assess the effects of aging, natural developmental processes, or one or more other independent variable on one or more dependent variables over time.

LONG-TERM CARE (LTC): Comprehensive long-term social, personal, and health care services given to individuals who have lost some degree of functioning (i.e., due to a functional impairment, they have limited ability to perform important activities of daily living). LTC may be provided in nursing homes or in the community and is provided by professionals, volunteers, and family members.

LOOSE ASSOCIATIONS (DERAILMENT OF THOUGHT): Involve abrupt shifts from one fragmented thought to another with little if any logical connection between the thoughts.

LOW-CONTEXT COMMUNICATION: See *high-context vs. low-context communication*.

LOW-INCOME HOME ENERGY ASSISTANCE: Through LIHEAP, the federal government provides grants to states, territories, Indian tribes, and tribal organizations to help low-income households meet home heating and cooling costs and to weatherize and make energy saving repairs.

MACRO ORIENTATION: Orientation to social work that emphasizes the sociopolitical, economic, historical, and environmental factors that affect the human condition. These factors either cause problems for people or afford them opportunities for growth, satisfaction, and justice.

MACRO PRACTICE: Social work activities undertaken to benefit large groups such as a particular client population, the residents of a community, or the personnel at an agency, and designed to improve the quality of life for clients or communities served or the quality of work life for employees at an organization so that they can provide the best possible services to clients or communities.

MAHLER'S OBJECT-RELATIONS THEORY: Object-relations approaches emphasize the impact of early relationships with other people ("objects") on personality development; for object-relations theorists, maladaptive behavior is the result of abnormalities in early object relations. Mahler's version of this approach stresses events that occur during the separation-individuation process.

MAJOR AND MILD NEUROCOGNITIVE DISORDERS: Major neurocognitive disorder (formerly dementia) is diagnosed when there is evidence of significant decline from a previous level of functioning in one or more cognitive domains that interferes with the individual's independence in everyday activities and does not occur only in the context of delirium. Mild neurocognitive disorder (formerly cognitive disorder NOS) is the appropriate diagnosis when there is evidence of a modest decline from a previous level of functioning in one or more cognitive domains that does not interfere with the individual's independence in everyday activities and does not occur only in the context of delirium. Subtypes are based on etiology and include major and mild neurocognitive disorder due to Alzheimer's disease, vascular disease, traumatic brain injury, HIV infection, Parkinson's disease, and Huntington's disease.

MAJOR DEPRESSIVE DISORDER: A diagnosis of major depressive disorder requires the presence of at least five symptoms of a major depressive episode nearly every day for at least two weeks, with at least one symptom being depressed mood or loss of interest or pleasure. Symptoms are depressed mood (or, in children and adolescents, a depressed or irritable mood); markedly diminished interest or pleasure in most or all activities; significant weight loss when not dieting or weight gain or a decrease or increase in appetite; insomnia or hypersomnia; psychomotor agitation or retardation; fatigue or loss of energy; feelings of worthless or excessive guilt; diminished ability to think or concentrate; recurrent thoughts of death, recurrent suicidal ideation, or a suicide attempt. Symptoms cause clinically significant distress or impaired functioning. Treatment usually includes cognitive-behavioral therapy and an SSRI or other antidepressant.

MAJOR DEPRESSIVE DISORDER WITH PERIPARTUM ONSET: The peripartum onset specifier is applied to major depressive disorder, bipolar I disorder, and bipolar II disorder when the onset of symptoms is during pregnancy or within four weeks postpartum. Symptoms may include anxiety and a preoccupation with the infant's well-being or, in extreme cases, delusional thoughts about the infant.

MAJOR DEPRESSIVE DISORDER WITH SEASONAL PATTERN: The seasonal pattern specifier is applied to major depressive, bipolar I disorder, and bipolar II disorder when there is a temporal relationship between the onset of a mood episode and a particular time of the year. This condition is also known as seasonal affective disorder (SAD) and, in the Northern Hemisphere, most commonly occurs during the winter months. People with SAD usually experience hypersomnia, increased appetite and weight gain, and a craving for carbohydrates.

MAJOR DEPRESSIVE EPISODE: Characterized by a depressed mood and/or loss of interest or pleasure in nearly all activities. The episode lasts for at least two weeks, represents a noticeable change from the person's previous functioning, and includes at least five of the following symptoms (with at least one symptom being a depressed mood or loss of interest or pleasure): (a) depressed mood most of the day, nearly every day as reported by the client or observed by others (in children or adolescents, can be an irritable mood); (b) markedly diminished interest or pleasure in all or nearly all activities; (c) significant weight loss (without dieting) or weight gain and a decrease or increase in appetite nearly every day; (d) insomnia or hypersomnia nearly every day; (e) psychomotor agitation or retardation nearly every day; (f) fatigue or loss of energy nearly every day; (g) feelings of worthlessness or excessive or inappropriate guilt nearly every day; (h) impaired ability to think or concentrate or indecisiveness nearly every day; and/or (i) recurrent thoughts of death, suicidal ideation without a specific plan, or a suicide attempt or specific plan for committing suicide.

MALINGERING (in DSM-5): Malingering is included in the DSM-5 with other conditions that may be a focus of clinical attention. It involves the intentional production, faking, or gross exaggeration of physical or psychological symptoms to obtain an external reward (e.g., to avoid criminal prosecution or obtain financial compensation).

MALINGERING ("FAKING BAD"): A conscious effort by a client to present him/herself as being worse off than is really the case. Clients who "fake bad" during assessments are usually motivated by a specific external incentive for wanting to come off as more disturbed or less able than they actually are.

MALPRACTICE: The injurious or unprofessional treatment of a client/patient by a practitioner (social worker, psychotherapist, psychiatrist, physician, etc.). Malpractice is generally covered under tort law. A malpractice claim requires that three conditions be met: there must be a relationship between the practitioner and the client that implies a duty, there must have been a breach of that duty, and the breach must have caused the client some identifiable harm.

MANAGED CARE ORGANIZATION (MCO): A health plan that seeks to manage health care generally through contracting with health care providers to deliver health care services on a capitated (per-member per-month) basis.

MANAGEMENT BY OBJECTIVES (MBO, Administration): Management approach that focuses on results or outcomes. Emphasis is placed on producing clear statements about expectations for the coming year and making these statements available to all employees; breaking goals and objectives into tasks; and monitoring progress throughout the year. Success is measured by the extent to which objectives were achieved.

MANAGEMENT BY OBJECTIVES (MBO, Supervision): Participatory management approach in which a supervisor and worker jointly establish precise, measurable objectives and a timeframe for achieving them; monitor work toward the objectives; and then evaluate performance by determining the extent to which the worker achieved the objectives.

MANAGEMENT INFORMATION SYSTEMS (MIS): Systems used in social agencies to acquire, process, analyze, and disseminate data that are useful for carrying out the goals of the organization. May be used to track staff activity and the services provided to clients and are believed to enhance goal attainment.

MANIC EPISODE: A period, lasting at least one week, of abnormally and persistently elevated, expansive, or irritable mood. At least three characteristic signs are present: (a) inflated self-esteem or grandiosity; (b) decreased need for sleep; (c) more talkative or pressure to keep talking; (d) flight of ideas or the sense that one's thoughts are racing; (e) distractibility; (f) increase in goal-directed activity or psychomotor agitation; and/or (g) excessive involvement in pleasurable activities that have a high potential for painful consequences. The mood disturbance is severe enough to cause marked impairment in social or occupational functioning *or* to require hospitalization to prevent harm to self or others, *or* there are psychotic features.

MAOIs (MONOAMINE OXIDASE INHIBITORS): Antidepressant drugs that inhibit the enzyme that deactivates dopamine, norepinephrine, and serotonin. MAOIs appear to be most effective for treating non-endogenous and atypical depressions. Side-effects include anticholinergic effects, insomnia, agitation, confusion, and weight gain. When taken in conjunction with other drugs or foods containing tyramine, they can cause a hypertensive crisis.

MASKED DEPRESSION: A form of depression in which physical symptoms (pain, paresthesias, anorexia, etc.) predominate, and the individual often denies experiencing a depressed mood.

MATURATIONAL (DEVELOPMENTAL) CRISES: A crisis in which the origin is embedded in maturational processes – i.e., the person struggles with an anticipated transition from one life stage or role to another.

MCKINNEY ACT: Federal response to homelessness which called for the establishment of programs providing specific services to homeless individuals to help them regain their independence (e.g., emergency shelter, transitional and permanent housing, job training, primary health care, education).

MEANS TEST: Process used to evaluate a person's financial means or well-being based on his/her income, debts, health, number of dependents, etc. The results are used to determine the person's eligibility to receive a benefit. A person who has the "means" to pay for the services he/she is seeking will be turned down. Examples of mean-tests federal programs and services include Temporary Assistance to Needy Families (TANF), the Food Stamp Program, and Medicaid.

MECHANICAL ANALOGY: A way of viewing social systems that compares them to machines. All parts of the system work closely together – they are integrated and well coordinated. Practice models that derive from this analogy aim to organize the community or organization to make conditions more pleasant and restore order.

MEDIAN: The measure of central tendency that is the middle score in a distribution of scores when scores have been ordered from lowest to highest.

MEDIATOR: A role of social workers. As a mediator in direct practice, a social worker settles disputes between conflicting parties and restores communication between them (e.g., disputes between a client and provider or between the members of a family). As a mediator in indirect practice, a social worker helps factions within a community or organization resolve their differences or disagreements. A mediator stays neutral, tries to understand the positions of both parties, help the parties clarify their respective positions, etc.

MEDICAID: Social security program providing medical and health related services for individuals and families with low incomes through direct payment to suppliers of the program. Low income is only one test for Medicaid eligibility; assets and resources also are tested against established thresholds determined by each state (i.e., means testing). Within federal guidelines, states have discretion in determining which groups their Medicaid programs will cover and the financial criteria for eligibility. States must cover categorically needy individuals, however, which usually includes recipients of SSI and families with dependent children receiving cash assistance, as well as other mandatory low-income groups such as pregnant women, infants, and children with incomes less than a specified percent of the federal poverty level. States must also cover certain low-income Medicare beneficiaries.

MEDICARE: Social security program providing health care benefits (health insurance coverage) to most people over age 64 (i.e., those who are eligible for monthly social security benefits and are U.S. citizens or permanent residents of the U.S. who have lived in the U.S. for at least five years); to some people with disabilities under age 65; and to people of all ages with end-stage renal disease (permanent kidney failure treated with dialysis or a transplant). Part A of Medicare is a compulsory Hospital Insurance (HI) program, and Part B is a voluntary program of Supplementary Medical Insurance (SMI). Part A covers inpatient hospital services, care in skilled nursing facilities, home health services, and hospice care.

MENTAL STATUS EXAM: Evaluation of a client's current mental functioning. Most MSEs include evaluation of behavioral and cognitive aspects. Information is collected through observation and questioning. Using a mental status exam can help a social worker recognize key symptoms and when to refer clients for psychiatric evaluations and evaluations of medical problems (including neurological problems) that affect psychological functioning.

METHYLPHENIDATE (RITALIN): Psychostimulant drug used to treat ADHD. Common side-effects include dysphoria, decreased appetite, insomnia, and growth suppression.

MEZZO PRACTICE: Level of social work practice that usually takes place with small groups and families. Activities emphasize facilitating communication, mediation, and negotiation, educating, and bringing people together.

MICRO PRACTICE: Level of social work practice that usually takes place on a case-by-case basis or in a clinical setting. Micro social workers use their technical skills to help solve the psychosocial problems of individuals, families, or small groups.

MILLON CLINICAL MULTIAXIAL INVENTORY (MCMI-III): Self-report inventory used to assess lasting personality traits and acute clinical states. Is appropriate for individuals age 18 and over with at least an 8th-grade reading comprehension level. For adolescents (ages 13 to 19) whose reading ability is at or above the 6th-grade level, the MACI is available.

MIMESIS: Literally means imitation. A family therapist uses mimesis to accommodate to a family's style, tempo, and affective range; he/she joins the family by imitating the style or content of its communication. Like other methods that allow the therapist to join a family, mimesis establishes a common base with the family from which the therapist may intervene. Associated with structural family therapy.

MINNESOTA MULTIPHASIC PERSONALITY INVENTORY (MMPI-2): Self-report personality test that reports an examinee's performance in terms of clinical scales and validity scales. Although originally intended as a tool for deriving psychiatric diagnoses, is now more commonly interpreted in terms of score profiles to derive information about an examinee's personality characteristics. For adolescents (ages 14 to 18), the MMPI-A is available.

MOBILIZER: A role of social workers. As a mobilizer, a social worker identifies and brings together community members and resources and makes them responsive to unmet community needs. The goal may be to match resources to needs in the community, to make services more accessible to residents who need them, or to initiate and develop services to meet needs that previously have been unmet. This role applies in communities only.

MODE: The measure of central tendency that represents the most frequently occurring category or score in a distribution.

MODELING: Describes observational learning, or the process by which learning occurs as the result of observing the behavior of others.

MODELS OF INDIVIDUAL DECISION-MAKING (Simon): (a) The "rational-economic model" proposes that decision-makers attempt to maximize benefits by systematically searching for the best solution. (b) The "bounded rationality (administrative) model" proposes that rational decision-making is limited by internal and external constraints so that decision-makers often "satisfice" rather than optimize (i.e., consider solutions until a fairly good one is encountered and then stop searching due to limited time and resources).

MOOD STABILIZING DRUGS (LITHIUM, ANTICONVULSANT DRUGS): Mood stabilizing drugs are used to alleviate mania and mood swings in bipolar disorder and include lithium and anticonvulsants (e.g., carbamazepine). Lithium is usually the drug-treatment-of-choice for classic bipolar disorder, while an anticonvulsant drug may be more effective for patients who experience rapid mood swings or who have dysphoric mania.

MORPHOGENIC ANALOGY: A way of viewing social systems that applies when change is ongoing and the structure of the system is continually emerging. Under these circumstances, fundamental change can occur because there is no chance of returning to how things were before. Change is likely to be unpredictable, and social workers should be open to a wide variety of solutions and interventions.

MOTIVATIONAL INTERVIEWING: An approach developed specifically for clients who are ambivalent about changing their behaviors that combines the transtheoretical (stages of change) model with client-centered therapy and self-efficacy. The goal is to increase a client's intrinsic motivation to change so that change and the reasons for change come from the client rather than being imposed by a therapist, a spouse, employer, etc.

MOTIVATION, CAPACITY, AND OPPORTUNITY: A client's motivation to change, capacity for change, opportunity to change have a significant impact on the success of the planned change process. Motivation refers to a state of readiness to take action; capacity refers to the abilities and resources that the client or people in his/her environment bring to the change process; and opportunity refers to conditions and circumstances within the client's immediate environment that support positive change.

MULTIPLE BASELINE DESIGN: A single-subject design that involves sequentially applying a treatment to different "baselines" (e.g., to different behaviors, settings, or subjects). Useful when a reversal design would be impractical or unethical.

MULTISYSTEMS APPROACH: An approach that, according to many experts, is appropriate for clients from non-white-Anglo cultures because the concept underlying it is familiar and acceptable to many non-dominant cultural groups (i.e., "it takes a community to raise a child"). It entails taking full advantage of all appropriate resources available in the community, and its goals are to increase a client's awareness of all available support systems and resources and to empower the client to use them.

MUTUALITY: Mutual efforts by the social worker and a client to work on the problem. Establishing mutuality with a client requires the worker to both adopt a posture of professional competence and convey that he/she and the client are equal partners in the helping relationship who are both responsible for what happens in the helping process.

NARCISSISTIC PERSONALITY DISORDER: Narcissistic personality disorder involves a pervasive pattern of grandiosity, need for admiration, and lack of empathy as indicated by at least five characteristic symptoms (e.g., has a grandiose sense of self-importance; is preoccupied with fantasies of unlimited success, power, beauty, love; believes he/she is unique and can be understood only by other high-status people; requires excessive admiration; has a sense of entitlement; lacks empathy; is often envious of others or believes others are envious of him/her).

NARCOTIC-ANALGESICS: The drugs classified as narcotic-analgesics (opioids) have both sedative and analgesic properties. Chronic use of a narcotic-analgesic results in tolerance and psychological and physical dependence. Withdrawal symptoms resemble those associated with a bad case of the flu.

NARROWING THE FOCUS (FUNNELING): A helping skill that involves asking a series of questions designed to help the client describe his/her concerns or situation with more specificity.

NATIONAL SCHOOL LUNCH PROGRAM: A federally assisted meal program that operates in public and private schools and residential child care institutions and provides nutritionally balanced low-cost or free lunches to children.

NATURAL HELPING NETWORK: Informal linkages and relationships between people who voluntarily provide services to people in need and those to whom they provide the services. For example, this type of network often includes the needy person's friends and family, neighbors, fellow employees and church (or other religious body) members, altruistic community members, etc.

NATURAL SOCIAL NETWORKS: Consist of family, friends, neighbors, and coworkers who exchange emotional support and other resources in times of need. When effective, they make it unnecessary for an individual to turn to institutionalized services offered by social agencies. Because geographically dispersed social networks depend on linkages such as transportation, they may be vulnerable in times of crisis.

NEED HIERARCHY THEORY (Maslow): Maslow's theory of motivation, which proposes that five basic needs are arranged in a hierarchical order such that a need higher in the hierarchy doesn't serve as a source of motivation until all lower needs have been fulfilled. From the lowest level to the highest level, the five basic needs defined by Maslow are survival and physiological needs; safety and security needs; social (belonging) needs; esteem (ego) needs; and self-actualization needs.

NEEDS ASSESSMENT: Technique used to identify the nature, incidence, and prevalence of a condition or problem in a community in order to determine the adequacy of existing services and resources for addressing the condition or problem. Results should provide information about the quantity (does the level of service meet the need?), quality (are the services effective?), and direction of existing services (e.g., are service delivery approaches appropriate to the real needs of clients?). The most useful approach for needs assessment is survey research.

NEGATIVE FEEDBACK LOOP: See *positive and negative feedback loops*.

NEGATIVE PUNISHMENT: In operant conditioning, the withdrawal of a stimulus contingent on the performance of a behavior in order to decrease the likelihood that the behavior will occur again.

NEGATIVE REINFORCEMENT: In operant conditioning, the withdrawal of a stimulus following a behavior in order to increase the likelihood that the behavior will occur again.

NEGATIVE SYMPTOMS OF SCHIZOPHRENIA: These involve a restriction in the range and intensity of emotions and other functions. Examples include affective flattening (reduced body language, expressionless, unresponsive face, poor eye contact); alogia (poverty of thought and speech); and avolition (restricted initiation of goal-directed behavior). See also *positive symptoms of schizophrenia*.

NEGLIGENCE: Failure to meet one's responsibility to protect or help another person or failure to practice reasonable care or caution to the extent that another person is harmed or placed at unnecessary risk of harm.

NEGOTIATOR: A role of social workers. As a negotiator, a social worker acts as an intermediary who attempts to settle disputes and/or resolve disagreements between various parties. The worker takes the side of one of the parties (i.e., the client system) and seeks to resolve the conflict on behalf of that party.

NETWORK: Any informal or formal linkage of people or organizations that share resources, skills, knowledge, and contacts with one another.

NETWORKING: Efforts to develop and enhance the social linkages between people by (a) strengthening the quality of existing networks, (b) establishing new networks, (c) creating linkages among various networks to engender more competent support, and (d) mobilizing networks.

NEUROCOGNITIVE DISORDER DUE TO ALZHEIMER'S DISEASE: This disorder is diagnosed when the criteria for major or mild neurocognitive disorder are met, there is an insidious onset and gradual progression of impairment in one or more cognitive domains (or at least two domains for major neurocognitive disorder), and the criteria for probable or possible Alzheimer's disease are met. It involves a slow, progressive decline in cognitive functioning.

NEUROIMAGING TECHNIQUES: Techniques that make it possible to study both the structure and function of the living brain. Computed tomography (CT) and magnetic resonance imaging (MRI) are structural techniques. Positron-emission tomography (PET), single proton emission computed tomography (SPECT), and functional magnetic resonance imaging (fMRI) provide information on the functional activities of the brain.

NEUROLEPTIC MALIGNANT SYNDROME (NMS): A rare, but potentially fatal side-effect of the antipsychotic drugs. It involves a rapid onset of motor, mental, and autonomic symptoms including muscle rigidity, tachycardia, hyperthermia, and altered consciousness. To avoid a potentially fatal outcome, the drug must be stopped as soon as symptoms of NMS develop.

NEURON: The nerve cell specialized for the conduction of electrochemical signals that carry information from one part of the body to another (e.g., from the brain to the muscles, from the sensory organs to the brain). Is made up dendrites, the soma (cell body), and an axon.

NEUROPSYCHOLOGICAL TESTS: Used when brain degeneration or damage is suspected and to determine the nature of the impairment produced by brain pathology.

NEUROTRANSMITTERS (ACETYLCHOLINE, DOPAMINE, SEROTONIN, GABA): Neurotransmitters are chemical substances that are released from axon terminals, diffuse across synapses, and excite or inhibits receptor sites on postsynaptic nerve cells. (a) Acetylcholine mediates neuromuscular transmission, parasympathetic arousal, and memory (e.g., memory loss in neurocognitive disorder due to Alzheimer's disease). (b) Dopamine is involved in inhibitory motor regulation and motivational/emotional functions. Excessive activity at dopamine receptors has been linked to schizophrenia and Tourette's disorder. (c) Serotonin ordinarily inhibits behavior and is involved in the regulation of mood, hunger, arousal, sleep, temperature, and pain. Elevated levels contribute to schizophrenia and autism spectrum disorder. Low levels play a role in depressive disorders, suicide, PTSD, obsessive-compulsive disorder, and aggression. (d) GABA is the most common inhibitory neurotransmitter and is believed to be involved in anxiety, sleep, and seizures. Low levels of GABA in the motor region are associated with Huntington's disease.

NEWBORN REFLEXES: Reflexes are unlearned responses to particular stimuli in the environment. Early reflexes include the Babinski reflex (toes fan out and upward when soles of the feet are tickled) and the Moro reflex (flings arms and legs outward and then toward the body in response to a loud noise or sudden loss of physical support).

NOMINAL SCALE: A scale of measurement in which the variable is divided into unordered groups or categories. When a variable is measured on a nominal scale (or is treated as though it were measured on a nominal scale), the data to be described or analyzed are frequency data (i.e., the frequency of observations in each group or category). The primary limitation of this measurement scale is that the only mathematical operation that can be performed on nominal data is to count the number (frequency) of cases in each category.

NONPROFIT PRIVATE AGENCY: A social agency operated to achieve a service provision goal rather than to make a financial profit for its owners.

NON-RAPID EYE MOVEMENT SLEEP AROUSAL DISORDERS: This disorder involves recurrent episodes of incomplete awakening that usually occur during the first third of the major sleep episode and are accompanied by sleepwalking (getting out of bed during sleep and walking around) and/or sleep terror (an abrupt arousal from sleep that often begins with a panicky scream and is accompanied by intense fear and signs of autonomic arousal). The individual has limited or no recall of an episode upon awakening, and the disturbance causes significant distress or impaired functioning.

NORMALIZING: A form of information giving used to place a client's problem in a new context by defining it as expectable or predictable rather than pathological. With the parents of a defiant toddler, for example, a social worker could explain the behaviors that are expected during this developmental stage.

NORMS (Groups): The standard rules of conduct used by groups to maintain uniformity of behavior among group members. Norms may be formal (codified or written) or informal (unwritten but "understood" by group members). Norms do not govern all aspects of behavior, only those considered by the group to be important for effective group functioning. In addition, norms usually apply to behavior not to personal feelings and thoughts.

NOTICE OF PRIVACY PRACTICES (NPP): A consent form required under HIPAA's privacy rule that must be given to clients on or before the beginning of treatment. The NPP informs clients of their rights and indicates how health information may be used and disclosed.

OBJECT CONSTANCY (Mahler): A permanent sense of self and object (other) that develops at about age 3.

OBJECTIVES (Direct Practice): See *goals and objectives*.

OBJECT PERMANENCE (OBJECT CONCEPT): The understanding that objects continue to exist when they are no longer detectable by the senses (e.g., when they are out of sight). Object permanence emerges at the end of Piaget's sensorimotor stage of development.

OBSERVATIONAL LEARNING (GUIDED PARTICIPATION): Bandura's observational learning theory predicts that behaviors can be acquired simply by observing someone else (a model) perform those behaviors (i.e., the acquisition of behavior is due largely to social influences) and that learning is cognitively mediated and involves four processes: attention, retention, production, and motivation. The research suggests that guided participation (participant modeling) is the most effective type of observational learning, especially for treating phobic reactions.

OBSESSIONS: Persistent thoughts, impulses, or images that an individual experiences as senseless or intrusive and that cause marked distress. The thoughts are not simply excessive worries about real-life problems, and the person may attempt to ignore, suppress, or neutralize them with other thoughts or actions.

OBSESSIVE-COMPULSIVE DISORDER (OCD): OCD is characterized by recurrent obsessions and/or compulsions that are time-consuming or cause clinically significant distress or impairment in functioning. Obsessions are persistent thoughts, impulses, or images that the person experiences as intrusive and unwanted and that he/she attempts to ignore or suppress, and compulsions are repetitious and deliberate behaviors or mental acts that the person feels driven to perform either in response to an obsession or according to rigid rules. A combination of exposure with response prevention and the tricyclic clomipramine or an SSRI is usually the treatment-of-choice for OCD.

OBSESSIVE-COMPULSIVE PERSONALITY DISORDER: Obsessive-compulsive personality disorder is characterized by a persistent preoccupation with orderliness, perfectionism, and mental and interpersonal control that severely limits the individual's flexibility, openness, and efficiency. At least four characteristic symptoms must be present (e.g., exhibits perfectionism that interferes with task completion, is excessively devoted to work and productivity to the exclusion of leisure activities and friendships, is reluctant to delegate work to others unless they are willing to do it his/her way, adopts a miserly spending style toward self and others).

OLD-AGE, SURVIVORS, AND DISABILITY INSURANCE (OASDI): The OASDI program (commonly known as "social security") is the largest income-maintenance program in the U.S. The program provides monthly benefits designed to replace, in part, the loss of income due to retirement, disability, or death. Coverage is nearly universal (approximately 96 percent of jobs in the United States are covered). Workers finance the program through a payroll tax that is levied under the Federal Insurance and Self-Employment Contribution Acts (FICA and SECA).

OMBUDSPERSON: (a) An advocate or spokesperson for the people who are served by an organization to ensure that the organization's obligations, ethical duties, and rule are being followed, or (b) an individual employed by an organization to investigate potential illegal and/or unethical activities or unintended harmful consequences stemming from the organization's activities and to facilitate fair negotiations or actions toward satisfactory solutions.

OPEN-ENDED QUESTIONS: Interview questions that define a topic area but allow a client to respond in whatever way he/she chooses. Effective for encouraging a client to self-disclose or expand on personal information and, thus, tend to elicit valuable data.

OPEN GROUP (OPEN-ENDED GROUP): Therapy group in which members join and leave the group at different times. Also identified as a group without a pre-set number of sessions or ending date.

OPERANT CONDITIONING: A type of learning in which behaviors are increased or decreased as the result of the consequences (reinforcements or punishments) that follow them.

OPERANT EXTINCTION AND EXTINCTION BURSTS: In operant conditioning, extinction refers to the elimination of a previously reinforced response through the consistent withholding of reinforcement following that response. Operant extinction is usually associated with a temporary increase in the response (an "extinction burst").

OPIOID WITHDRAWAL: Opioid withdrawal occurs following cessation or reduction in opioid use that has been heavy and prolonged or after administration of an opioid antagonist following a period of opioid use. The diagnosis requires at least three characteristic symptoms – dysphoric mood; nausea or vomiting; muscle aches; lacrimation (excessive secretion of tears) or rhinorrhea (excessive mucus secretion from the nose); pupillary dilation, piloerection ("goose bumps" or erection of hair on the skin), or sweating; diarrhea; yawning; fever; and/or insomnia.

OPPOSITIONAL DEFIANT DISORDER: Oppositional defiant disorder involves a recurrent pattern of an angry/irritable mood, argumentative/defiant behavior, or vindictiveness as evidenced by at least four characteristic symptoms that are exhibited during interactions with at least one person who is not a sibling. Examples of symptoms include often loses temper, often argues with authority figures, often actively refuses to comply with requests from authority figures or with rules, and often blames others for his/her mistakes.

ORDINAL SCALE: The scale of measurement in which the variable is divided into ordered categories, scores, or levels. A limitation of ordinal scores is that they do not lend themselves to determining just how much difference there is between scores. For example, we can't say that the person with a rank of 10 has twice as much of the characteristic as the person with a rank of 5, only that he/she is ranked higher.

ORGANISMIC ANALOGY: A way of viewing social systems that compares social systems to living organisms. Each part of the system has a special function, and, if each part performs its function as intended, the parts work together for the common good. This analogy may apply if key people in a community or an organization can agree on how to resolve a problem.

ORIENTATION (DISORIENTATION): An accurate awareness of person, place, time, situation, familiar objects, and other people. Marked disorientation may be associated with severe mental illness, substance intoxication, or a pathological brain syndrome (e.g., delirium).

OUTCOME MODEL: Approach to social program evaluation that emphasizes the evaluation of expected results. If productivity is being evaluated, a "quantitative outcome model" is used to measure, in numbers, program factors such as activity, revenue, and so forth. If clients' perceptions of a program are being evaluated, a "qualitative outcome model" is used.

OUTLINE FOR CULTURAL FORMULATION: The DSM-5's Outline for Cultural Formulation provides guidelines for assessing four factors: the client's cultural identity; the client's cultural conceptualization of distress; the psychosocial stressors and cultural factors that impact the client's vulnerability and resilience; and cultural factors relevant to the relationship between the client and therapist.

OUTREACH: Public relations approach in which efforts are made to bring an agency's services and information about its services to people in their homes or other natural environments. Avenues used to achieve outreach include case finding, public speaking, interagency collaboration, and written material.

OVERCORRECTION: An operant technique used to eliminate an undesirable behavior. It involves having the individual correct the consequences of his/her behavior (restitution) and/or practice corrective behaviors (positive practice). Overcorrection may require constant supervision and/or physical guidance.

PANIC ATTACK: A sudden surge of intense fear or discomfort that peaks within minutes and includes four or more symptoms (e.g., palpitations, pounding heart, or accelerated heart rate; sweating; trembling; shortness of breath; chest pain or discomfort; nausea; feeling unsteady, light-headed, or faint; chills or heat sensations; numbness or tingling; derealization or depersonalization; fear of losing control; fear of dying). Panic attacks can occur in the context of any anxiety disorder as well in the context of some other mental disorders (e.g., depressive disorders, PTSD, substance use disorders) and other medical conditions. Panic disorder requires at least two unexpected panic attacks. Unexpected (uncued) panic attacks are not associated with any internal or external trigger (they occur "out of the blue").

PANIC DISORDER: Panic disorder is characterized by recurrent (at least two) unexpected panic attacks with at least one attack being followed by one month of persistent concern about having additional attacks or about their consequences and/or involving a significant maladaptive change in behavior related to the attack. Cognitive behavioral interventions that incorporate exposure are the treatment-of-choice for this disorder.

PARADOXICAL INTERVENTIONS (THERAPEUTIC DOUBLE-BIND): Therapeutic interventions in which the therapist deliberately gives the client a directive that the therapist wants the client to resist; the resulting change in the client is then the result of defying the therapist's directive. Examples include prescribing the symptom and restraining.

PARALLEL PROCESS: (A.k.a. reflection process.) Phenomenon in supervisory interactions in which a worker unconsciously reenacts certain client behavior in an effort to understand it better and get help from the supervisor in dealing with it.

PARANOID PERSONALITY DISORDER: Paranoid personality disorder involves a pervasive pattern of distrust and suspiciousness that entails interpreting the motives of others as malevolent. The diagnosis requires the presence of at least four characteristic symptoms (e.g., suspects that others are exploiting, harming, or deceiving him/her without a sufficient basis for doing so; reads demeaning content into benign remarks or events; persistently bears grudges; is persistently suspicious about the fidelity of his/her spouse or sexual partner without justification).

PARAPHILIC DISORDERS: The paraphilic disorders include voyeuristic, exhibitionistic, frotteuristic, sexual sadism, pedophilic, fetishistic, and transvestic disorders. These disorders are characterized by an "intense and persistent sexual interest other than sexual interest in genital stimulation or preparatory fondling with phenotypically normal, physically mature, consenting human partners …[that] is currently causing distress or impairment to the individual or … has entailed personal harm, or risk of harm, to others" (APA, 2013, pp. 685-686).

PARAPHRASE: A selective restatement of the main idea of a client's message that resembles his/her message but is not identical to it. A paraphrase emphasizes the literal meaning of the client's message (the content rather than affect) and is expressed in fewer words than the client has used.

PARASYMPATHETIC DIVISION: The division of the autonomic nervous system involved in the conservation of energy and relaxation. Activation of the parasympathetic division is associated with a slowing of heart rate, lowered blood pressure, contraction of pupils, reduction of sweat gland output, and increased activity of the digestive system.

PARENTIFICATION: Process within a family system in which a spouse, or more typically, a child, is expected to take on a significant parenting role in the family. Represents a subjective distortion of family relationships in which a family member acts as though his/her spouse or child were actually his/her parent (e.g., a child assumes excessive responsibility in a pseudo-adult role by emotionally or physically caring for a weak parent or a vulnerable marriage).

PARENTING STYLE (Baumrind): Baumrind distinguishes between four styles that reflect various combinations of responsivity and demandingness: authoritarian, authoritative, permissive, and rejecting-neglecting. High parental responsivity mixed with moderate control (an "authoritative style") is associated with the best outcomes including greater self-confidence and self-reliance, achievement-orientation, and social responsibility.

PARKINSON'S DISEASE: Movement disorder involving bradykinesia (slowness of movement), rigidity, and resting tremor. About 20-60 percent of patients eventually develop neurocognitive disorder due to Parkinson's disease.

PARTIALIZATION: The method of temporarily considering a client's interconnected problems as separate issues so that planning and doing the work toward resolving them can be more manageable. After a client's problems have been partialized, the social worker and client will ordinarily first deal with those that need immediate attention.

PARTICIPANT MODELING: A technique based on observational learning theory in which a model demonstrates the desired behavior and then helps the individual to gradually imitate the modeled behavior.

PARTICIPATORY ADMINISTRATION: An approach to social agency administration that allows democratic involvement in the formulation of agency policies and procedures. When agency staff are part of participatory administration, they tend to perform better, which, in turn, improves the performance of the agency.

PARTICIPATORY (PARTICIPATIVE) MANAGEMENT: Decision-making strategy in which administrators involve all those who are likely to be affected by a proposed organizational decision or change. Includes building voluntary consensus and commitment among personnel, clientele, sponsors, and other interested parties to achieve organizational goals.

PATTERNS OF ATTACHMENT (Ainsworth): Research using Ainsworth's "strange situation" revealed four patterns of attachment: secure, insecure/ambivalent, insecure/avoidant, and disorganized/disoriented. Each is associated with different caregiver behaviors and different personality and behavioral outcomes.

PEER GROUP SUPERVISION: Supervision approach in which a group of workers at an agency meets regularly without a leader to review cases and treatment approaches and share expertise. The workers take responsibility for their own and each other's professional development and for maintaining standards of agency service.

PEER REVIEW: A formal evaluation by a peer group of a professional's specific actions or overall competence. Peer review is used primarily for the purposes of quality assurance. Often, it is used as an alternative to the legal system to settle disputes between practitioners, consumers, and third-party payers.

PERIPHERAL NERVOUS SYSTEM (PNS): The nervous system elements lying outside of the spinal cord and brain. The PNS consists of the spinal and cranial nerves and is divided into the somatic and autonomic nervous systems.

PERMANENCY PLANNING: Child welfare strategy used to provide alternatives to temporary foster care placement through organized efforts to provide long-term continuity in the care of dependent children.

PERSISTENT DEPRESSIVE DISORDER (DYSTHYMIA): Persistent depressive disorder is characterized by a depressed mood (or in children and adolescents, a depressed or irritable mood) on most days for at least two years in adults or one year in children and adolescents as indicated by the presence of at least two characteristic symptoms (i.e., poor appetite or overeating, insomnia or hypersomnia, low energy or fatigue, low self-esteem, poor concentration or difficulty making decisions, feelings of hopelessness). During the two- or one-year period, the individual has not been symptom-free for more than two months, and symptoms cause clinically significant distress or impaired functioning.

PERSONAL RESPONSIBILITY AND WORK OPPORTUNITY RECONCILIATION ACT (PRWORA): PRWORA (1996) was designed to reform the nation's welfare system into one that requires work in exchange for time-limited assistance. The law either eliminated or placed new restrictions on many national programs and established the Temporary Assistance to Needy Families (TANF) program.

PERSONAL SOCIAL SERVICES: Social services that address individualized needs involving interpersonal relationships and the ability to function within one's immediate environment.

PERSON-CENTERED THERAPY: Therapeutic approach based on the assumptions that people possess an inherent ability for growth and self-actualization and that maladaptive behavior occurs when "incongruence between self and experience" disrupts this natural tendency. The therapist's role in person-centered therapy is to provide the client with three facilitative conditions (empathy, genuineness, and unconditional positive regard), which enable the client to return to his/her natural tendency for self-actualization.

PERSON-IN-ENVIRONMENT FRAMEWORK: A framework that views the client as part of an environmental system and is concerned with the reciprocal relationships and other influences between a client and his/her physical and social environment.

PERSON-IN-ENVIRONMENT (PIE) SYSTEM: A diagnostic taxonomy used to describe, classify, and code problems in adult social functioning. Problems are grouped into four factors: factor I, problems in social role functioning; factor II, problems in the environment; factor III, mental health problems; and factor IV, physical health problems.

PERSON-IN-ENVIRONMENT (PIE) THEORY: PIE theory assumes that human problems have their roots in both individual and situational factors and that understanding and treating human problems requires a dual focus on the individual and environmental forces.

PERT (PROGRAM EVALUATION REVIEW TECHNIQUE): Program management technique used to systematically relate goals to the means of achieving them. PERT assesses program objectives, the activities, resources, and time needed to achieve the objectives, and the order in which the activities should be performed.

PHENOTYPE: See *genotype vs. phenotype*.

PHENYLKETONURIA (PKU): Potential cause of intellectual disability due to an inability to metabolize the amino acid phenylalanine. Can be prevented by providing a diet low in phenylalanine.

PHYSICAL ABUSE (Children): The nonaccidental physical injury to a child caused by a parent or other caregiver. May result from an act of commission or from an act of omission (e.g., failure to protect the child). Occurs across all socioeconomic classes but a disproportionate number of known cases (i.e., reported cases, or those that come to the attention of authorities) involve low-income families. Perpetrators of child physical abuse are more often female than male; and young, low-income, single mothers with young children are at greatest risk of abusing their children.

PHYSICAL NEGLECT (Children): A parent's or other caregiver's persistent lack of attention to the child's basic physical needs (e.g., food, shelter, clothing, supervision, health care). Types of neglect include abandonment/lack of supervision; nutritional neglect; hygiene neglect; medical neglect; shelter neglect; educational neglect; and some cases of failure to thrive (signs of chronic undernutrition). Any acts of commission or omission that put a child in danger constitute child endangerment, and physical neglect is the most common type of child endangerment.

PIAGET'S THEORY OF COGNITIVE DEVELOPMENT: Proposes that knowledge is actively constructed by the individual from elements provided by both maturation and experience. According to Piaget, cognitive development involves four universal and invariant stages: sensorimotor, preoperational, concrete operational, and formal operational.

PLANNED CHANGE PROCESS: A deliberate series of actions directed toward improving a client's social functioning or well-being. Includes five phases (intake and engagement; data collection and assessment; planning and contracting; intervention and monitoring; and final evaluation and termination) and the involvement of four main systems (change agent system, client system, target system, and action system).

PLEASURE PRINCIPLE: According to Freud, the function of the id that reduces tension by gratification of instinctual needs without regard for logic, reality or morality.

POSITIVE AND NEGATIVE FEEDBACK LOOPS: A key feature of cybernetics is its concept of the feedback loop through which a system receives information. A negative feedback loop reduces deviation and helps a system maintain its status quo, while a positive feedback loop amplifies deviation or change and thereby disrupts the system.

POSITIVELY SKEWED DISTRIBUTION: A distribution in which scores are "piled up" in the negative (low score) side of the distribution, but a few scores are located in the distribution's positive tail.

POSITIVE PUNISHMENT: In operant conditioning, the application of a stimulus following a response with the goal of reducing or eliminating the response.

POSITIVE REINFORCEMENT: In operant conditioning, the application of a stimulus following a response with the goal of increasing the occurrence or strength of the response.

POSITIVE REINTERPRETATION: A method for reducing resistances. Involves attributing positive intentions to what normally would be regarded as undesirable behavior by a group member or the group.

POSITIVE SYMPTOMS OF SCHIZOPHRENIA: These include delusions, hallucinations, disorganized speech, and grossly disorganized behavior. The active phase symptoms of schizophrenia include delusions, hallucinations, and/or disorganized speech and may also include grossly disorganized behavior or negative symptoms. See also *negative symptoms of schizophrenia.*

POSTCONVENTIONAL MORALITY: For Kohlberg, the final level of moral development. At this level, moral judgments are independent of personal consequences and social convention and are based on social contracts, democratically determined laws, and universal principles. Many adults do not reach this stage of moral development.

POSTPARTUM DEPRESSION (PPD): Depression that may affect women after childbirth. Early-onset PPD ("baby blues") begins right after delivery, lasts about 10 to 12 days without medical intervention, and is relatively mild. Later-onset PPD is more serious and is typically recognized several weeks after delivery. Indicators include severe mood swings; a lack of joy in life; intense irritability and anger; withdrawal from family and friends; feelings of shame, guilt, or inadequacy; loss of appetite; insomnia; overwhelming fatigue; loss of interest in sex; thoughts of harming oneself or one's baby; and difficultly bonding with one's baby.

POSTTRAUMATIC STRESS DISORDER (PTSD): The diagnosis of PTSD requires exposure to actual or threatened death, serious injury, or sexual violence; presence of at least one intrusion symptom related to the event; persistent avoidance of stimuli associated with the event; negative changes in cognition or mood associated with the event; and marked change in arousal and reactivity associated with the event. Symptoms must have a duration of more than one month and must cause clinically significant distress or impaired functioning. The treatment-of-choice is a comprehensive cognitive-behavioral intervention that incorporates exposure, cognitive restructuring, and anxiety management or similar techniques.

POVERTY LINE: Index of the amount of money necessary to enable a person to live at a minimum standard of living. Revised regularly to reflect changes in the cost-of-living index.

POWER GROUP: The individuals in a community who have the greatest access to resources and who, due to their social status, influence the decisions made on behalf of the community. These individuals are often political leaders, financial and industrial executives, clergy members, and indigenous community leaders.

PPBS (PROGRAM PLANNING AND BUDGETING SYSTEMS): Planning and budgeting technique that relates spending to outputs (services) rather than inputs (capital, etc.) and specifies objectives and measures progress in terms of end products. The essential concept is that each program component included in a budget must carry a stated objective; this way, spending can be justified in terms of how a program's various activities contribute to its overall objectives. The focus is on a program's individual components and how each fits in terms of a cost-benefit analysis into an overall, long-range plan. Agencies using this process must analyze their goals, priorities, and capabilities every year.

PRACTICE GUIDELINES: Systematically developed statements to facilitate practitioner and patient decisions about appropriate health care for specific clinical circumstances. Developed on the basis on empirical (observed) evidence of efficacy and serve several purposes including standardizing and improving the quality of client care; helping clinicians identify the most effective treatment approaches for specific disorders; and reducing the costs of health care.

PRECIPITATING FACTOR (Crisis): The final stressful event in a series of events that moves a person from a state of acute vulnerability into crisis. The precipitating factor is often a minor event but it can assume catastrophic proportions in the context of other stressful events and the person's inability to use his/her usual problem-solving strategies.

PRECONVENTIONAL MORALITY: According to Kohlberg, the first level of moral development in which judgments of right and wrong are based on consequences and personal needs. Includes the punishment-obedience and instrumental hedonism stages. Characteristic of childhood.

PREJUDICE: *See discrimination vs. prejudice.*

PREMACK PRINCIPLE: An application of positive reinforcement that involves using a high-frequency behavior as a positive reinforcer for a low-frequency behavior.

PREMATURITY: Infants born before 37 weeks are considered premature. Risk factors for prematurity include low SES, teen motherhood, malnutrition, and drug use. In the absence of significant abnormalities and with appropriate medical attention and a supportive environment, most premature infants catch up to their nonpremature peers in terms of cognitive, language, and social skills by 2 or 3 years of age.

PREOPERATIONAL STAGE: Second stage in Piaget's model of cognitive development (age 2 through 7 years). Children at this age can think symbolically but haven't mastered logical operations (e.g., mental addition, classification, conservation).

PRESCRIBING THE SYMPTOM: One of the original paradoxical interventions. It forces a patient to either give up the symptom or admit that it is under voluntary control. The prescription of the symptom – for example, telling an overprotective mother to take better care of her child – is thought to create the possibility of unbalancing the family situation, which would make the family more available for change.

PRESENTING PROBLEM: Consists of the perceived symptoms and overt issues or difficulties that, according to the client, constitute the problem for which he/she has sought help. May not be the actual problem, or the problem that needs attention (i.e., may be a distortion of the actual problem or a matter that the client feels safer disclosing or a client and his/her family may misunderstand the problem or not understand it fully). Nevertheless, a social worker should "start where the client is" during assessment and focus initially on eliciting the presenting problem.

PREVENTION (Community Mental Health): An approach to the alleviation of mental disorders that is associated with both community mental health and public health. Preventions are classified as primary, secondary, or tertiary: Primary preventions make an intervention available to all members of a target group or population in order to keep them from developing a disorder. Secondary preventions identify at-risk individuals and offer them appropriate treatment. Tertiary preventions are designed to reduce the duration and consequences of an illness that has already occurred.

PRIMARY GAIN AND SECONDARY GAIN: Two mechanisms used to explain the development of symptoms: With primary gain, the symptom keeps an internal conflict or need out of conscious awareness; with secondary gain, the symptom helps the individual avoid a noxious activity or obtain otherwise unavailable support from the environment.

PRIMARY PREVENTION: Community mental health intervention aimed at reducing the prevalence of mental disorders by reducing the incidence of new cases. Examples include prenatal nutrition programs for lower SES mothers and public education programs on drug abuse.

PRIMARY (UNCONDITIONED) REINFORCER: A stimulus that has reinforcing value without conditioning (learning). Examples include food and water.

PRIVACY: A general legal term that refers to an individual's right to have information about his/her life withheld from others. While privacy originated from laws guaranteeing individuals freedom from invasion (of privacy) by governmental agencies, it now applies in situations involving nongovernmental agencies as well.

PRIVATE (VOLUNTARY) AGENCY: A social agency that is privately owned and is operated by people who are not employed by a government. A board of directors has ultimate responsibility for a private agency's programmatic and financial operations.

PROBLEM-FOCUSED COPING: See *emotion-focused coping vs. problem-focused coping*.

PROBLEM SYSTEM: The client, other people, and elements in the environment that interact to produce and/or maintain the client's problem situation. Consists of three systems that interact to produce and maintain human problems: the intrapersonal system (biophysical, emotional, psychological); the interpersonal system (family, other relationships); and the environmental system (support system, resources).

PROCESS RECORDING: A detailed case recording procedure that emphasizes recording objective and subjective information about social worker-client interactions during treatment. It is frequently used to help new social workers and social work students learn practice skills; more experienced workers may use it when they are having unusual problems with a client and want to maintain a detailed record that can be examined by a supervisor, consultant, or peers.

PROGRAM EVALUATION: In social work, assessments carried out to obtain information that can be used to improve social programs and social service accountability. Involves using applied social research to discover the extent to which social programs are carried out efficiently and effectively.

PROGRAM EVALUATION CRITERIA: (a) Effort: Evaluates the resources needed to reach program objectives. (b) Impact: Examines the program's effect on broad social change. (c) Effectiveness: Determines how well the objectives of the program were met in terms of client change. (d) Efficiency: Assesses the economics of program operation in relation to its accomplishments (the ideal is maximum performance using minimal resources). (e) Quality: Examines professional competence and standards of service.

PROGRAMMING (Small Group Work): Involves selecting and planning activities (drama, art, dance, music, sports, parties, work tasks, etc.) to create opportunities for clients to learn new behaviors and experience positive interactions with others and to guide the group process in desired directions.

PROJECTION: A defense mechanism. Involves attributing one's own unacceptable instinctual needs and drives to another person. Projection is derived from the primitive thought process of egocentrism.

PROJECTIVE IDENTIFICATION: A concept associated with object-relations theories. Consists of three steps: An aspect of the self is projected onto someone else; the projector tries to coerce the other person to identify with what has been projected; and the projector and the recipient of the projection feel a sense of oneness or union. In object-relations family therapy, is considered a common source of dysfunction – i.e., a family member projects old introjects onto another family member and then reacts to that person as though he/she actually has the projected characteristics or provokes the person to act in ways consistent with the projected characteristics.

PROJECTIVE PERSONALITY TESTS: Relatively unstructured personality tests (e.g., Rorschach, TAT) in which the stimuli are ambiguous and the responses required are open-ended. Their development and use are based on the "projective hypothesis," which proposes that a person's interpretation of ambiguous stimuli provides information about his/her personality traits, needs, feelings, conflicts, etc.

PROPRIETARY (FOR-PROFIT) AGENCY: A social agency that provides designated social services that often are similar to those provided by nonprofit private social agencies, but one of its major purposes is to make a financial profit for it owners.

PROPRIETARY PRACTICE: The delivery of social services for profit, typically by self-employed professionals in nonclinical settings. The term "private practice" has a similar meaning but usually refers to clinical practice. Social workers in private practice assume responsibility the services they provide in exchange for direct payment or third-party reimbursement.

PROTECTIVE FACTORS: Protective factors coexisting with risks are personal, social, and institutional factors that promote personal competence and successful development and, thereby, decrease the likelihood of a problem occurring. Examples include adequate prenatal care, active coping mechanisms, and low family stress.

PROTECTIVE SERVICES: Intervention on behalf of individuals who are or may be in danger of harm from others or who are unable to care for themselves (e.g., children, older adults, the disabled). The main activities include investigating situations in which a person is alleged to be at risk, minimizing further risk, improving current conditions, accessing resources, and facilitating placement in alternative environments when necessary.

PSYCHIC DETERMINISM: The doctrine that all actions, thoughts, verbalizations, etc., are meaningful and obey the law of cause and effect (e.g., slips of the tongue reflect unconscious material).

PSYCHOACTIVE (PSYCHOTROPIC) DRUGS: Agents that interact with the central nervous system in a way that produces changes in mood, consciousness, perception, and/or behavior. The psychoactive drugs exert their effects in various ways but all have one of two basic effects: They either increase or decrease the effectiveness of transmission at nerve synapses. Psychoactive drugs also have side-effects that may interfere with a person's physical, psychological, and/or social functioning or well-being.

PSYCHODRAMA: A therapeutic technique that involves having clients dramatically act out (role-play) the conflicts they are having with other people or other situations. Psychodrama involves a protagonist (the client), auxiliary egos (individuals trained to act out aspects of the client's situation), and the director (therapist).

PSYCHODYNAMIC THERAPIES: (i.e., classical psychoanalysis, the therapeutic approaches of the ego-analysts, the object-relations theorists, and the neo-Freudians, Adler's individual psychology, Jung's analytical psychotherapy.) These therapies view human behavior as being motivated largely by unconscious processes, regard early development as having a profound effect on adult functioning, propose that there are general (universal) principles that explain personality development and behavior, and consider insight into unconscious processes to be a key component of psychotherapy. They generally give more attention to clients' thoughts and feelings than to social and environmental factors and seek to improve clients' social functioning by helping them understand their conflicting thoughts and feelings.

PSYCHOEDUCATION: A form of information giving that involves teaching a client and his/her family about the nature of the client's disorder or condition, including its etiology, progression, consequences, prognosis, treatment, and alternatives.

PSYCHOLOGICAL REACTANCE: The tendency to resist being influenced or manipulated by others, usually by doing the opposite of what is desired or expected.

PSYCHOSEXUAL DEVELOPMENT: Freud's theory of personality development, which proposes that development involves five invariant stages (oral, anal, phallic, latency, and genital), in which the libido shifts from one area of the body to another.

PSYCHOSOCIAL DEVELOPMENT: Erikson's theory of personality development, which proposes that an individual faces different social crises at different points (stages) throughout the life span. These stages are trust vs. mistrust, autonomy vs. shame and doubt, initiative vs.

guilt, industry vs. inferiority, identity vs. role confusion, intimacy vs. isolation, generativity vs. stagnation, and integrity vs. despair.

PSYCHOTHERAPIST-PATIENT PRIVILEGE: A legal term referring to a client's statutory right not to have confidential information disclosed (without his/her permission) especially during legal proceedings. The legal requirements with regard to privilege vary from state to state.

PUBLIC AGENCY: An agency established by legislation adopted by elected officials at the federal, state, county, or city level; funded by tax dollars; run by a unit of government; and generally regulated by laws that directly affect policy.

PUBLIC ASSISTANCE: Government funded financial assistance to individuals who cannot support themselves.

PUBLIC HOUSING: Social security program established to provide decent and safe rental housing for eligible low-income families, older adults, and persons with disabilities. Public housing ranges from single family houses to high-rise apartments for older adults. The Department of Housing and Urban Development (HUD) administers federal aid to local public housing authorities (PHAs) that manage and operate the housing program for low-income residents at rents they can afford. Public housing is limited to low-income families and individuals. The PHA determines the individual's eligibility based on annual gross income; whether the applicant qualifies as elderly, a person with a disability, or a family; and U.S. citizenship or eligible immigration status.

PUNISHMENT: In operant conditioning, a method used to decrease a behavior by applying or withdrawing a stimulus following the behavior. A major disadvantage of punishment is that it suppresses rather than eliminates a behavior.

PURCHASE OF SERVICE (POS) CONTRACT: A financial arrangement between two or more social agencies or between an agency and a government organization. When the agreement is between a private agency and a public (governmental) agency, the private agency is paid to provide particular services (i.e., the private agency is funded, in part, by tax dollars); the government retains control over financing and decision-making functions but the delivery of services is moved to the private sector.

QUALITY ASSURANCE (QA): (A.k.a. Quality control.) Procedures and steps undertaken by an organization to determine whether its goods and services meet the standards established for them. Quality assurance programs usually examine whether professionals complied with standards, rather than the outcome of their services. Quality assurance procedures for social workers include the requirement for adequate education from an accredited school of social work, supervision, licensing and certification, and continuing education requirements. For the profession, sample procedures include a code of ethics, peer review, utilization review, program evaluation, professional sanctions, and lawsuits.

QUASI-EXPERIMENTAL RESEARCH: Experimental research in which an investigator's experimental control is limited; especially his/her ability to assign subjects to groups because intact groups must be used, the variable of interest is an organismic variable, or the study includes only one group that will be compared to itself. A limitation of quasi-experimental research is that it does not allow an investigator to conclude that an observed relationship between variables is a causal one.

RACIAL/CULTURAL IDENTITY DEVELOPMENT MODEL (Atkinson, Morten, & Sue): Distinguishes between five stages that people experience as they attempt to understand themselves in terms of their own culture, the dominant culture, and the oppressive relationship between the two cultures. The five stages are: conformity, dissonance, resistance and immersion, introspection, and integrative awareness.

RACISM (LEVELS OF RACISM): Racism is a system of power and privilege that may be manifested in attitudes, behaviors, and/or institutional structures based on people's skin color. Levels of racism include institutional racism (denial or restriction of material conditions and access to power to members of minority groups); personally mediated racism (prejudice and discrimination at the individual level); and internalized racism (acceptance by members of the stigmatized races of negative messages about their own abilities and intrinsic worth).

RAPID ASSESSMENT INSTRUMENTS (RAIS): Relatively short, self-administered, and easily scored instruments useful for demonstrating that a client's condition warrants treatment because of its effects on his/her functioning. Examples include the SF-36 Health Survey and SF-12 Health Survey.

RAPPORT: Consists of a sense of trust between a social worker and client, a comfortable atmosphere, and a mutual understanding of the purpose of an interview. Many experts believe that rapport must start to develop in the first face-to-face interview because a client's sense of trust and comfort are vital for facilitating a productive assessment.

RATIONAL EMOTIVE BEHAVIOR THERAPY (REBT): (A.k.a. Rational emotive therapy or RET.) From the perspective of REBT, behavior is a chain of events – A, B, and C – where A is the external event to which the individual is exposed; B is the belief the individual has about A; and C is the emotion or behavior that results from B. In other words, an emotional or behavioral response to an external event is due to beliefs about that event rather than to the event itself. According to Ellis, the founder of REBT, the primary cause of neurosis is the continual repetition of certain common irrational beliefs and these beliefs are the appropriate target of therapy.

RATIONALIZATION: A defense mechanism. Occurs when an individual interprets his/her behaviors in a way that makes them seem more rational, logical and/or socially acceptable. Rarely appears before adolescence.

RATIO SCALE: The scale of measurement that has equal intervals between successive points on the measurement scale and an absolute zero point. An absolute zero point makes it possible to multiply and divide ratio scores and to determine more precisely how much more or less of a characteristic one subject has compared to another.

REACTION FORMATION: A defense mechanism in which a person avoids an anxiety-evoking instinct by actively expressing its opposite.

REACTIVE ATTACHMENT DISORDER: Reactive attachment disorder is characterized by a pattern of inhibited and emotionally withdrawn behavior toward adult caregivers as manifested by a lack of seeking or responding to comfort when distressed and a persistent social and emotional disturbance. The diagnosis requires evidence that the child has experienced extreme insufficient care that is believed to be the cause of the disturbed behavior. Symptoms must be apparent before the child is 5 years of age, and the child must have a developmental age of at least 9 months.

REACTIVITY: The response of research subjects that is caused by their awareness of being participants in a research study and/or the knowledge that their behaviors are being observed. Can threaten a study's internal and external validity. Reactivity may also refer more generally to the tendency for people behave differently because they know they are being observed; this tendency can compromise the validity of a formal or informal observational procedure.

REALITY PRINCIPLE: According to Freud, the ego function that gratifies id needs in a manner consistent with the realistic demands of the environment.

REALITY THERAPY: The primary goal of reality therapy is to help clients identify responsible and effective ways to satisfy their needs and thereby to develop a success identity. Reality therapy rejects the medical model and the concept of mental illness; focuses on current behaviors and beliefs; views transference as detrimental to therapy progress; stresses conscious processes; emphasizes value judgments, especially the client's ability to judge what is right and wrong in his/her daily life; and teaches clients specific behaviors that will enable them to fulfill their needs.

REASONABLE ACCOMMODATION (Americans With Disabilities Act): Under the Americans with Disabilities Act, a "qualified person with a disability" is someone with a disability who, with or without "reasonable accommodation," can perform the essential functions of the job he/she holds or has applied for. Reasonable accommodation involves, among other things, making existing workplace facilities readily accessible to and usable by the person with a disability and the acquisition or modification of needed equipment.

RECIPROCAL EMPATHIC RESPONDING: A form of empathic responding used to build trust and understanding. At the reciprocal level, the social worker's verbal and nonverbal responses convey understanding, but are more or less interchangeable with the client's basic messages: They accurately reflect factual aspects of the client's messages and his/her surface feelings.

RECIPROCAL INHIBITION: A form of counterconditioning developed by Wolpe to alleviate anxiety reactions by pairing a stimulus that produces anxiety (CS) with a stimulus that produces relaxation or other incompatible response (US).

REFERENT POWER: A source of power for supervisors and other leaders that derives from a subordinate's identification with the leader and eagerness to be like him/her and liked by him/her. See also *bases of social power*.

REFLECTION (OF CONTENT AND FEELING): An active listening skill that involves restating or repeating something a client has just said with an emphasis on the part of the message that is most helpful. Its key purpose is to build understanding. In reflecting content, a social worker considers what elements of a client's message are most likely to promote achievement of the interview's goals and then uses that content in the reflection; a simple reflection of content will then repeat, verbatim, a key word or phrase from the client's message. In reflecting feeling, a social worker expresses the emotional component of the client's message: Rather than responding to only the client's words, the worker also infers from those words, other verbal cues, and nonverbal cues what the client is feeling about the information being disclosed.

REFRAMING (REDEFINING): A technique used to help clients change the negative meaning they give to an event, behavior, or life experience through gently persuading them that it can be viewed in a different and more positive light. For example, the social worker may offer a new perspective, encourage a client to come up with a new perspective, or redefine a problem behavior as a positive behavior that has been taken to an extreme.

REGRESSION: A defense mechanism. Occurs when a person retreats to an earlier, safer stage of development and behaves in ways characteristic of that stage.

RELABELING AND REFRAMING (Family Therapy): In family therapy, relabeling is used to offer family members an alternative way of perceiving and understanding a symptom, behavior, or problem; the idea is that, when family members view the problem from a different perspective, they may begin responding to it in a different, often healthier, way. Reframing is also used to help family members perceive and understand symptoms or behaviors in a new light; the goal of reframing, however, is usually to change a family's understanding of a symptom from one individual's problem to a family problem.

RELAPSE PREVENTION (RP): A self-management approach emphasized at all stages of addiction treatment. The most common precipitant of relapse among people recovering from substance-use disorders is the experience of anxiety, frustration, depression, or other negative emotional states. According to Marlatt and Gordon, the potential for future relapse is reduced when the client is encouraged to view the episode of drinking as a mistake resulting from specific, external, and controllable factors. Their relapse prevention program combines behavioral and cognitive techniques that are aimed at helping clients deal effectively with situations that elicit negative emotions and other high-risk situations.

RELATIONAL CRISIS (Gilligan): A theory proposing that, in early adolescence, girls experience a relational crisis due to pressures to conform to cultural stereotypes of femininity. As a result, they become disconnected from themselves (e.g., experience a "loss of voice").

RELATIVE POVERTY: An individual's standard of living is well below that of the mainstream community but higher than the subsistence level. See also *absolute poverty*.

RELIABILITY: The degree of accuracy (repeatability, consistency) of a test.

REPRESSION: A defense mechanism. Occurs when the id's drives and needs are excluded from conscious awareness by maintaining them in the unconscious. Considered the most "basic" defense mechanism because it is also the goal of all other defense mechanisms and the foundation of all neuroses.

RESILIENCE: A person's ability to function adaptively despite exposure to risks.

RESILIENCE (Werner and Smith): Longitudinal research by Werner and Smith suggests that exposure to early (prenatal and perinatal) stress may be ameliorated when the baby experiences fewer stressors following birth, exhibits good communication skills and social responsiveness, and receives stable support from a parent or other caregiver.

RESISTANCE (Psychoanalysis): The client's reluctance to bring into conscious awareness repressed, threatening unconscious material. May be manifested as missed appointments, silence during free association, or hostility toward the therapist. Interpretation of a client's resistance leads to insight.

RESOURCE SYSTEMS (SOCIETAL, FORMAL, AND INFORMAL): Resource systems in communities include (a) societal resource systems (e.g., social service agencies and programs and health-care and educational systems) that provide specific kinds of assistance to community residents; (b) formal resource systems (e.g., voluntary membership organizations such as congregations and civic groups); and (c) informal resources systems that perform mutual support activities and include family, friends, neighbors, and coworkers.

RESPONDEAT SUPERIOR DOCTRINE: The legal liability of supervisors (or other employers) for the job-related actions of their supervisees (or employees). When a worker engages in a practice that harms a client, the worker's supervisor can be held liable along with the worker.

RESPONSE COST: A form of negative punishment that involves removing a reinforcer (e.g., a specific number of tokens or points) following a behavior in order to reduce that behavior.

RETROGRADE AMNESIA: A loss of memory for events that occurred or information that was acquired prior to the trauma or other event that caused the amnesia.

REVERSAL (WITHDRAWAL) DESIGN: A type of single-subject design that includes, at a minimum, two baseline phases and one treatment phase (e.g., an ABA or ABAB design). The treatment is withdrawn ("reversed") during the second and subsequent baseline phases.

REWARD POWER: A source of power for supervisors and other leaders involving the ability to control tangible rewards (raises, work assignments, etc.) and psychic rewards (e.g., praise). See also *bases of social power.*

RISKS: Hazards within a person or in the environment that increase the likelihood of a problem occurring. Examples include genetic predisposition for a mental disorder, insecure attachment pattern, and living in poverty.

RISK TECHNIQUE: Technique used to facilitate committee or group members in expressing their concerns about an issue or proposed action.

ROLE (SOCIAL ROLE): A social role is defined in terms of fulfilling an established and regulated position in society (e.g., child, parent, sibling, spouse, employee, organization member, neighbor, immigrant, patient, parolee).

ROLE CONCEPTION: An individual's own beliefs and assumptions about how he/she is supposed to behave in a particular social role. What an individual expects of him/herself may not conform to the role expectations defined by others and the wider society.

ROLE DEMANDS (ROLE REQUIREMENTS): The knowledge, skills, physical and mental abilities, and other personal attributes an individual must have in order to successfully perform a given social role.

ROLE EXPECTATIONS: Beliefs held by relevant others (family, cultural models, society, etc.) regarding how a person in a particular social role should behave. A person's patterned behaviors are often influenced by his/her various social roles.

ROLE INDUCTION: A part of the contracting process with clients when the roles of the client(s) and the social worker are defined. This process tends to reduce the ambiguity of the helping process and the anxiety of clients.

ROLE PERFORMANCE (ROLE ENACTMENT): An individual's actual behavior while performing a social role. A person's role performance may be consistent with his/her role conception but not conform to others' role expectations.

ROLE-PLAYING: A technique in which a client rehearses behaviors that will be useful in a particular situation so that he/she can meet a goal or fulfill an expectation. For example, the client practices the behavior in the social worker's presence and then receives feedback from the worker. When used in this way, as a part of behavioral rehearsal, role-playing is effective for increasing a client's sense of self-efficacy.

ROLE-REVERSAL: A technique used to help clients understand the perceptions and feelings of significant others. It involves having one person (e.g., a spouse, a parent) take on the perspective of another person (e.g., the other spouse, the child) in an effort to better understand him/her. Is particularly useful in couples and family therapy and is indicated whenever one or both parties in a relationship have little or no awareness of how the other one feels.

ROLE THEORY: Set of concepts that define how the behaviors of individuals are influenced by the different social positions they hold and the expectations that accompany those positions.

RUTTER'S INDICATORS: Rutter argues that the greater the number of risk factors a baby is exposed to, the greater the risk for negative outcomes. He concludes that the following six family risk factors are particularly accurate predictors of child psychopathology: severe marital discord, low socioeconomic status, overcrowding or large family size, parental criminality, maternal psychopathology, and the placement of a child outside the home.

SANCTIONS (By Supervisors): Corrective or disciplinary actions a supervisor may take in response to worker noncompliance, listed from least to most severe, include a review of the situation with the worker; a warning; a verbal reprimand if the behavior continues; a written reprimand placed in the worker's file; a lower-than-average evaluation rating; suspension for a limited period; demotion; and dismissal. Other guidelines for taking disciplinary action include the following: (a) The supervisor's objective in applying a sanction should be preventative and corrective, not punitive. (b) The supervisor should respond in a timely way the first time a worker chooses to be noncompliant. (c) The supervisor should discuss in private with a worker any behavior that calls for a reprimand. (d) When delivering a reprimand, the supervisor should be impersonal, consistent, specific, and factual. (e) A reprimand tends to be more effective when the supervisor also communicates concern for the worker, listens to the worker's explanation of the situation and tries to understand how the worker sees it, and conveys a desire to help the worker improve or change.

SATIATION VS. HABITUATION: Satiation is the condition of being satisfied or gratified with regard to a particular reinforcer. Satiation is a problem with continuous reinforcement and with the use of primary (unconditioned) reinforcers. Satiation must be distinguished from habituation, which is the process of becoming accustomed (physiologically nonreactive) to a stimulus as the result of prolonged exposure to that stimulus. Habituation may occur when using punishment if the punishment is initially delivered at low intensity and thereafter gradually increased in intensity.

SCALES OF MEASUREMENT (Statistics): The first consideration when choosing a statistical technique is usually the scale of measurement of the data that is to be described or analyzed. There are four different measurement scales – nominal, ordinal, interval, and ratio – and each involves dividing a set of observations into mutually exclusive and exhaustive categories. The differences between the four scales are that each provides a different kind of information and allows different mathematical operations to be performed.

SCAPEGOATING: The process by which a family designates a member to be the object of displaced conflict or criticism. This family member is typically the identified patient.

Commonly a child may become depressed or engage in delinquent behavior as a way of acting out stress in his/her parents' marriage.

SCHEMA: A knowledge structure or framework about a particular topic or process that influences how information and events are interpreted and responded to.

SCHIZOAFFECTIVE DISORDER: Schizoaffective disorder is a psychotic disorder involving an uninterrupted period of disturbance during which there are concurrent symptoms of a mood disorder and the active-phase symptoms of schizophrenia, with at least a two-week period in which hallucinations and delusions are present *without* predominant mood symptoms.

SCHIZOID PERSONALITY DISORDER: Schizoid personality disorder involves a pervasive pattern of detachment from interpersonal relationships and a restricted range of emotional expression in social settings with at least four characteristic symptoms – doesn't desire or enjoy close relationships; almost always chooses solitary activities; has little interest in sexual relationships; takes pleasure in few activities; lacks close friends or confidents other than first-degree relatives; seems indifferent to praise or criticism; exhibits emotional coldness or detachment.

SCHIZOPHRENIA: A diagnosis of schizophrenia requires the presence of at least two active phase symptoms (i.e., delusions, hallucinations, disorganized speech, grossly disorganized behavior, negative symptoms) for at least one month, with at least one symptom being delusions, hallucinations, or disorganized speech. There must be continuous signs of the disorder for at least six months, and symptoms must cause significant impairment in functioning. Treatment usually includes an antipsychotic drug, cognitive-behavioral therapy, psychoeducation, social skills training, supported employment, and other interventions for the individual with schizophrenia and psychosocial interventions for his/her family.

SCHIZOPHRENIFORM DISORDER: The diagnostic criteria for schizophreniform disorder are identical to those for schizophrenia except that the disturbance is present for at least one month but less than six months and impaired social or occupational functioning may occur but is not required.

SCHIZOTYPAL PERSONALITY DISORDER: Schizotypal personality disorder is diagnosed in the presence of (a) pervasive social and interpersonal deficits involving acute discomfort with and reduced capacity for close relationships and (b) eccentricities in cognition, perception, and behavior as manifested by the presence of at least five symptoms (e.g., ideas of reference, odd beliefs or magical thinking that influence behavior, bodily illusions and other unusual perceptions, is suspicious or has paranoid ideation, inappropriate or constricted affect, lacks close friends or confidents other than first-degree relatives, excessive social anxiety).

SCHOOL BREAKFAST PROGRAM: A federal program that provides states with cash assistance for nonprofit breakfast programs in schools and residential child care institutions.

SCHOOL PHOBIA/SCHOOL REFUSAL: Intense anxiety about going to school or being in school, usually accompanied by a stomachache, headache, nausea, and other physical symptoms.

SCHOOL SOCIAL WORK: Social work practice in school settings that emphasizes enabling students to learn and function in the school environment. The school social worker mobilizes all facets of a student's life situation in an effort to foster a supportive learning environment for the student and serves as a vital link between the student's school, home, and community. School social workers adopt a strengths-based and empowerment approach to their practice;

they seek to identify and build on existing strengths within students and the social systems in which students must function.

SCIENTIFIC MANAGEMENT: As described by Taylor, involves scientifically analyzing jobs into their component parts and then standardizing those parts; scientifically selecting, training, and placing workers in jobs for which they are mentally and physically suited; fostering cooperation between supervisors and workers to minimize deviation from scientific methods of work; and having managers and workers assume responsibility for their own share of their work. Taylor believed that employees are motivated primarily by economic self-interest and argued that money is the most effective motivator.

SCULPTING: An adaptation of psychodrama in which family members position themselves (or objects that represent them) in a way that reflects their relations and roles within the family system. Can be useful for revealing family members' differing perceptions and feelings.

SECONDARY GAIN: See *primary gain and secondary gain.*

SECONDARY PREVENTION: Community mental health intervention that attempts to reduce the prevalence of mental disorders by reducing their duration through early detection and intervention (e.g., training teachers to recognize the early signs of behavior disorders and 24-hour emergency services such as walk-in clinics and hotlines).

SECONDARY (CONDITIONED) REINFORCER: Reinforcers that are not inherently reinforcing but that acquire their reinforcing value through association with a primary reinforcer (e.g., tokens are reinforcing only because they can be exchanged for primary reinforcers).

SECOND GENERATION (ATYPICAL) ANTIPSYCHOTICS (CLOZAPINE): Clozapine and other atypical (newer) antipsychotic drugs affect receptors for several neurotransmitters including dopamine, serotonin, and glutamate. These drugs are effective for both positive and negative symptoms of schizophrenia and are less likely to produce tardive dyskinesia than the traditional antipsychotics. However, they can produce agranulocytosis (loss of the white blood cells that fight infection) and other blood dyscrasias, as well as neuroleptic malignant syndrome. Their use requires careful blood monitoring.

SECOND ORDER CHANGE: Basic changes in the structure and functioning of a system that alter its fundamental organization. A symptomatic family can be said to undergo second order change when a therapeutic intervention fundamentally disrupts the pattern of symptomatic interaction so that it ceases.

SECTION 8 PROGRAMS: A social security program. Section 8 rental voucher and rental certificate programs are the federal government's major programs for assisting very low-income families, older adults, and the disabled to rent decent, safe, and sanitary housing in the private market. Because the rental assistance is provided on behalf of the family or individual, participants are able to find and lease privately owned housing, including single-family homes, townhouses, and apartments. The participant is free to choose any housing that meets the requirements of the program and is not limited to units located in subsidized housing projects. Eligibility for a rental voucher or certificate is determined by the local public housing authority based on total annual gross income and family size and is limited to U.S. citizens and specified categories of noncitizens who have eligible immigration status. Generally the family's income cannot exceed 50 percent of the median income for the county or metropolitan area in which the family chooses to live.

SECTION 8 SINGLE ROOM OCCUPANCY (SRO): SRO housing assistance seeks to bring more standard single-room dwelling units into the local housing supply and to use those units to assist homeless individuals. The Department of Housing and Urban Development (HUD) contracts with public housing authorities (PHAs) to rehabilitate residential properties for SRO housing. PHAs make Section 8 rental assistance payments to participating owners on behalf of homeless individuals who rent the rehabilitated dwellings. The rental assistance payments cover the difference between a portion of the tenant's income (normally 30 percent) and the unit's rent, which must be within the fair market rent established by HUD. Rental assistance for SRO units is provided for a period of 10 years.

SEDATIVE-HYPNOTICS (BENZODIAZEPINES): The sedative-hypnotics include the barbiturates, anxiolytics, and alcohol. These drugs are generalized CNS depressants, and their effects, for the most part, are dose dependent: At low doses, these drugs reduce arousal and motor activity; at moderate doses, they induce sedation and sleep; and at high doses, they can produce anesthesia, coma, and death. The benzodiazepines are a type of anxiolytic. Their side-effects include drowsiness, ataxia, slurred speech, and other signs of CNS depression; abrupt cessation can cause rebound hyperexcitability. The benzodiazepines are the most commonly prescribed anxiolytic and are used to alleviate anxiety and treat sleep disturbances, seizures, cerebral palsy, and alcohol withdrawal. Common side-effects include drowsiness, dizziness, lethargy, slurred speech, and impaired psychomotor ability. They can also produce paradoxical agitation, impaired sexual functioning, confusion, and sleep disturbances.

SEEKING CONCRETENESS: Interview technique used to determine the specific meaning of vague words that a client has used or to elicit specific information that might not otherwise be revealed. Having a client define or explain certain words helps the social worker understand the problem and prevents the worker from making assumptions.

SELECTIVE ELIGIBILITY: Social service delivery policy in which benefits and services are provided to only persons who meet specific, pre-established criteria; eligibility is often determined by using a means test. The amount of the benefit varies based on special needs, circumstances, or economic status.

SELF-CONTROL PROCEDURES: Techniques administered by the client him/herself and most commonly used to increase behaviors that occur less frequently than desired or to decrease self-injurious behaviors. Include self-monitoring, stimulus control, self-reinforcement, and self-punishment.

SELF-DETERMINATION: Principle in social work practice that recognizes clients' need and right to make their own decisions and choices.

SELF-EFFICACY BELIEFS: Positive beliefs about one's self-efficacy (personal mastery) include feeling competent, effective, and in control of one's life. A person's self-efficacy beliefs determine how much effort he/she is willing to exert and how long he/she will continue to act when faced with obstacles.

SELF-FULFILLING PROPHECY: An expectation about a certain group, person, etc., that influences the way that group, person, etc. is perceived. Can occur when social workers or other therapists have biases about certain groups and may adversely affect treatment. For example, if a therapist believes the poor have low incomes because they are too lazy to work, he/she might not follow through on a poor client's request for vocational assistance.

SELF-HELP GROUPS: Groups intended to improve members' social functioning through a group experience and discussions with others who have, or had, similar problems or concerns. Examples of self-help groups include those through self-help organizations such as

Alcoholics Anonymous, Overeaters Anonymous, and Parents Without Partners. Many self-help groups rely on leaders who are also members of the group but some are led by professionals or by members who have received training on how to conduct and lead meetings.

SELF-INSTRUCTIONAL TRAINING: A cognitive-behavioral technique in which the individual learns to modify maladaptive thoughts and behaviors through the use of covert self-statements. It was originally developed as a way to help impulsive and hyperactive children slow down their behaviors and guide themselves through academic and other types of tasks.

SELF-MONITORING (Behavior Therapy): Observational technique in which a client is asked to record information about the frequency and conditions surrounding a target behavior; the client may also be instructed to keep a journal of other important information such as his/her feelings and thoughts before, during, and after each occurrence of the behavior. Results provide detailed information about the behavior and the variables that influence it so that an appropriate intervention strategy can be developed and the effects of the intervention can be evaluated.

SELF-MONITORING (Social Psychology): The need for and ability to manage the impression that others form of us. High self-monitors are most concerned about their "public self" and, consequently, strive to match their attitudes and behaviors to the situation. Low self-monitors are guided primarily by their own beliefs and values and attempt to alter the situation to match their "private self."

SELF-REPORT INVENTORIES AND CHECKLISTS: Tools used to assess and diagnose specific client problems, determine the need for further assessment in specific areas, and facilitate treatment planning, monitoring, and outcome assessment. A useful alternative to longer psychological tests when the presence or severity of one problem, condition, or symptom is of particular concern. Are easy to administer and allow a social worker to learn a client's own perception of his/her problem; however, are susceptible to response sets on the part of the client, yield limited information, and must be supplemented with data from other sources.

SENSATE FOCUS: Technique used in sex therapy to reduce performance anxiety and increase sexual excitement. Involves "nongenital pleasuring" initially, gradually building to genital stimulation with a ban on intercourse.

SENSORIMOTOR STAGE: First stage in Piaget's model of cognitive development (the first two years of life). During this stage, knowledge is acquired through the senses and motor behaviors. The end of this stage is marked by the emergence of symbolic thought and object permanence.

SEPARATION ANXIETY: A normal fear response exhibited by a young child when he/she is separated from his/her mother or other primary caregiver. Begins at about 6 to 8 months, increases in intensity at about 14 to 18 months, and thereafter declines.

SEPARATION ANXIETY DISORDER: Separation anxiety disorder involves developmentally inappropriate and excessive fear or anxiety related to separation from home or attachment figures as evidenced by at least three symptoms (e.g., recurrent excessive distress when anticipating or experiencing separation from home or major attachment figures, persistent excessive fear of being alone, repeated complaints of physical symptoms when separation from an attachment figure occurs or is anticipated). The disturbance must last at least four weeks in children and adolescents or six months in adults and must cause clinically significant distress or impaired functioning.

SEPARATION-INDIVIDUATION (Mahler): According to Mahler, the development of object relations occurs during a developmental stage termed separation-individuation, which begins at about age 4 months. Separation refers to the development of limits or the differentiation between the infant (self) and the mother; and individuation refers to the development of the infant's ego, sense of identity, and cognitive abilities.

SERVICE DELIVERY SYSTEMS: Means of delivering health and human services within communities. Informal service-delivery units include household units and social networks; mediating service-delivery units include self-help groups, grassroots associations, and voluntary associations; and formal service-delivery units include nonprofit and for-profit private agencies and public agencies.

SEXUAL ABUSE (Children): The initiation of an interaction with a child by an adult or older child for the purpose of sexually gratifying or stimulating the adult or older child or another person (e.g., genital fondling, molestation, rape, incest, sexual exploitation, exhibitionism, pedophilia). The majority of victims are assaulted by someone they know and trust (e.g., a parent, parent surrogate, other relative, friend). Only a small minority of sexual abusers use physical violence; most use bribes, threats, and other forms of coercion and/or the existing relationship with the child to gain the child's cooperation.

SEXUAL PREJUDICE, SEXUAL STIGMA, HETEROSEXISM (Herek): Herek (2004) argues that sexual prejudice is a more precise term than homophobia and describes sexual prejudice as all negative attitudes based on sexual orientation, whether the target is homosexual, bisexual, or heterosexual. Herek also uses the term heterosexism, which he defines as cultural ideologies or "systems that provide the rationale and operating instructions" that promote and perpetrate antipathy, hostility, and violence against homosexuals. Furthermore, stigma refers to "the shared knowledge of society's negative regard for any nonheterosexual behavior, identity, relationship, or community."

SHAPING: (A.k.a. the method of "successive approximations.") Behavioral technique that involves teaching a new behavior through prompting and reinforcing behaviors that come closer and closer to the target behavior.

SINGLE-SUBJECT DESIGNS: (e.g., AB, ABA, ABAB and multiple baseline designs.) Research designs that involve obtaining repeated measurements from a single subject over a specific period of time to measure changes in behaviors, attitudes, or beliefs. Each single-subject design includes at least one baseline (no treatment) phase and one treatment phase. As a result, the subject acts as his/her own no-treatment "control." In most single-subject designs, the dependent variable (behavior, attitude, or belief) is measured repeatedly at regular intervals throughout the baseline and treatment phases. If status on the dependent variable is stable within each phase of the study and changes only at the same time that the independent variable (treatment) is applied or removed, then it is likely that any observed change in the dependent variable is due to the effects of the independent variable rather than to history, maturation, or another extraneous factor.

SITUATIONAL CRISES: A crisis in which the origin is a sudden, random, shocking, and often catastrophic event that cannot be anticipated or controlled. Factors that determine whether a person will experience such an event as a crisis include his/her perception or interpretation of the event and available coping mechanisms and social supports.

SLIDING FEE SCALE: Practice in which clients are charged for services according to their ability to pay rather than on a flat-fee basis.

SOAP CHARTING: Charting system used in many medical and mental health professions that entails classifying client information according to the acronym, SOAP (Subjective information, Objective information, Assessments, and Plan).

SOCIAL ACTION: An organized effort to bring about institutional change; the goal is usually to meet a certain need, address a social problem, correct an injustice, or improve quality of life. An effort may be organized by professionals or by the people who are directly affected by the desired change or the problem.

SOCIAL ACTION MODEL: Community organizing model that focuses on redistributing power and resources through institutional change. The client system is a segment of the community that has experienced social injustice and, therefore, has difficulty making demands in the larger society. Community power centers are the targets of social change.

SOCIAL AGENCY: An organization or facility that delivers social services under the auspices of a board of directors and provides a range of social services for members of a population group that has or is vulnerable to a specific social problem.

SOCIAL ANXIETY DISORDER (SOCIAL PHOBIA): Social anxiety disorder involves intense fear or anxiety about one or more social situations in which the individual may be exposed to scrutiny by others. The individual fears that he/she will exhibit anxiety symptoms in these situations that will be negatively evaluated; he/she avoids the situations or endures them with intense fear or anxiety; and his/her fear or anxiety is not proportional to the threat posed by the situations. The fear, anxiety, and avoidance are persistent and cause clinically significant distress or impaired functioning. Exposure with response prevention is an effective treatment, and its benefits may be enhanced when it is combined with social skills training or cognitive restructuring and other cognitive techniques.

SOCIAL ASSESSMENT REPORTS: Professional reports that describe the social aspects of a client's functioning and his/her situation (i.e., social history) with a particular focus on the match or lack of match between a client's needs and the resources available to meet his/her needs. Used by social workers to communicate to other professionals (e.g., interdisciplinary teams, doctors, psychologists, school personnel, judges) relevant social information about a client (or family) and are particularly useful when decisions are being made about the type of service or program that would be most appropriate for a client and/or when attempting to facilitate a client's adjustment to a new environment (e.g., foster home, nursing home).

SOCIAL CAPITAL: The collection of values, beliefs, and behaviors that are followed by the members of a society and that contribute to the well-being of all. Social capital tends to be higher when people's sense of community is strong.

SOCIAL CLASS: A social category of persons based on wealth, status, power, educational attainment and background.

SOCIAL DARWINISM: Ideology that assumes that income differences between the wealthy and the poor occur because the wealthy inherently are "more fit."

SOCIAL EXCHANGE THEORY: Proposes that social behavior is the result of an exchange process. The purpose of exchange is to maximize benefits and minimize costs – people weigh the potential benefits and risks of social relationships, and when risks outweigh rewards, people end or abandon a relationship.

SOCIAL FUNCTIONING: A person's motivation, capacity, and opportunity to (a) meet his/her basic needs (including performing tasks necessary for daily living such as obtaining food, shelter, and transportation) and (b) perform his/her major social roles as defined by his/her community and culture. Information about a client's need-meeting activities and social role performance provides valuable information about his/her current level of social functioning, including strengths and deficits.

SOCIAL NETWORK GRID: Assessment tool used to identify a client's potential social supports with an emphasis on his/her perceptions and beliefs about them. Results can be used to help the client use his/her social supports more effectively.

SOCIAL NETWORKS: Networks that include individuals or groups linked by a common bond, shared social status, similar or shared functions, or geographic or cultural connection. They develop and discontinue on an ad hoc basis, depending on specific need and interest. Types of social networks include support systems, natural social networks, self-help groups, and groups of formal organizations.

SOCIAL PLANNING: The use of organized procedures to achieve improved socioeconomic structures and manage social change in a rational way. Usually includes assigning an individual or organization to collect facts, defining several courses of action, and making recommendations to those with the power to carry out the plan.

SOCIAL PLANNING MODEL: Community organizing model that focuses on providing needed goods and services through a technical process that emphasizes fact-gathering, rational decision-making, and regulated change by experts, usually with the backing of an existing organization. The client system may include all residents of a geographic-spatial community or one of its segments. Community power centers are regarded as potential sponsors of social programs.

SOCIAL POLICY: Laws and regulations established by a government that determine which social programs exist, what categories of clients are served, and who qualifies for a program. Social policy also sets standards regarding the type of services to be provided, the qualifications of service providers, etc., and rules for how money can be spent to help people and how these people will be treated.

SOCIAL (PRAGMATIC) COMMUNICATION DISORDER: Social (pragmatic) communication disorder involves persistent difficulties in the social use of language and nonverbal communication that limit effective communication, social participation, social relationships, academic achievement, or work performance. Autism spectrum disorder (ASD) includes similar social communication deficits: If these deficits are present, a diagnosis of social (pragmatic) communication disorder can be made only if the person has never displayed the restricted/repetitive patterns of behavior, interests, or activities that are associated with ASD.

SOCIAL SECURITY ACT: Federal legislation passed in 1935 and designed to help meet the economic needs of older people, dependent survivors, people with disabilities, and needy families. The two major provisions of the Act, in its original form, were a mandatory insurance program for workers funded by payroll taxes and matching employer contributions and a public assistance program financed by both federal and state treasuries.

SOCIAL SECURITY DISABILITY INSURANCE (SSDI): See *Disability Insurance*.

SOCIOCULTURAL RISK: Exists when a child lacks the basic material, social, and psychological necessities of life (e.g., food, water, shelter, love and affection, medical care, educational stimulation, positive social interactions). Children (and adults) who lack all or some of these necessities are at risk for impaired development and other deficiencies. Two key sources of sociocultural risk are "social impoverishment" (lack of critical social resources in a child's life) and "cultural impoverishment" (values that undermine a child's healthy development).

SOCIOECONOMIC CLASS (OR STATUS; SES): Categorization of groups of people according to level of income or education, value orientation, location of residence, etc. (e.g., upper, middle, and working classes).

SOLUTION-FOCUSED THERAPY: Solution-focused therapists believe that understanding the etiology or attributes of problem (maladaptive) behavior is irrelevant and focus, instead, on solutions to problems. In therapy, the client is viewed as the "expert," while the therapist acts as a consultant/collaborator who poses questions designed to assist the client in recognizing and using his/her strengths and resources to achieve specific goals (e.g., the miracle question, exception questions, scaling questions).

SOMATIC NERVOUS SYSTEM (SNS): Consists of sensory nerves that carry information from the body's sense receptors to the central nervous system (CNS) and motor nerves that carry information from the CNS to the skeletal muscles. The SNS governs activities that are ordinarily considered voluntary.

SPECIAL SUPPLEMENTAL NUTRITION PROGRAM FOR WOMEN, INFANTS, AND CHILDREN (WIC): See *WIC*.

SPECIFIC LEARNING DISORDER: Specific learning disorder is diagnosed when a person exhibits difficulties related to academic skills as indicated by the presence of at least one characteristic symptom that persists for at least six months despite the provision of interventions targeting those difficulties. The diagnosis requires that the individual's academic skills are substantially below those expected for his/her age, interfere with academic or occupational performance or activities of daily living, began during the school-age years, and are not better accounted for by another condition or disorder or other factor such as uncorrected visual or auditory impairment or psychosocial adversity.

SPECIFIC PHOBIA: Specific phobia is characterized by intense fear of or anxiety about a specific object or situation, with the individual either avoiding the object or situation or enduring it with marked distress. The fear or anxiety is not proportional to the danger posed by the object or situation, is persistent (typically lasting for at least six months), and causes clinically significant distress or impaired functioning. The treatment-of-choice is exposure with response prevention (especially in vivo exposure).

SSRIs (SELECTIVE SEROTONIN REUPTAKE INHIBITORS): Antidepressant drugs that include Prozac and Zoloft. Exert their effects by blocking the reuptake of serotonin. Side-effects include gastrointestinal disturbances, sexual dysfunction, insomnia, anxiety, headache, and anorexia. In comparison to the TCAs, the SSRIs are less cardiotoxic, safer in overdose, and less likely to produce cognitive impairments.

STAFF DEVELOPMENT: The procedures used by an agency to improve the job-related knowledge, skills, and attitudes of its staff. In-service training and educational supervision are examples of staff development procedures.

STAKEHOLDERS: People in a community with a particular interest in what happens with a social agency or program; they may be for or against the service or program. For a typical social service, there are usually three kinds of stakeholders: (a) patrons (those who provide support and/or legitimacy for the service or program), (b) agents and the social service agency (those who carry out the patrons' wishes and provide the services), and (c) clients (those who receive the services).

STARTING WHERE THE CLIENT IS: Entails focusing on a client's priorities, including his/her primary concerns (what he/she considers important or wants to talk about) and current emotional state.

STEREOTYPES: Schemas about entire groups that contain oversimplified, rigid, and generalized impressions of members of those groups; these impressions are held despite the existence of individual differences among members of the group. A serious consequence of stereotyping is the devaluation of the individual which occurs when the people belonging to another group are no longer viewed as unique individuals – instead, all members of the group are presumed have the same, often negative or inferior, characteristics.

STIMULUS CONTROL: In operant conditioning, the process by which a behavior does or does not occur due to the presence (or absence) of discriminative stimuli. Positive discriminative stimuli signal that a behavior will be reinforced; negative discriminative stimuli (S-delta stimuli) signal that a behavior will not be reinforced.

STIMULUS DISCRIMINATION AND EXPERIMENTAL NEUROSIS: In classical conditioning, stimulus discrimination training is used to teach an organism to respond with a CR only in the presence of certain stimuli – i.e., in the presence of the original CS. Sometimes, when discriminations are difficult, the organism will exhibit "experimental neurosis" (i.e., it will exhibit unusual behaviors such as restlessness, aggressiveness, or fear).

STIMULUS GENERALIZATION: In operant and classical conditioning, stimulus generalization refers to responding with a particular response to similar stimuli. In classical conditioning, it refers to responding to stimuli similar to the CS with the CR; in operant conditioning, the term is used to describe responding to stimuli similar to the discriminative stimuli with the target behavior.

STRANGER ANXIETY: A normal fear response to strangers exhibited by young children. Begins at about 8 to 10 months of age and declines during the second year.

STRATEGIC FAMILY THERAPY (Haley): Family therapy approach that focuses on transactional patterns and views symptoms as interpersonal events that serve to control relationships; focuses on symptom relief (rather than insight); and involves the use of specific strategies, especially paradoxical techniques and homework assignments. Influenced by structural family therapy, the communication/interaction school, and the work of Milton Erickson.

STRENGTHS PERSPECTIVE: An approach that requires attention to a client's (or community's) strengths and resources during assessment and intervention and serves as a counterbalance to the focus on problems, deficiencies, and pathology that characterizes many commonly used practice theories and models.

STRESS INOCULATION: A cognitive-behavioral technique used to help individuals cope with stressful and other aversive states by enhancing their coping skills. It includes three stages: cognitive (education), skills acquisition, and application.

STRUCTURAL FAMILY THERAPY (Minuchin): Family therapy approach that emphasizes altering the family's structure (rigid triangles, power hierarchies) in order to change the behavior patterns of family members. Involves joining the family system, evaluating the family structure, and then restructuring the family using several techniques such as enactment and reframing. Focus is on behavior change rather than achieving insight.

SUBLIMATION: A defense mechanism. A type of displacement in which an unacceptable impulse is diverted into a socially acceptable, even admirable, activity. Considered to be a "mature" defense mechanism (i.e., it is common in "healthy" adults).

SUBPOENA: A written legal document requiring a person to appear in court to testify at a certain time and/or to produce certain written records.

SUBPOENA DUCES TECUM: Subpoena requiring a witness who is called to bring to court, or to a deposition, any relevant documents he/she possesses.

SUBSTANCE-INDUCED DISORDERS: The substance-induced disorders include substance intoxication, substance withdrawal, and substance/medication-induced mental disorders. The latter "are potentially severe, usually temporary, but sometimes persisting central nervous system (CNS) syndromes that develop in the context of the effects of substances of abuse, medications, or toxins" (APA, 2013, p. 487) and include, among others, substance/medication-induced psychotic disorder, substance/medication-induced depressive disorder, and substance/medication-induced neurocognitive disorders.

SUBSTANCE USE DISORDERS: The substance use disorders are characterized by "a cluster of cognitive, behavioral, and physiological symptoms indicating that the individual continues using the substance despite significant substance-related problems" (APA, 2013, p. 483) as manifested by at least two symptoms during a 12-month period. The characteristic symptoms can be categorized in terms of four groups: (a) impaired control (e.g., substance used in larger amounts or for a longer period of time than intended, persistent desire or unsuccessful efforts to cut down or control use, craving for the substance); (b) social impairment (e.g., recurrent substance use despite persistent social problems caused or worsened by substance use, important activities given up due to substance use); (c) risky use (e.g., continued substance use despite knowing that doing so creates a physical or psychological problem); and (d) pharmacological criteria (tolerance, withdrawal).

SUBSYSTEM: An element or functional component that, is itself, a system but also plays a specialized role in the operation of a larger system. The family system differentiates and carries out its functions through the subsystems. In a family, subsystems include the individual, spouse, parent, and sibling.

SUBTLE RACISM: Term used to describe a less blatant (more covert) form of racism, which some authors contend has replaced "old-fashioned" (overt) prejudice and discrimination. Typically refers to the beliefs, attitudes, and actions of individuals rather than institutions.

SUDDEN INFANT DEATH SYNDROME (SIDS): The unexpected death of an infant for which no physical cause can be found. Although the cause of SIDS is unknown, SIDS occurs more often in low-birth-weight infants, premature infants, infants with low Apgar scores, infants who sleep on their stomachs, infants with a sibling who previously died of SIDS, and male infants. Maternal risk factors include young age, low SES, smoking, drug abuse during pregnancy, closely spaced pregnancies, and inadequate prenatal care.

SUMMARIZATION (SUMMARIZING): A verbal message from a social worker that ties together functionally related elements that occur at different times in the helping process.

SUMMATIVE EVALUATION (Direct Practice Evaluation): An assessment of the final outcome of an intervention; also identifies factors that contributed to the relative success or failure of an intervention.

SUMMATIVE EVALUATION (Program Evaluation): Describes the research goal once a program has been developed and implemented – i.e., the goal is to evaluate the program's effects. Summative evaluation is most useful when it involves a true or quasi-experimental research approach. Summative evaluation results may be generalized to other programs, situations, and populations and used to make decisions about closing programs or opening other programs similar to the one that was evaluated.

SUPEREGO: For Freud, the structure of the psyche that represents society's standards of right and wrong (the conscience) and the individual's own aims and aspirations (ego ideal). Develops at age 4 or 5 years, primarily as the result of identification with one's parents.

SUPERORDINATE GOALS: Goals that can be achieved only when individuals or members of different groups work together cooperatively. These have been found useful for reducing intergroup conflict.

SUPPLEMENTAL SECURITY INCOME (SSI): A social security program. A federal income supplement program funded by general tax revenues (not social security taxes). SSI is designed to help aged, blind, and disabled people who have little or no income and provides cash to meet basic needs for food, clothing, and shelter. Basic requirements for SSI eligibility involve citizenship, income, financial resources, age, and disability. Since the passage of the Personal Responsibility and Work Opportunity Reconciliation Act of 1996, SSI eligibility is generally restricted to U.S. citizens living in one of the 50 States, the District of Columbia, or the Northern Mariana Islands. However, eligibility is still possible for noncitizen members of certain classes of refugees or asylees, active duty or retired military personnel and their families, and lawful permanent residents who have earned or can be credited with 40 quarters of social security covered employment.

SUPPORTIVE COUNSELING: Counseling in which the emphasis is on providing reassurance, guidance, support, encouragement, explanation, and opportunities to express emotions and reinforcing a client's healthy and adaptive patterns of thought and behavior.

SUPPORTIVE SUPERVISION: Supervision function concerned with providing the psychological and interpersonal resources that enable workers to function effectively on an emotional level.

SUPPORT SYSTEM: An interrelated group of people, resources, and organizations that provide an individual with emotional, informational, material, and affectional support and can be called on in times of need. The members of a person's support system may include his/her family members, friends and other peers, coworkers, membership organizations, and institutions.

SUSTAINMENT INTERVENTIONS: Relationship-building activities used primarily in the initial phases of the change process to reduce a client's feelings of anxiety or guilt, increase his/her self-esteem, and instill a sense of hope. Examples include acceptance, reassurance, and encouragement.

SYMBOLIC (MODERN) RACISM: A theory about current, less blatant forms of racism that reflect a combination of anti-African-American attitudes, strong support for traditional American values (e.g., the work ethic), and a belief that African-Americans violate those values.

SYMBOLIC (REPRESENTATIONAL) THOUGHT: The ability to use words, actions, and other symbols to represent objects and experiences. Emerges at the end of Piaget's sensorimotor stage of development. Also referred to as "symbolic capacity."

SYMMETRICAL COMMUNICATION: Communication that occurs between equals and may escalate into a competitive one-upsmanship game.

SYMPATHETIC DIVISION: The division of the autonomic nervous system involved in the mediation of flight or fight (emergency) reactions. Activation produces increased heart rate, pupil dilation, increased blood sugar, and inhibition of the digestive processes.

SYSTEMATIC DESENSITIZATION: A classical conditioning procedure based on counterconditioning (reciprocal inhibition). It involves pairing hierarchically-arranged anxiety-evoking stimuli with relaxation in order to eliminate the anxiety response.

SYSTEMATIC ECLECTICISM: An approach to selecting intervention strategies for a client that entails choosing interventions from different practice perspectives, theories, and models based on how well they match a client's problem and the empirical research showing the interventions to be effective.

TANF (TEMPORARY ASSISTANCE FOR NEEDY FAMILIES): Social security program that provides assistance and work opportunities to needy families by granting states federal funds and flexibility to develop and implement their own welfare programs. TANF places restrictions on recipients (e.g., most recipients must work after no more than two years on cash assistance, families receiving assistance for five cumulative years may become ineligible for cash aid).

TARDIVE DYSKINESIA: Potentially irreversible extrapyramidal side-effect associated with long-term use of a first-generation (traditional) antipsychotic drug. Symptoms include rhythmical, stereotyped movements of the muscles of the face, limbs, and trunk (similar to Huntington's chorea). In some cases, symptoms are alleviated by a GABA agonist or by gradual withdrawal of the drug.

TASK GROUPS (TASK FORCES): Temporary groupings created to achieve a specific, predefined goal or function. At an agency, for example, task group meetings of various forms provide a forum for staff to exchange information and give and receive feedback and support, for tasks to be distributed, and for planning, decision-making, and problem-solving.

TEAM SERVICE DELIVERY: Participatory management approach in which a team of workers is given responsibility for performing the primary tasks of supervision. The supervisor is just another member of the team, but has somewhat higher status – he/she acts as consultant, coordinator, and resource person and, when necessary, as a team leader. The group is authorized to make decisions but final decisions must be approved by the supervisor.

TELEMENTAL HEALTH SERVICES: Mental health services that are delivered to a client not in a face-to face setting. This can include email, internet therapy, videoconferencing, chat rooms, social media, etc.

TEMPORARY ASSISTANCE FOR NEEDY FAMILIES: See *TANF*.

TERATOGENS: Substances (e.g., alcohol, nicotine, lead, amphetamines and other drugs, certain medications) that cross the placental barrier and cause defects in the embryo or fetus. The different organs are most susceptible to the effects of teratogens at different times but, overall, exposure during the embryonic stage is most likely to cause major structural abnormalities.

TERTIARY PREVENTION: Community mental health intervention that attempts to reduce the duration of mental disorders by reducing their duration and consequences (e.g., rehabilitation programs and halfway houses).

THEORY X AND THEORY Y: According to McGregor, Theory X managers believe that employees dislike work and avoid it whenever possible and, as a result, must be directed and controlled. In contrast, Theory Y managers view work as being "as natural as play" and assume that employees are capable of self-control and self-direction.

THERAPEUTIC PARADOX: When a therapist uses a therapeutic paradox, he/she uses an intervention that may seem contradictory to the therapeutic objectives. Yet, the goal of the therapeutic paradox is to bring about desired change that is consistent with the goals of therapy. Prescribing the symptom is an example of a therapeutic paradox.

THERAPIST-CLIENT MATCHING: Research on therapist-client matching in terms of race, ethnicity, or culture has shown that it increases the duration of treatment but does not have consistent effects on other therapy outcomes.

THINNING VERSUS FADING (Behavioral Therapy): Thinning refers to the process of reducing the proportion of reinforcements. Fading refers to the gradual removal of prompts.

THIRD-PARTY PAYMENT: Monetary reimbursement made to the social worker, agency, or other provider of services to a client by an insurance company or government funding agency.

TIME-OUT: A form of negative punishment in which the individual is removed from all opportunities for reinforcement for a prespecified period of time following a misbehavior in order to decrease the occurrence of that behavior.

TIME-SERIES COMPARISON: Technique for collecting and displaying data that provides data from repeated observations over time. It displays trends in the variable(s) of interest, which can help predict future needs and cost based on assumptions about these trends.

TITLE XX OF THE SOCIAL SECURITY ACT: An amendment to the Social Security Act designed to prevent, reduce, or eliminate dependency on welfare and change how social services were delivered to low-income people. Under Title XX ("Social Services Block Grant," 1974), states started receiving funding for social service programs through block grants from the federal government which increased their flexibility in determining where to allocate the funds.

TOURETTE'S DISORDER: Tourette's disorder is characterized by the presence of at least one vocal tic and multiple motor tics that may appear simultaneously or at different times, may wax and wane in frequency, have persisted for more than one year, and began prior to age 18.

TRACKING (Family Therapy): Structural family therapy technique in which the therapist helps the family elaborate the details of behaviors in order to clarify the nature of its problem. Permits the family a new and expanded version of reality, thereby taking the focus off of the identified or index patient.

TRANSFERENCE: A client's experience of feelings, attitudes, fantasies, etc., toward the therapist, which represent a projection or displacement and repetition of reactions to a significant other person in the client's past. Freud considered transference to be a form of resistance and the cornerstone of psychoanalysis.

TRANSFERENCE NEUROSIS: The "artificial neurosis" that occurs during the course of psychoanalysis and that involves the development of transference.

TRANSFER PAYMENTS: Used to fund some social security programs. Involve taking cash benefits from one group and redirecting them to another group (i.e., through withholding payroll money and placing it in the federal treasury, which then disburses the funds to the eligible group).

TRANSGENDER: Refers to a person whose gender identity differs from assigned sex at birth. May choose to participate in hormone treatment and reconstructive surgery to change genital or secondary sex characteristics.

TRANSTHEORETICAL MODEL: Prochaska and DiClemente's model of behavior change that proposes that change involves six stages: precontemplation (the person is unaware of his/her problem or unwilling to change it); contemplation (the person is considering the possibility of change but remains ambivalent); determination (a person's decisional balance tips in favor of change and he/she becomes ready and determined to change); action (the person takes action to make the desired change); maintenance (the goals are to sustain the change accomplished through action and to prevent relapse); and relapse (may occur before the person achieves stable change and is considered a normal part of the change process, especially when a person is attempting to change a longstanding behavior or pattern).

TRAUMA-INFORMED CARE: "A strengths-based framework that is responsive to the impact of trauma, emphasizing physical, psychological, and emotional safety for both service providers and survivors; and creates opportunities for survivors to rebuild a sense of control and empowerment" (Mental Health Coordinating Council, 2017).

TREATMENT MANUALS: Originally developed to assist in research and training but are now considered a means of delivering empirically supported treatments (ESTs) to clients with specific disorders. Manuals have several advantages: They provide a theoretical framework for understanding a client's symptoms/disorder; offer concrete descriptions of therapy techniques; and present case examples that illustrate the appropriate application of the techniques. However, like practice guidelines, treatment manuals do not take into account a client's unique characteristics or the nonspecific factors that have been linked to positive treatment outcomes.

TRIANGLING: The process in which a third person is introduced into a dyadic relationship to balance either excessive intimacy or distance and, thereby, provide stability in the system. Associated with the work of Bowen.

TRIANGULATION: According to Minuchin, a form of rigid triad involving usually two parents and a child. In triangulation, the two parents avoid conflict by involving the child, thereby stabilizing their own relationship. For example, each parent may demand that the child side with him/her in a conflict with the other. The child is then paralyzed, for no matter how he/she responds, he/she is defined by one of the parents as attacking. Although originally defined by Minuchin and others as it relates to the parents and a child, triangulation can refer to any triad in which the conflict of two individuals involves a third person in a way that immobilizes the third person in a loyalty conflict.

TRICYCLICS (IMIPRAMINE, CLOMIPRAMINE): The tricyclic antidepressants (TCAs) are believed to work by blocking the reuptake of norepinephrine, dopamine, and/or serotonin. They are most effective for alleviating somatic, vegetative symptoms. Side-effects include anticholinergic effects, confusion, drowsiness, weight gain, and cardiovascular symptoms.

Imipramine has also been found useful for treating enuresis, while clomipramine is an effective treatment for panic disorder, agoraphobia, bulimia nervosa, and OCD.

TRUE EXPERIMENTAL RESEARCH: Experimental research that provides the investigator with maximal experimental control. Most important, when conducting a true experimental research study, an investigator can randomly assign subjects to groups, which makes it easier to determine if observed variability in the dependent variable was actually caused by the different levels of the independent variable.

UNCOMPLICATED BEREAVEMENT: Uncomplicated bereavement is included in the DSM-5 with other conditions that may be a focus of clinical attention and is described as "a normal reaction to the death of a loved one" (APA, 2013, p. 716). Uncomplicated bereavement may include symptoms of a major depressive episode, but the individual usually experiences the symptoms as normal and may be seeking treatment for insomnia, anorexia, or other associated symptoms.

UNCONDITIONED RESPONSE (UR): In classical conditioning, the response naturally elicited by the unconditioned stimulus (US) without conditioning.

UNCONDITIONED STIMULUS (US): In classical conditioning, the stimulus that naturally elicits the target response (unconditioned response, UR) without conditioning. In Pavlov's original studies, meat powder was the US and salivation was the UR.

UNDOING: A defense mechanism. Occurs when a person repeatedly engages in a behavior to undo the effects of a past action that he/she has found to be unacceptable. The behavior is typically the opposite of the unacceptable action.

UNDOCUMENTED STATUS: A person is a non-citizen residing in the United States with expired or nullified immigration documents or no documents at all. Also known as an undocumented alien, this individual entered the United States illegally and is deportable if apprehended. The term also refers to a person who entered the United States legally but has fallen "out of status" and is therefore deportable.

UNEMPLOYMENT INSURANCE: Social security program designed to provide partial income replacement to regularly employed members of the labor force who become involuntarily unemployed. Unemployment benefits are available as a matter of right (i.e., without a means test) to unemployed workers who have demonstrated their attachment to the labor force by a specified amount of recent work and/or earnings in covered employment. All workers whose employers contribute to or make payments in lieu of contributions to state unemployment funds are eligible if they become involuntarily unemployed and are able to work, available for work, and actively seeking work, and register at a public employment office. Workers must also meet the eligibility and qualifying requirements of their state's law. Workers who meet these eligibility conditions may be denied benefits if they are found to be responsible for their own unemployment. The benefit may be reduced if the worker is receiving certain types of income – pension, back pay, or workers' compensation for temporary partial disability. Unemployment benefits are subject to federal income taxes.

UNIVERSAL ELIGIBILITY: Social service delivery policy in which benefits or services are provided in the same amount to all individuals in the nation rather than on the basis of need, circumstance, or economic status. This policy can take the form of universal programs, such as OASDI ("social security") and Medicare. Universal programs are open to everyone who falls into a certain category; people are not required to undergo tests of need or income.

UNIVERSALIZATION: A form of reassurance that involves explaining to the client that his/her thoughts, feelings, or behavior are similar to those of other people in similar circumstances. The purpose is to counteract the client's perception that his/her feelings or behaviors are strange or abnormal.

UTILIZATION REVIEW: Method of service evaluation that assesses the kind and amount of service that exists and is provided in order to determine if the service is warranted. May be used to determine the over- or underutilization of services. Most often conducted when an agency receives governmental or other outside funding.

VALIDITY: The usefulness of a test – i.e., the extent to which a test measures what it purports to measure.

VALUES (OF THE SOCIAL WORK PROFESSION): Principles and standards of conduct for social workers, which include the following: (a) a commitment to the primary importance of the individual in society; (b) respect for the confidentiality of relationships with clients; (c) a commitment to social change to meet socially recognized needs; (d) a willingness to keep personal feelings and needs separate from professional relationships; (e) a willingness to transmit knowledge and skills to others; (f) respect and appreciation for individual and group differences; (g) a commitment to develop clients' ability to help themselves; (h) a willingness to persist in efforts on behalf of a client despite frustration; (i) a commitment to social justice and the economic, physical, and mental well-being of all persons in society; and (j) a commitment to a high standard of personal and professional conduct.

VARIABLE INTERVAL (VI) SCHEDULE: In operant conditioning, an intermittent reinforcement schedule in which the reinforcer is applied after a varying amount of time (with the average time interval being predetermined). Associated with a smooth rate of responding.

VARIABLE RATIO (VR) SCHEDULE: In operant conditioning, an intermittent reinforcement schedule in which the reinforcer is applied after a varying number of responses (with the average number of responses being predetermined). Associated with a high, stable rate of responding and the greatest resistance to extinction.

VASCULAR NEUROCOGNITIVE DISORDER: Vascular neurocognitive disorder is diagnosed when the criteria for major or mild neurocognitive disorder are met, the clinical features are consistent with a vascular etiology, and there is evidence of cerebrovascular disease from the individual's history, a physical examination, and/or neuroimaging that is considered sufficient to account for his/her symptoms. This disorder often has a stepwise, fluctuating course with a patchy pattern of symptoms that is determined by the location of the brain damage.

VEGETATIVE SYMPTOMS: Consist of sleep disturbances, changes in appetite or weight, loss of energy or frequent fatigue, and changes in sexual function. Useful for diagnostic screening purposes because they may indicate a serious mental disorder. If a client reports vegetative symptoms, the social worker should find out whether they reflect a change from the client's previous functioning.

VENTILATION PROCEDURES: Techniques used to assist clients to identify and appropriately express their feelings (e.g., techniques that encourage verbalization). Effective for establishing a foundation for self-exploration and rational discussion in work with a client because, once verbalized, a client's emotions become more accessible to support and reassurance from the social worker.

VERTICAL COMMUNITY: Consists of external linkages that connect community units (people, groups, organizations) to units outside the community and provide a way for local communities to reach out to other systems (groups, organizations, other communities). Decisions made by organizations outside the boundaries of a local community may not always be in the best interests of the community.

VETERANS' BENEFITS: Provided under the Social Security Act. Eligibility for most veterans benefits is based on discharge from active military service under other than dishonorable conditions for a minimum period specified by law. Many of the benefits and services provided to veterans were adopted to help war veterans readjust to civilian life. These benefits include, but are not limited to, disability compensation, benefits for survivors, health care, and educational assistance and training.

VICARIOUS LIABILITY: The legal principle that civil liability may extend to a defendant's employer, supervisor, etc. A client who sues a social worker for malpractice may include the worker's agency and/or supervisor as co-defendants. In other words, by delegating tasks, a supervisor shares some of his/her authority with a supervisee who may be empowered to make decisions and take action when doing an assigned task. The supervisor, however, retains ultimate responsibility for the work he/she assigns and delegates (i.e., if the work is performed incompetently, the supervisor is responsible for having delegated it to a worker who was not competent to perform it).

VINELAND ADAPTIVE BEHAVIOR SCALES (VINELAND-II): Appropriate for individuals from birth to age 90 and designed to evaluate personal and social skills of individuals with intellectual disability, autism spectrum disorder, ADHD, brain injury, or major neurocognitive disorders (i.e., dementia), and for assisting in the development of educational and treatment plans.

VIRAL LOADS AND CD4 COUNTS (HIV/AIDS): HIV viral load is the number of copies of the human immunodeficiency virus in a person's blood and other parts of his/her body. Keeping the viral load low can reduce complications of HIV disease and extend a person's life. The CD4 count measures the number of CD4 cells in a sample of blood and is a good indicator of how strong a person's immune system is. The CD4 count is also useful for identifying the stage of a person's HIV disease. Keeping the CD4 count high can reduce complications of HIV disease and extend a person's life. (CD4 cells, also called T-helper cells, are a type of white blood cell that fights infection.)

VULNERABLE STATE (Crisis): A person's subjective response to stressful events. Is marked by an increase in anxiety, which the person attempts to relieve by using his/her customary coping strategies. If these are unsuccessful, the person's tension continues to rise and eventually he/she is unable to function effectively.

VYGOTSKY'S SOCIOCULTURAL THEORY: Proposes that cognitive development is always first interpersonal (when the child interacts with an adult or other teacher) and then intrapersonal (when the child internalizes what he/she has learned). Additionally, cognitive development is fostered when instruction targets the "zone of proximal development," which is defined by what a child can currently do alone and what he/she can accomplish with assistance from a parent, teacher, or more experienced peer.

WARM-UP PERIOD: A brief period of "small talk" that may be used at the beginning of an interview to help a client feel more comfortable before he/she begins self-disclosing. Is most appropriate to use when a client appears resistant or defensive and is also useful with many adolescent clients.

WIC PROGRAM: Social security program that provides a combination of food, nutrition counseling, and access to health services to low-income women, infants, and children who are at nutritional risk. Among its goals are to improve fetal development and reduce the incidence of low birth-weight, short gestation, and anemia through intervention during the prenatal period. Participants receive food supplements, nutrition education, and access to health care services to maintain and improve their health and development. Most states provide WIC vouchers that can be used at authorized retail food stores for specific foods that are rich sources of nutrients. Pregnant and postpartum women, infants, and children up to age 5 are eligible. They must meet income guidelines and a state residency requirement and be determined to be at "nutritional risk" by a health professional.

WORKERS' COMPENSATION: Social security program that provides benefits to individuals with injuries or diseases traceable to industrial accidents and with certain occupational diseases. The benefits provided include periodic cash payments and medical services to the worker during a period of disablement, and death and funeral benefits to the worker's survivors. Lump-sum settlements are permitted under most programs.

ZERO-BASED BUDGETING: Budgeting system in which an agency starts from scratch, or with a "clean slate," at the beginning of each year (i.e., it starts with no money) and must describe and justify every financial request it makes for the coming year.

PREPARATORY COURSE FOR THE ASWB BACHELORS LEVEL EXAM

References

**Association for Advanced Training
in the Behavioral Sciences**
212 W. Ironwood Drive, Suite D #168 Coeur d'Alene, ID 83814
(800) 472-1931

© Association for Advanced Training in the Behavioral Sciences. All rights reserved. No part of these materials may be reproduced in any form, or by any means, mechanical or electronic, including photocopying, without the written permission of the publisher. To reproduce or adapt, in whole or in part, any portion of these materials is not only a violation of copyright law, but is unethical and unprofessional. As a condition of your acceptance of these materials, you agree not to reproduce or adapt them in any manner or license others to do so. The unauthorized resale of these materials is prohibited. The Association for Advanced Training in the Behavioral Sciences accepts the responsibility of protecting not only its own interests, but to protect the interests of its authors and to maintain and vigorously enforce all copyrights on its material. Your cooperation in complying with the copyright law is appreciated.

BACHELORS LEVEL

REFERENCES

AARP. (2003). *Standing ahead of the curve: AARP working in retirement study.* Washington, DC: Author.

Abramson, J. S. (2002). Interdisciplinary team practice. In A. R. Roberts & G. J. Greene (Eds.), *Social workers' desk reference.* New York: Oxford University Press.

Abramson, L. Y., Metalsky, G. J., & Alloy, L. B. (1989). Hopelessness depression: A theory-based subtype of depression. *Psychological Review, 96*(2), 358-372.

Abramson, L. Y., Seligman, M. E. P., & Teasdale, J. D. (1978). Learned helplessness in humans: Critique and reformulation. *Journal of Abnormal Psychology, 87,* 49-74.

Achenbach, T. M., & Edelbrook, C. (1983). *Manual for the Child Behavior Checklist and Revised Child Behavior Profile.* Burlington: University of Vermont Department of Psychiatry.

Adler, S. R., et al. (2000). Conceptualizing menopause and midlife: Chinese-American and Chinese women in the U.S. *Maturitas, 35,* 11-23.

Administration on Aging. (2003). *A Profile of older Americans.* Washington, DC: Author.

Administration on Aging. (2004). *Elder Abuse.* Washington, DC: Author.

Agras, W. S., et al. (1992). Pharmacologic and cognitive-behavioral treatment for bulimia nervosa: A controlled comparison. *American Journal of Psychiatry, 1,* 82-87.

AHRQ (Agency for Healthcare and Quality). (2007). Newer class of antidepressants similar in effectiveness, but side effects differ. Retrieved from: http://www.ahrq.gov/news/press/pr2007/antideppr.htm

Ainsworth, M. D. S., et al. (1978). *Patterns of attachment: Observations in the Strange Situation and at home.* Hillsdale, NJ: Erlbaum.

Alderman, A. (1997). *The scarred soul: Understanding and ending self-inflicted violence.* New York: Harbinger.

Alejandro-Wright, M. N. (1985). The children's conception of racial classification: A socio-cognitive developmental model. In M. B. Spencer et al. (Eds.), *Beginnings: The social and affective development of Black children.* Hillsdale, NJ: Lawrence Erlbaum.

Alkin, M. C. (1992). *Encyclopedia of educational research.* New York: Macmillan Publishing Co.

Al-Krenawi, A. (1999). Culturally sensitive mental health therapy with Arabs. In C. Rabin (Ed.), *Being different in Israel: Ethnicity, gender, and therapy* (pp. 65-82). Tel-Aviv: Ramot, Tel-Aviv University Press (in Hebrew).

Al-Krenawi, A., & Graham, J. R. (2000). *Culturally sensitive social work practice with Arab clients in mental health settings.* Retrieved from NASW.org/pressroom, November 2010.

Allport, G. W. (1954). *The nature of prejudice.* Reading, MA: Addison-Wesley.

Allport, G. W. (1968). The historical background of social psychology. In G. Lindzey & E. Aronson (Eds.), *Handbook of social psychology (Vol. 1)*, New York: Random House.

Althof, S. E., et al. (2010). International Society for Sexual Medicine's guidelines for the diagnosis and treatment of premature ejaculation. *Journal of Sexual Medicine, 7*(9), 2947-2969.

Amato, P. R. (2000). The consequences of divorce for adults and children. *Journal of Marriage and the Family, 62,* 1269-87.

Amato, P. R. (2001). Children of divorced in the 1990s: An update of the Amato and Keith (1991) meta-analysis. *Journal of Family Psychology, 15*(3), 355-370.

Amato, P. R., & Keith, B. (1991). Parental divorce and the well-being of children: A meta-analysis. *Psychological Bulletin, 110,* 26-46.

Amato, P. R., & Rezac, S. J. (1994). Contact with nonresident parents, interparental conflict, and children's behavior. *Journal of Family Issues, 15,* 191-207.

American Academy of Pediatrics. (1999). Adolescent pregnancy: Current trends and issues. *Pediatrics, 103,* 516-20.

American Association of State Social Work Boards Model Law Task Force. (1997). *Model State Social Work Practice.* Culpepper VA: AASWB.

American Psychiatric Association. (1996). *Practice guidelines for the treatment of patients with nicotine dependence.* Washington, DC: Author.

American Psychiatric Association. (2000). *Diagnostic and statistical manual of mental disorders – Text revision (DSM-IV-TR).* Washington, DC: Author.

American Psychiatric Association. (2000). Practice guidelines for the treatment of patients with major depressive disorder. *American Journal of Psychiatry, 157*(4), 1-52.

American Psychiatric Association. (2004). *Practice guidelines for the treatment of patients with schizophrenia.* Washington, DC: Author.

American Psychiatric Association. (2006). *Practice guidelines for the treatment of psychiatric disorders: Compendium 2006.* Arlington, VA: Author.

American Psychiatric Association. (2013). *Diagnostic and statistical manual of mental disorders, 5th Edition* (DSM-5). Washington, DC: Author.

American Psychological Association. (1994). Guidelines for providers of services to ethnic, linguistic, and culturally diverse populations. *American Psychologist, 48(1),* 45-48.

American Psychological Association, Committee on Legal Issues. (2006). Strategies for private practitioners coping with subpoenas or compelled testimony for client records or test data. *Professional Psychology: Research and Practice, 37*(2), 215-222.

Anderson, M. L., & Collins, P. H. (1995). *Race, class and gender: An anthology.* Belmont, CA: Wadsworth.

Anderssen, N., Amlie, C., & Ytteroy, E. A. (2002). Outcomes for children of lesbian or gay parents: A review of studies from 1978 to 2000. *Scandinavian Journal of Psychology, 43,* 335-351.

Aponte, H. (1994). *Bread and spirit: Therapy with the new poor.* New York: Morton Press.

Aronson, E., & Linder, O. (1965). Gain and loss of esteem as determinants of interpersonal attractiveness. *Journal of Experimental Social Psychology, 1,* 156-171.

Aronson, E., & Mills, J. (1959). The effect of severity of initiation on liking for a group. *Journal of Abnormal and Social Psychology, 59,* 177-181.

Ashford, J. B., et al. (2013). *Human behavior in the social environment: A multidimensional perspective, 5th Edition.* Belmont, CA: Thomson-Brooks/Cole.

Atchley, R. C. (1976). *The sociology of retirement.* Cambridge, MA: Schenkman.

Atkinson, D. R., Morten, G., & Sue, D. W. (1993). *Counseling American minorities: A cross-cultural perspective.* Madison, WI: Brown & Benchmark.

Avis, N. E., et al. (2002). Menopause. In G. M. Wingood & R. J. DeClemente (Eds.), *Handbook of women's sexual and reproductive health.* New York: Kluwer.

Ballew, J. R., & Mink, G. (1996). *Case management in social work: Developing the Professional skills needed for work with multiproblem clients.* Springfield, IL: Charles C. Thomas Publishing, LTD.

Bandler, R., Grinder, J., & Satir, V. (1976). *Changing with families.* Palo Alto, CA: Science & Behavior Books.

Bandura, A. (1969). *Principles of behavior modification.* New York: Holt, Rinehart & Winston.

Bandura, A. (1977). Self-efficacy: Toward a unifying theory of behavior change. *Psychology Review, 84,* 191-215.

Bandura, A. (1983). Psychological mechanisms of aggression. In R. G. Geen & E. I. Donnerstein (Eds.), *Aggression: Theoretical and empirical reviews.* New York: Academic Press.

Barinaga, M. (1998). Neurobiology: New leads to brain neuron regeneration. *Science 282,* 1018b-19b.

Barker, R. L. (2003). *Social work dictionary, 5th Edition.* Washington, DC: NASW Press.

Barkley, R. A. (2002a). Major life activity and health outcomes associated with attention-deficit/hyperactivity disorder. *Journal of Clinical Psychiatry, 63*(Suppl. 12), 10-15.

Barkley, R. A. (2002b). Psychosocial treatments for attention-deficit/hyperactivity disorder in children. *Journal of Clinical Psychiatry, 63*(Suppl. 12), 36-43.

Barnes, H., & Parry, J. (2004). Renegotiating identity and relationships: Men and women's adjustments to retirement. *Aging and Society, 24,* 213-33.

Barnett, W. S. (1993). Benefit-cost analysis of preschool education: Findings from a 25-year follow-up. *American Journal of Orthopsychiatry, 63,* 500-08

Baumrind, D. (1971). Current patterns of parental authority. *Developmental Psychology Monographs, 4.*

Baumrind, D. (1991). Parenting styles and adolescent development. In R. M. Lerner, et al. (Eds.), *Encyclopedia of adolescence.* New York: Garland.

Beck, A. T. (1967). *Depression: Causes and treatment.* Philadelphia: University of Pennsylvania Press.

Beck, A. T. (1976). *Cognitive therapy and emotional disorders.* New York: International Universities Press.

Beck, A. T. (1984). Cognition and therapy. *Archives of General Psychiatry, 41,* 1112-1114.

Beck, A. T., et al. (1985). Treatment of depression with cognitive therapy and amitriptyline. *Archives of General Psychiatry, 42,* 142-148.

Beck, J. S. (1995). *Cognitive therapy: Basics and beyond.* New York: Guilford Press.

Beck, A. T., & Weishaar, M. E. (2000). Cognitive therapy. In R. J. Corsini & D. Wedding (Eds.), *Current psychotherapies.* Itasca, IL: F. E. Peacock Publishers.

Belsky, J., & Rovine, M. (1988). Nonmaternal care in the first year of life and infant-parent attachment security. *Child Development, 59,* 157-67.

Bem, S. L. (1981). Gender schema theory: A cognitive account of sex typing. *Psychological Review, 88,* 354-64.

Bem, S. L. (1993). *The lenses of gender.* New Haven, CT: Yale University Press.

Bennett, D. (2004). Mild cognitive impairment. *Clinics in Geriatric Medicine, 20,* 15-25.

Berg-Weger, M. (2016). *Social Work and Social Welfare An Invitation 4th Edition.* New York, NY: Routledge.

Berk, L. (1998). *Development through the lifespan.* Needham Heights, MA: Allyn & Bacon.

Berk, L. (2004). *Development through the lifespan.* Boston, MA: Allyn & Bacon.

Berkowitz, L. (1971). The contagion of violence: An S-R mediational analysis of some effects of observed aggression. In W. Arnold & M. Page (Eds.), *Nebraska symposium on motivation (Vol. 18).* Lincoln: University of Nebraska Press.

Berry, J. W., et al. (1987). Comparative studies of acculturative stress. *International Migration Review,* 21, 491-511.

Bierman, K. L. (1983). Cognitive development and clinical interviews with children. In B. B. Lahey & A. E. Kazdin (Eds.), *Advances in clinical and child psychology, (Vol. 6).* New York: Plenum.

Blasey, C., Belanoff, J. K., DeBattista, C., & Schatzberg, A. F. (2013). Adult psychopharmacology. In G. P. Koocher, J. C. Norcross, & B. A. Greene (Eds.), *Psychologists' desk reference* (pp. 441-448). New York: Oxford University Press.

Bloom, S., & Farragher, B. (2013). Restoring sanctuary: A new operating system for trauma-informed systems of care . New York: Oxford University Press.

Borduin, C. M., et al. (1995). Multisystemic treatment of juvenile offenders: Long-term prevention of criminality and violence. *Journal of Consulting and Clinical Psychology, 63,* 569-578.

Borland, J. J. (1981). Burnout among workers and administrators. *Health and Social Work,* 6, Feb., 73-78.

Bornstein, R. F. (1992). Subliminal mere exposure effects. In R. F. Bornstein & T. S. Pittman (Eds.), *Perception without awareness: Cognitive, clinical, and social perspectives.* New York: Guilford.

Boscolo, L., et al. (1987). *Milan systemic family therapy.* New York: Basic Books, Inc.

Bowlby, J. (1973). *Attachment and loss.* New York: Basic Books.

Bowlby, J. (1980). *Attachment and loss (Vol. 3): Loss, sadness, and depression.* New York: Basic Books.

Boyd-Franklin, N. (1989). *Black families in therapy: A multisystems approach.* New York: Guilford Press.

Brager, G., Specht, H., & Torczyner, J. L. (1987). *Community organizing.* New York: Columbia University Press.

Brammer, L. (1985). *The helping relationship: Process and skills.* Englewood Cliffs, NJ: Prentice-Hall.

Braun, D. L., et al. (2004). Attention-deficit/hyperactivity disorder in adults: Clinical information for primary care physicians. *Primary Psychiatry, 11*(9), 56-65.

Brehm, J. W. (1972) *Responses to loss of freedom: A theory of psychological reactance.* Morristown, NJ: General Learning Press.

Bremmer, J. (1998). *Infancy.* Norwich, UK: Page Bros.

Brent, D. A., et al. (1988). Risk factors for adolescent suicide: A comparison of adolescent suicide victims with suicidal inpatients. *Archives of General Psychiatry, 45,* 581-588.

Breton, M. (2001). Neighborhood resiliency. *Journal of Community Practice, 9*(1), 21-36.

Brewaeys, A., Ponjaert, I., Van Hall, E. V., & Golombok, S. (1997). Donor insemination: Child development and family functioning in lesbian mother families. *Human Reproduction, 12,* 1349-1359.

Broadhurst, D. D., Edmunds, M., & MacDicken, R. A. (1979). *Early childhood programs and the prevention of treatment of child abuse and neglect.* DHEW Publ. No. (OHDS) 79-30198. Washington, DC: U.S. DHEW, National Center on Child Abuse and Neglect.

Bromwich, R. (1985, Dec.). Vulnerable infants and risky environments. *Zero to Three,* 7-12.

Bronfenbrenner, U. (2004). *Making human beings human.* Thousand Oaks, CA: Sage.

Brown, B. B., Clasen, D. R., & Eicher, S. A. (1986). Perception of peer pressure, peer conformity dispositions, and self-reported behavior among adolescents. *Developmental Psychology, 22,* 521-530.

Brownell, P., & Wolden, A. (2002). Elder abuse intervention strategies: Social service or criminal justice? *Journal of Gerontological Social Work, 40*(1/2) 83-100.

Buchanan, C. M., Maccoby, E. E., & Dornbusch, S. M. (1996). *Adolescents after divorce.* Cambridge, MA: Harvard University Press.

Buell, S. J., & Coleman, P. D. (1979). Dendritic growth in the aging human brain and failure of growth in senile dementia. *Science, 206,* 854-56.

Buelow, G., & Hebert, S. (1995). *Counselor's resource on psychiatric medications.* Pacific Grove, CA: Brooks/Cole Publishing Co.

Bulik, C. M. (2002). Anxiety, depression, and eating disorders. In C. G. Fairburn & K. D. Brownell (Eds.), *Eating disorders and obesity: A comprehensive handbook* (pp. 193-198). New York: Guilford.

Burgess, E. (2004). Sexuality in midlife and later life couples. In J. H. Harvey, A. Wenzel, & S. Sprecher (Eds.), *The handbook of sexuality in close relationships* (pp. 437-454). Mahwah, NJ: Erlbaum.

Burke, E. M. (1968). Citizen participation strategies. *Journal of the American Institute of Planners, 34*(5), 293.

Butler, R. N. (1963). The life review: An interpretation of reminiscence in the aged. *Psychiatry, 26,* 65-76.

Butzlaff, R. L., & Hooley, J. M. (1998). Expressed emotion and psychiatric relapse: A meta-analysis. *Archives of General Psychiatry, 55,* 547-552.

Cammaert, L. P., & Larsen, C. C. (1988). Feminist frameworks of psychotherapy. In M. A. Dutton-Douglas & L. E. A. Walker (Eds.), *Feminist psychotherapies: Integration of therapeutic and feminist systems.* Norwood, NJ: Ablex Publishing Corp.

Campbell, D. T., & Stanley, J. C. (1963). *Experimental and quasi-experimental designs for research.* Boston: Houghton Mifflin Co.

Campbell, D. T., & Stanley, J. C. (1966). *Experimental and quasi-experimental designs for research.* Chicago: Rand McNally.

Cannon, T. D., Barr, C. E., & Mednick, S. A. (1991). Genetic and perinatal factors in the etiology of Schizophrenia. In E. F. Walker (Ed.), *Schizophrenia: A life-course developmental perspective.* New York: Academic Press.

Cannon, T. D., et al. (1994). Developmental brain abnormalities in the offspring of schizophrenic mothers: 2. Structural brain characteristics of schizophrenia and schizotypal personality disorder. *Archives of General Psychiatry, 51,* 955-962.

Canter, M. B., et al. (1994). *Ethics for psychologists: A commentary on the APA Ethics Code.* Washington, DC: American Psychological Association.

Carlson, V. et al. (1989). Contributions of the study of maltreated infants to the development of disorganized type of attachment relationship. In D. Cicchetti & V. Carlson (Eds.), *Child maltreatment: Theory and research on the causes and consequences of child abuse and neglect.* Cambridge: Cambridge University Press.

Carkhuff, R. (1969). *Helping and human relations: Practice and research.* New York: Holt, Rinehart & Winston.

Carter, B., & McGoldrick, M. (1980). *The family life cycle: A framework for family therapy.* New York: Gardner.

Casas, J. M., & Vasquez, M. J. T. (1989). Counseling the Hispanic client: A theoretical and applied perspective. In P. B. Pedersen, et al. (Eds.), *Counseling across cultures.* Honolulu: University of Hawaii Press.

CDC. (2007). Suicide: Facts at a glance. Retrieved from: http://www.cdc.gov/ncipc/dvp/suicide/SuicideDataSheet.pdf

CDC. (2012). Suicide facts at a glance. Retrieved from: http://www.cdc.gov/violenceprevention/pdf/suicide_datasheet_2012-a.pdf

CDC. (2014). Trends in suicide rates among both sexes, by age group, United States, 1991-2009. Retrieved from: http://www.cdc.gov/violenceprevention/suicide/statistics/trends02.html

Ceci, S. J., et al. (1992). *Cognitive and social factors in early deception.* Hillsdale, NJ: Erlbaum.

Center for American Progress. (2011). Domestic violence in the LGBT community: A fact sheet. Retrieved from http://www.americanprogress.org/issues/lgbt on March 9, 2015.

Chambers, C. A. (1985). The historical role of the volunteer sector. In G. A. Tobin (Ed.), *Social planning and human service delivery in the voluntary sector* (pp. 3-28). Westport, CT: Greenwood Press.

Chambers, D. E. (2000). *Social policy and social programs: A method for the practical public policy analyst, 3rd Edition.* Boston: Allyn & Bacon.

Chase-Lansdale, P. L., & Hetherington, E. M. (1990). The impact of divorce on lifespan development: Short- and long-term effects. In D. Featherman & R. M. Lerner (Eds.), *Lifespan development and behavior, Vol. 10.* Orlando: Academic Press.

Chassin, L. et al. (1993). Relation of parental alcoholism to early adolescent substance use: A test of three mediating mechanisms. *Journal of Abnormal Psychology, 102,* 3-19.

Chehil, S., & Kutcher, S. (2012). *Suicide risk management: A manual for health professionals.* West Sussex, UK: John Wiley & Sons.

Cherlin, A., et al. (1991). Longitudinal studies of the effects of divorce on children in Great Britain and the U.S. *Science, 252*(5011), 1386-89.

Chess, S., & Thomas, A. (1987). *Know your child.* New York: Basic Books.

Chomsky, N. (1968). *Language and mind.* New York: Harcourt, Brace, & World.

Cillessen, A. H. N., et al. (2000). Stability of sociometric categories. In A. H. N. Cillessen & W. M. Bukowski (Eds.). *Recent advances in the measurement of acceptance and rejection in the peer system: New directions for child and adolescent development.* San Francisco: Jossey-Bass.

Clark, D. C. (1973). The concept of community: A reexamination. *Sociological Review, 21,* 397-416.

Clark, M. L., & Bittle, M. L. (1992). Friendship expectations and the evaluation of present friendships in middle childhood and early adolescence. *Child Study Journal, 22,* 115-35.

Clark, M. S., & Mills, J. (1993). The difference between communal and exchange relationships: What it is and is not. *Personality and Social Psychology Bulletin, 19,* 684-691.

Cloninger, C. R., Bohman, M., Sigvardsson, S., & Von-Knorring, A. L. (1985). Psychopathology in adopted-out children of alcoholics: The Stockholm Adoption Study. In M. Galanter (Ed.) *Recent developments in alcoholism, Vol. 3, High-risk studies prostaglandins and leukotrienes, cardiovascular effects, cerebral function in social drinkers.* New York: Plenum Press.

Cochran, S., & Maya, V. (2006). Estimating prevalence of mental and substance-using disorders among lesbians and gay men from existing national health data. In A. Omoto & H. Kurtzman (Eds.), *Sexual orientation and mental health.* Washington, DC: American Psychological Association.

Cohen, A. P. (1985). *The symbolic construction of community.* London: Routledge & Kegan Paul.

Cohen, B. Z. (1999). Intervention and supervision in strengths-based social work practice. Families in Society: *The Journal of Contemporary Social Services,* 80(5), 460-466.

Cohen, S., et al. (1991). Psychological stress and susceptibility to the common cold. *New England Journal of Medicine, 325,* 606-12.

Coie, J. D., & Kupersmidt, J. B. (1983). A behavior analysis of emerging social status in boys' groups. *Child Development, 54,* 1400-16.

Coleman, E. (1985). Developmental stages of the coming out process. In J. C. Gonsiorek (Ed.), *A guide to psychotherapy with gay and lesbian clients.* New York: Harrington Park Press.

Collin-Vézina, D., Coleman, K., Milne, L., Sell, J., & Daigneault, I. (2011). Trauma experiences, maltreatment-related impairments, and resilience among child welfare youth in residential care. *International Journal of Mental Health and Addiction,* 9(5), 577-589.

Collins, R. (1974). *Conflict sociology.* New York: Academic Press.

Collins, W. A., & Gunnar, M. R. (1990). Social and personality development. *Annual Review of Psychology, 41,* 387-46.

Colvin, T. J., & Kilmann, R. H. (1989). *A profile of large scale change programs.* Proceedings, Southern Management Association.

Conger, J. J. (1956). Reinforcement theory and the dynamics of alcoholism. *Quarterly Journal of Studies on Alcohol, 17,* 296-305.

Connidis, I., & McMullin, J. (2002). Sociological ambivalence and family trees: A critical perspective. *Journal of Marriage and the Family, 64,* 558-67.

Coon, D. (1995). *Introduction to psychology: Exploration and application, 7th Edition.* New York: West Publishing Company.

Corey, G. (1991). *Theory and practice of counseling and psychotherapy.* Pacific Grove, CA: Brooks/Cole.

Corey, G., Corey, M., & Callanan, P. (1988). *Issues and ethics in the helping professions.* Pacific Grove, CA: Brooks/Cole Publ.

Cormier, W. H., & Cormier, L. S. (1991). *Interviewing strategies for helpers: Fundamental skills and cognitive-behavioral interventions, 3rd Edition.* Pacific Grove, CA: Brooks/Cole.

Council on Social Work Education. (2012). Advanced practice in social work practice in trauma. Retrieved from
https://cswe.org/getattachment/Publications-and-multimedia/CSWE-Full-Circle-(1)/Newsletters

-Archive/CSWE-Full-Circle-November-2012/Resources-for-Members/Traumabrochurefinalfor Web.pdf.aspx

Cowan, C. P., & Cowan, P. A. (1987). A preventive intervention for couples becoming parents. In C. F. Z. Boukydis (Ed.), *Research in support for parents and infants in the postnatal period.* New York: Ablex.

Craighead, W. E., Miklowitz, D. J., Frank, E., & Vajk, F. C. (2002). Psychosocial treatments for bipolar disorder. In P. E. Nathan & J. M. Gorman (Eds.), *A guide to treatments that work* (pp. 263-275). New York: Oxford University Press.

Crick, N. R., & Grotpeter, J. K. (1995). Relational aggression, gender, and social-psychological adjustment. *Child Development, 66,* 710-22.

Crittenden, P. M. (1985). Social networks and quality of childrearing and child development. *Child Development, 56,* 1299-1313.

Crnic, K. (1984). Maternal stress and social support: Effects on the mother-infant relationship from birth to 18 months. *American Journal of Orthopsychiatry, 54,* 224-35.

Croen, L. A., Grether, J. K., & Selvin, S. (2001). The epidemiology of mental retardation of unknown cause. *Pediatrics, 107,* 1410-1414.

Csoti, M. (2003). *School phobia, panic attacks, and anxiety in children.* New York: Jessica Kingsley.

Cummings, J. L. (1992). Depression and Parkinson's disease: A review. *American Journal of Psychiatry, 149,* 443-54.

Daft, R. L. (2004). *Organization theory and design, 8th Edition.* Cincinnati, OH: Southwestern.

Dahl, R., & Lewin, D. S. (2002). Pathways to adolescent health: Sleep regulation and behavior. *Journal of Adolescent Health, 31,* 175-84.

Damon, W. (1988). *The moral child.* New York: Free Press.

Damon, W., & Hart, D. (1988). *Self-understanding in childhood and adolescence.* New York: Cambridge University Press.

Dao, J., & Frosch, D. (2009.) Military rules said to hinder therapy. Retrieved from http://www.nytimes.com/2009/12/07/us/07therapists.html on Feb 23, 2015.

Davidson, J. R. T., et al. (2001). Efficacy of sertraline in preventing relapse of posttraumatic stress disorder: Results of a 28-week double-blind, placebo-controlled study. *American Journal of Psychiatry, 158,* 1974-1981.

Davidson, K. (2001). Late life widowhood and new partnership choices: A gendered perspective. *Ageing and Society, 21*(3) 297-317.

Davies, D. (2011). Child development: A practitioner's guide. Guilford Press.

Davis, V. E., & Walsch, M. J. (1970). Alcohol, amines and alkaloids: A possible biochemical basis for alcohol addiction. *Science, 167,* 1005-1007.

Davison, G. C. (1991). Construction and morality in therapy for homosexuality. In J. C. Gonsiorek & J. D. Weinrich (Eds.), *With compassion toward some: Homosexuality and social work in America* (pp. 115-136). New York: Harrington Press.

DeAngelis, T. (1997, Nov.). Menopause symptoms vary among ethnic groups. *APA Monitor*, 16-17.

Demo, D. H., & Acock, A. C. (1988). The impact of divorce in children. *Journal of Marriage and the Family, 50*, 619-48.

Denham, S., et al. (2002). Emotional and social development in childhood. In P. K. Smith & C. H. Hart (Eds.). *Blackwell handbook of childhood social development.* Malden, MA: Blackwell.

deShazer, S. (1985). *Keys to solution in brief therapy.* New York: W. W. Norton.

Diaz, R. M. (1983). Thought and two languages: The impact of bilingualism on cognitive development. *Review of Research in Education, 10*, 23-54.

Dishion, T. J., et al. (1991). Family, school, and behavioral antecedents to early adolescent involvement with antisocial peers. *Developmental Psychopathology, 27*, 172-80.

Dodge, K. A., et al. (1990). Mechanisms in the cycle of violence. *Science, 250*, 1678-83.

Dominelli, L. (2010). Globalization, contemporary challenges and social work practice. *International Social Work, 53*(5), 599-612.

Doremus, B. (1976). The four R's: Social diagnosis in health care. *Health and Social Work 1*, 121-139.

Dorfman, R. A. (1996). *Clinical social work: Definition, practice, and vision.* New York: Brunner/Mazel.

Dougherty, A. M. (1990). *Consultation: Practice and perspectives.* Pacific Grove, CA: Brooks/Cole.

Downar, J., & Kapur, S. (2008). Biological theories. In K. T. Mueser & D. V. Jeste (Eds.), *Clinical handbook of schizophrenia* (pp. 25-34). New York: Guilford Press.

Downey, D. B., & Powell, B. (1993). Do children in single-parent households fare better living with same-sex parents? *Journal of Marriage and the Family, 55*(1), 55-71.

Drachman, D., & Halberstadt, A. (1993). A stage of migration framework as applied to recent Soviet emigres. *Journal of Multicultural Social Work, 2*(1), 63-78.

Dreikurs, R. (1951). The unique social climate experienced in group psychotherapy. *Group Psychotherapy, 3*, 292-299.

Dryfoos, J. G. (1990). *Adolescents at risk: Prevalence and prevention.* New York: Oxford University Press.

Dubovsky, S. L., Davies, R., & Dubovsky, A. N. (2003). Mood disorders. In S. C. Yudofsky & R. E. Hales (Eds.). *The American Psychiatric Publishing textbook of clinical psychiatry* (pp. 439-542). Washington, DC: American Psychiatric Publishing, Inc.

Dugas, M. J., Freeston, M. H., Ladouceur, R., Rheaume, J., Provencher, M., & Boisvert, J. M. (1998). Worry themes in primary GAD, secondary GAD, and other anxiety disorders. *Journal of Anxiety Disorders, 12*, 253-261.

Dupper, D. R. (2003). *School social work: Skills and interventions for effective practice.* Hoboken, NJ: John Wiley & Sons.

Dutton-Douglas, M. A., & Walker, L. E. A. (1988). Introduction to feminist therapy. In M. A. Dutton-Douglas and L. E. A. Walker (Eds.), *Feminist therapies: Integration of therapeutic and feminist systems.* Norwood, NJ: Ablex Publishing Corp.

Dyck, M. J. (1987). Assessing logotherapeutic constructs: Conceptual and psychometric status of Purpose in Life and Seeking of Noetic Goals tests. *Clinical Psychology, 7,* 439-447.

Dziegielewski, S. F., et al. (2002). Midlife changes: Utilizing a social work perspective. *Journal of Human Behavior in the Social Environment, 6,* 65-86.

Eisenberg, N. (Ed.) (1982). *The development of prosocial behavior.* New York: Wiley.

Eisenberg, N. (1992). *The caring child.* Cambridge, MA: Harvard University Press

Eisenberg-Berg, N., & Mussen, P. (1978). Empathy and moral development in adolescence. *Developmental Psychology, 14*(2), 185-186.

Eisler, I., et al. (2000). Family therapy for adolescent anorexia nervosa: The results of a controlled comparison of two family interventions. *Journal of Child Psychology and Psychiatry, 41,* 727-736.

Ekman, P. (1993). Facial expressions and emotion. *American Psychologist, 48,* 384-92.

Eliot, T. D. (1955). Handling family strains and shocks. In H. Backer & R. Hill (Eds.), *Family, marriage, and parenting.* Boston: Heath & Company.

Elliot, J. G. (1999). School refusal: Issues of conceptualization, assessment, and treatment. *Journal of Child Psychology and Psychiatry, 40,* 1001-1012.

Elliott, D. E., Bjelajac, P., Fallot, R. D., Markoff, L. S., & Reed, B. G. (2005). Trauma-informed or trauma-denied: principles and implementation of trauma-informed services for women. *Journal of Community Psychology, 33*(4), 461-477.

Elkind, D. (1967). Egocentrism in adolescence. *Child Development, 38,* 1025-34.

Ellis, A. (1985). Expanding the ABCs of RET. In M. Mahoney & A. Freeman (Eds.), *Cognition and psychotherapy.* New York: Plenum Press.

Emde, R. (1987). Infant mental health: Clinical dilemmas, the expansion of meaning and opportunities. In J. Osofsky (Ed.), *Handbook of infant development.* New York: Wiley.

Enright, R. D. (2001). *Forgiveness is a choice: A step-by-step process for resolving anger and restoring hope.* Washington, DC: APA Lifebooks.

Erwin, P. (1993). *Friendship and peer relationships in children.* New York: Wiley.

Esposito, T., Chabot, M., Rothwell, D. W., Trocmé, N., & Delaye, A. (2017). Out-of-home placement and regional variations in poverty and health and social services spending: A multilevel analysis. Children and Youth Services Review, 72, 34-43.

Etzioni, A. (1964). *Modern organizations.* Englewood Cliffs, NJ: Prentice-Hall.

Etzioni, A. (1993). *The spirit of community: Rights, responsibilities, and the communitarian agenda.* New York: Crown Publishers.

Fahlberg, V. (1991). *A child's journey through placement.* Indianapolis: Perspectives Press.

Faraone, S. V., Biederman, J., & Mick, E. (2005). The age-dependent decline of attention deficit hyperactivity disorder: A meta-analysis of follow-up studies. *Psychological Medicine, 36*, 159-165.

Favazza, A. (1987). *Bodies under siege.* Baltimore: Johns Hopkins University Press.

Feigenbaum, W. (1988). Long-term efficacy of ungraded versus graded mass exposure in agoraphobics. In I. Hand & H. Wittchen (Eds.), *Panic and phobias: Treatments and variables affecting course and outcome.* Berlin: Springer-Verlag.

Feldman, M., & Khademian, A. (2004). *Inclusive management: Building relationships with the public.* Irvine, CA: Center for the Study of Democracy, U.C. Irvine.

Fellin, P. (1995). *The community and the social worker, 2nd Edition.* Itasca, IL: F. E. Peacock.

Fellin, P. (2001). Understanding American communities. In J. Rothman, J. L. Erlich, & J. E. Tropman (Eds.), *Strategies of community intervention, 6th Edition.* Itasca, IL: F. E. Peacock.

Fenton, C., Brooks, F., Spencer, N. H., & Morgan, A. (2010). Sustaining a positive body image in adolescence: an assets-based analysis. *Health & social care in the community, 18*(2), 189-198.

Fernald, A. (1987). Acoustic determinants of infant preference for motherese speech. *Infant Behavior and Development, 10*, 279-93.

Festinger, L. (1957). *A theory of cognitive dissonance.* Stanford, CA: Stanford University Press.

Festinger, L., & Carlsmith, J. (1959.) Cognitive consequences of forced compliance. *Journal of Abnormal and Social Psychology, 58*, 203-210.

Fine, S. F., & Glasser, P. H. (1996). *The first helping interview: Engaging the client and building trust.* Thousand Oaks, CA: Sage Publishing.

First, M. B., & Tasman, A. (2010). *Clinical guide to the diagnosis and treatment of mental disorders.* Chichester, UK: John Wiley & Sons, Ltd.

Flaks, D. K., et al. (1995). Lesbians choosing motherhood: A comparative study of lesbian and heterosexual parents and their children. *Developmental Psychology, 31*, 105-14.

Foa, E. B., & Meadows, E. A. (1997). Psychosocial treatments for posttraumatic stress disorder: A critical review. *Annual Review of Psychology, 48*, 449-480.

Forsyth, W. I., & Butler, R. J. (1989). Fifty years of enuretic alarms. *Archives of Disorders of Childhood, 64*, 879-885.

Fox, N. A., et al. (1991). Attachment to mother/attachment to father: A meta-analysis. *Child Development, 62*, 210-25.

Frankl, V. (1959). *Man's search for meaning.* Boston: Beacon Press.

Fraser, M. W., Galinsky, M. J., & Richman, J. M. (1999). Risk, protection, and resilience: Toward a conceptual framework for social work practice. Social work research, 23(3), 131-143.

Freiberg, H. J., & Stein, T. A. (1999). Measuring, improving, and sustaining healthy learning environments. In. H. J. Freiberg (Ed.), *School climate: Measuring, improving, and sustaining healthy learning environments.* London: Falmer Press.

French, J., & Raven, E. (1959). The bases of social power. In D. D. Cartwright (Ed.), *Studies on social power.* Ann Arbor: University of Michigan, Institute for Social Research.

Fried, L. P., et al. (2004). A social model for health promotion for an aging population: Initial evidence on the Experience Corps model. *Journal of Urban Health, 81*(1), 64-78.

Friedman, S. L., & Kalichman, M. A. (2014). Out-of-home placement for children and adolescents with disabilities. *Pediatrics, 134*(4), 836-846.

Gabel, S. G., & Healy, L. M. (2012). Introduction to the special issue: Globalization and social work education. *Journal of Social Work Education, 48*(4), 627-634.

Gager, C. T. (1998). The role of valued outcomes, justifications, and comparison referents in perceptions of fairness among dual-earner couples. *Journal of Family Issues, 19*(5), 622-648.

Gambrill, E. (2003). Evidence-based practice: Implications for knowledge development and use in social work. In A. Rosen & E. K. Proctor (Eds.), Developing practice guidelines for social work intervention: Issues, methods, and research agenda (pp. 37–58). New York: Columbia University Press.

Ganong, M. D., & Coleman, M. (2003). *Stepfamilies: Development, dynamics, and intervention.* New York: Plenum.

Gantt, H. (1919). *Organizing for work.* New York: Harcourt, Brace, & Howe.

Garland, A. F., & Zigler, E. (1993). Adolescent suicide prevention: Current research and social policy implications. *American Psychologist, 48*(2), 169-182.

Garland, J., Jones, H. & Kolondny, R. (1965). A model for stages in the development of social work groups. In S. Bernstein (Ed.) *Explorations in group work.* Boston: Milford House.

Garner, D. M., & Bemis, K. M. (1985) Cognitive therapy for anorexia nervosa. In D. M. Garner & P. E. Garfinkel (Eds.), *Handbook of psychotherapy for anorexia nervosa and bulimia.* New York: Guilford.

Garner, D. M., Vitousek, K., & Pike, K. M. (1997). Cognitive-behavioral therapy for anorexia nervosa. In D. M. Garner & P. E. Garfinkel (Eds.), *Handbook of treatments for eating disorders* (pp. 94-144). New York: Guilford Press.

Garrison, W. T., & McQuiston, S. (1989) *Chronic illness during childhood and adolescence.* Newbury Park, CA: Sage.

Gavin, N. I., et al. (2005). Perinatal depression: A systematic review of prevalence and incidence. *Obstetrics and Gynecology, 106*(5, Part 1), 1071-1083.

Gehlert, S., & Browne, T. A. (2006). *Handbook of health social work.* Hoboken, NJ: John Wiley & Sons.

Gelcer, E., McCabe, A., & Smith-Resnick, C. (1990). *Milan family therapy: Variant and invariant methods.* Northvale, NJ: Jason Aronson Inc.

Gelder, M. G., et al. (1996). *Oxford textbook of psychiatry.* New York: Oxford University Press.

Gelles, R. J. (1992). Poverty and violence toward children. *American Behavioral Scientist, 35*(3), 258-74.

Gergely, G. (1994). Self-recognition to theory of mind. In St. T. Parker et al. (Eds.), *Self-awareness in animals and humans.* Boston, Cambridge University Press.

Germain, C. B. (1984). *Social work practice in health care: An ecological perspective.* New York: The Free Press.

Gerson, A, Joyner, M., Fosarelli, P., Butz, A., Wissow, L., Lee, S., Marks, P., & Hutton, N. (2001). Disclosure of HIV diagnosis to children: When, where, why, and how. *Journal of Pediatric Health Care, 15*(4), 161-167.

Gerstein, F., & Pollack, F. (2016). Two Case Studies on Family Work with Eating Disorders and Body Image Issues. *Clinical Social Work Journal, 44*(1), 69-77.

Gesser, G. et al. (1987-88). Death attitude across the life-span: The development and validation of the Death Attitude Profile. *Omega, 18,* 113-28.

Gibson, M. (2015). Analysis of Social Work Practice: Foucault and Female Body Image in Therapy. *Journal of Social Work Practice, 29*(3), 287-299.

Gijsman, H. M., et al. (2004). Antidepressants for bipolar depression: A systematic review of randomized, controlled trials. *American Journal of Psychiatry, 161,* 1537-1547.

Gil, M. M. (1982). Analysis of transference. In H. J. Schlesinger (Ed.), *Psychological issues monograph series (No. 53).* New York: International Universities Press.

Gilbert, M.J. (2013). Transgender people. In T. Mizrahi & L. E. Davis (Eds.-in-Chief), Encyclopedia of social work (20th ed). [Electronic]. Washington, DC, and New York, NY: NASW Press and Oxford University Press. Retrieved from http://socialwork.oxfordre.com/view/10.1093/acrefore/9780199975839.001.0001/acrefore-9780199975839-e-399

Gilligan, C. (1991). Women's psychological development: Implications for psychotherapy. In C. Gilligan et al. (Eds.), *Women, girls, and psychotherapy: Reframing resistance.* New York: Haworth Press.

Gingerich, W. J. (2002). Online social work: Ethical and practical considerations. In A. R. Roberts & G. J. Greene (Eds.), *Social workers' desk reference.* New York: Oxford University Press.

Gitlin, M. J. (1996). *The psychotherapist's guide to psychopharmacology.* New York: The Free Press.

Glasser, W., & Zunin, L. M. (1979). Reality therapy. In R. J. Corsini (Ed.), *Current psychotherapies.* Itasca, NJ: F. E. Peacock.

Glisson, C., & Durick, M. (1988). Predictors of job satisfaction and organizational commitment in human service organizations. *Administrative Science Quarterly, 33,* 61-81.

Golan, N. (1978). *Treatment in crisis situations.* New York: The Free Press.

Golden, R. N., et al. (2005). The efficacy of light therapy in the treatment of mood disorders: A meta-analysis. *American Journal of Psychiatry, 162,* 656-662.

Goldenberg, I., & Goldenberg, H. (1991). *Family therapy: An overview.* Pacific Grove, CA: Brooks/Cole.

Goldenberg, I., & Goldenberg, H. (2004). *Family therapy: An overview, 6th Edition.* Pacific Grove, CA: Brooks/Cole.

Goldman, J., Salus, M. K., Wolcott, D., & Kennedy, K. Y. (2003). *A coordinated response to child abuse and neglect: The foundation for practice.* Office on Child Abuse and Neglect, Children's Bureau. Retrieved June 24, 2014 from the Child Welfare Information Gateway, U.S. Department of Health and Human Services Web site.

Goldstein, E. (1997). Clinical practice with lesbians. In J. R. Brandell (Ed.), *Theory and practice in clinical social work.* New York: The Free Press.

Gonsalves, C. (1992). Psychological stages of the refugee process: A model for therapeutic intervention. *Professional Psychology: Research and Practice, 23,* 382-389.

Goodwin, D. W. (1979). Alcoholism and heredity: A review and hypothesis. *Archives of General Psychiatry, 36,* 57-61.

Gopaul-McNicol, S., & Brice-Baker, J. *Cross-cultural practice.* New York: John Wiley & Sons.

Gorski, T. T. (1989). *Passages through recovery: An action plan for preventing relapse.* New York: Harper & Row.

Gottman, J. M. (1994). *What predicts divorce?* Hillsdale, NJ: Lawrence Erlbaum Associates.

Gottman, J. M., & Levenson, R. W. (2000). The timing of divorce: Predicting when a couple will divorce over a 14-year period. *Journal of Marriage and the Family, 62,* 737-745.

Gould, M. S. (1990). Suicide clusters and media exposure. In S. J. Blumenthal & D. J. Kupfer (Eds.), *Suicide over the life cycle: Risk factors, assessment, and treatment of suicidal patterns.* Washington, DC: American Psychiatric Press.

Greenberg, M. T., & Crnic, K. A. (1988) Longitudinal predictors of developmental status and social interactions in premature and full-term infants at age 2. *Child Development, 59,* 554-70.

Greenley, J. R., & Kirk, S. A. (1973). Organizational characteristics of agencies and the distribution of services to applicants. *Journal and Health and Social Behavior, 14,* 70-79.

Greenstein, T. N. (1993). Maternal employment and child behavioral outcomes. *Journal of Family Issues, 3,* 323-354.

Gregory, R. J. (1996). *Psychological testing: History, principles, and applications.* Boston: Allyn & Bacon.

Griswold, B. (January/February 2010). 10 easy ways to jeopardize your license: Surprisingly common forms of insurance fraud. The Therapist. Retrieved from http://www.camft.org/AM/Template.cfm?Section=Home&content=2010&template=/cm/contentdisplay.cfm&contentfileid=1290

Grove, W. R., & Zeiss, C. (1987). Multiple roles and happiness. In F. Crosby (Ed.), *Spouse, parent, worker.* New Haven, CT: Yale University Press.

Grusec, J. E., et al. (2002). Prosocial and helping behavior. In P. K. Smith & C. H. Hart (Eds.), *Blackwell handbook of childhood social development.* Malden, MA: Blackwell.

Gutierrez, L. M., & Lewis, E. A. (1999). *Empowering women of color.* New York: Columbia University Press.

Hakuta, K. (1987). Degree of bilingualism and cognitive ability in mainland Puerto Rican children. *Child Development, 58,* 1372-88.

Haldeman, D. C. (1994). The practice and ethics of sexual orientation conversion therapy. *Journal of Consulting and Clinical Psychology, 62,* 211–221.

Haley, J. (1984). *Ordeal therapy: Unusual ways to change behavior.* San Francisco: Jossey-Bass.

Hall, E. T. (1969). *The hidden dimension.* Garden City, New York: Doubleday.

Hall, J. A., & Halberstadt, A. G. (1980). Masculinity and femininity in children: Development of the Children's Personal Attributes Questionnaire, *Developmental Psychology, 16,* 270-80.

Halpern, C. F. (1997). Sex differences in intelligence. *American Psychologist, 52,* 1091-1102.

Hamilton, G. (1946). *Principles of social case recording.* New York: Columbia University Press.

Hann, D. M., et al. (1990). Maternal emotional availability in two risk groups. *Infant Behavior and Development, 13,* 404.

Harbeck-Weber, C,. & Peterson, L. (1996). Health-related disorders. In E. J. Mash & R. A. Barkley (Eds.), *Child psychopathology.* New York: Guilford Press.

Hardina, D. (2002). *Analytical skills for community organization practice.* New York: Columbia University Press.

Hare, R. T., & Frankena, S. T. (1972). Peer group supervision. *American Journal of Orthopsychiatry, 42,* 527-29.

Harlow, H. F., & Harlow, M. K. (1969). Effects of various mother-infant relationships on rhesus monkey behaviors. In B. M. Foss (Ed.), *Determinants of infant behavior.* London: Methuen.

Harris, E. C., & Barraclough, B. (1997). Suicide as an outcome for mental disorders: A meta-analysis. *British Journal of Psychiatry, 170,* 205-208.

Harrison, L., et al. (1991). Preterm infants; physiologic responses to early parent touch. *Western Journal of Nursing Research, 13,* 698-713.

Harrison, W. D. (1995). Community development. In *Encyclopedia of social work, 19th Edition (Vol. 1)* (pp. 555-562). Washington, DC: NASW.

Hart, E. L., et al. (1995). Developmental changes in attention-deficit hyperactivity disorder in boys: A four-year longitudinal study. *Journal of Abnormal Clinical Psychology, 23,* 729-750.

Harter, S. (1988). Developmental processes in the construction of self. In. T. D. Yawkey & J. E. Johnson (Eds.), *Integrative processes and socialization* (pp. 45-78). Hillsdale, NJ: Lawrence Erlbaum Associates.

Hartman, A., & Laird, J. (1983). *Family-centered social work practice.* New York: Free Press.

Hasenfeld, Y. (1983). *Human service organizations.* Englewood Cliffs, NJ: Prentice-Hall.

Hauser, S. T., et al. (1987). Family interiors of adolescent ego development trajectories. *Family Perspectives, 21,* 263-82.

Haviland, J. M., & Lelwica, L. (1987). The induced affect response: 10-week-old infants' responses to three emotional expressions. *Developmental Psychology, 23,* 97-104.

Haynes, K. S., & Mickelson, J. S. (2000). *Effecting change: Social workers in the political arena, 4th Edition.* Boston: Allyn & Bacon.

Hays D. (2010). Introduction to counseling outcome research and evaluation. Counseling Outcome Research and Evaluation, 1, 1–7.

Hepworth, D. H., et al. (2010). *Direct social work practice: Theory and skills, 8th Edition.* Pacific Grove, CA: Thomson-Brooks/Cole.

Herek, G. M. (2000). The psychology of sexual prejudice. *Current Directions in Psychological Science, 9,* 19-22.

Herek, G. M. (2004). Beyond "homophobia": Thinking about sexual stigma and prejudice in the twenty-first century. *Sexuality Research and Social Policy, 1*(2), 6-24.

Herzberg, F. (1966). *Work: The nature of man.* Cleveland: World Press.

Hetherington, E. M. (1988). The impact of the experience of divorce during childhood on women's adult adjustment. Unpublished manuscript, University of Virginia, Charlottesville.

Hetherington, E. M. (1989). Coping with family transitions: Winners, losers, and survivors. *Child Development, 60,* 1-14.

Hetherington, E. M., Bridges, M., & Insabella, G. M. (1998). What matters? What does not? Five perspectives on the association between marital transitions and children's adjustment. *American Psychologist, 53*(2), 167-184.

Hetherington, E. M., & Clingempeel, W. G. (1988, March). *Coping with remarriage: The first two years.* Symposium presented at the South. Conference on Human Development, Charleston, SC.

Hetherington, E. M., et al. (1985). Long-term effects of divorce and remarriage on the adjustment of children. *Journal of American Academy of Psychiatry, 24*(5), 518-30.

Hetherington, E. M., & Stanley-Hagan, M. (1986). Divorced fathers: Stress, coping, and adjustment. In M. Lamb (Ed.), *The father's role: Applied perspective.* New York: Wiley.

Hetherington, E. M., & Stanley-Hagan, M. (2000). Diversity among stepfamilies. In D. H. Demo, et al. (Eds.), *Handbook of family diversity.* New York: Oxford University Press.

Hewitt, P. L., Flett, G. L., & Ediger, G. (1996). Perfectionism and depression: Longitudinal assessment of a specific vulnerability hypothesis. *Journal of Abnormal Psychology, 105*(2), 276-280.

Hill, R. (1965). Generic features of families under stress. In H. Parad (Ed.), *Crisis intervention: Selected readings.* New York: Family Service Association of America.

Hinshaw, S. P., Owens, E. B., Sami, N., & Fargeon, S. (2006). Prospective follow-up of girls with attention-deficit/hyperactivity disorder into adolescence: Evidence for continuing cross-domain impairment. *Journal of Consulting and Clinical Psychology, 74,* 489-499.

Hodges, J., & Tizard, B. (1989). Social and family relationships of ex-institutionalized adolescents. *Journal of Child Psychology and Psychiatry, 30*, 77-97.

Hoff, L. A. (1978). *People in crisis: Understanding and helping.* Menlo Park, CA: Addison-Wesley Publishing Co.

Hoffman, K. S., & Sallee, A. L. (1994). *Social work practice.* Needham Heights, MA: Allyn & Bacon.

Hoffman, L. W. (1989). Effects of maternal employment in two-parent families. *American Psychologist, 44*(2), 283-92.

Hoffman, M. L. (1970). Moral development. In P. H. Mussen (Ed.), *Carmichael's manual of child psychology (Vol. 2).* New York: Wiley.

Hoffman, M. L. (1987). The contribution of empathy to justice and moral judgment. In N. Eisenberg & J. Strayer (Eds.), *Empathy and its development* (pp. 47-80). New York: Cambridge University Press.

Hollis, F. (1964). *Casework: A psychosocial approach.* New York: Random House.

Hollis, F. (1970). The psychosocial approach to the practice of casework. In R. Roberts & R. Nee (Eds.), *Theories of social casework.* Chicago: University of Chicago Press.

Hollis, F. (1972). *Casework: A psychosocial approach.* New York: Random House.

Holmes T. H., & Rahe R. H. (1967). The Social Readjustment Rating Scale. *Journal of Psychosomatic Research 11*(2), 213-8.

Hooyman, N. R., & Kiyak, H. A. (2002). *Social gerontology: A multidisciplinary approach.* Boston: Allyn & Bacon.

Hopper, K. (2003). *Reckoning with homelessness.* New York: Cornell University Press.

Horowitz M. J. (1983). Psychological response to serious life events. In S. Breznitz (Ed.), *The denial of stress.* New York: International Universities Press.

Howard, K. I., Kopta, S. M., Krause, M. S., & Orlinsky, D. E. (1986). The dose-effect relationship in psychotherapy. *American Psychologist, 41*, 159-164.

Howard, K. I., Moras, K., Brill, P. L., Martinovich, Z., & Lutz, W. (1996). Evaluation of psychotherapy: Efficacy, effectiveness, and patient progress. *American Psychologist, 51*(10), 1059-1064.

Hoyt, M. F., et al. (1992). Planned single-session psychotherapy. In S. H. Budman, M. F. Hoyt, & S. Friedman (Eds.), *The first session in brief therapy.* New York: The Guilford Press.

Hsu, L. K. G. (1993). *Eating disorders.* New York: Guilford.

Huff, R. G. (2001). *Gangs in America: III.* Thousand Oaks, CA: Sage.

Huyck, M. H. (1990). Gender differences in aging. In J. E. Birren & K. W. Schaie (Eds.), *Handbook of the psychology of aging.* San Diego: Academic Press.

Izard, C. (Ed.) (1982). *Measuring emotions in infants and children.* London: Cambridge University Press.

Jackson, S., et al. (2003). *Batterer intervention programs: Where do we go from here?* Washington, DC: The National Institute of Justice.

Jaimison, K. R. (1999). *Night falls fast: Understanding suicide.* New York: Knopf.

Jakob, M., Weck, F., & Bohus, M. (2013). Live supervision: From the one-way mirror to video-based online supervision. Retrieved from www.karger.com on February 21, 2015.

James, M., & Jongeward, D. (1971). *Born to Win: Transactional analysis with Gestalt experiments.* Reading, MA: Addison-Wesley.

James, R. K., & Gilliland, B. E. (2005). *Crisis intervention strategies.* Belmont, CA: Thomas Brooks/Cole.

Janis, I. (1982). *Groupthink.* Boston: Houghton-Mifflin.

Jellinek, E. M. (1960). *The disease concept of alcoholism.* New Haven, CT: College & University Press.

Jenson, J. M. (2005). Connecting science to intervention: Advances, challenges, and the promise of evidence-based practice. *Social Work Research, 29*(3), 131-135.

Johnson, D., & Johnson, S. (2003). *Real world treatment planning.* Pacific Grove, CA: Thomson-Brooks/Cole.

Johnson, K. W., et al. (1998). Serotonin in migraine: Theories, animal models, and emerging therapies. *Progress in Drug Research, 51,* 219-44.

Johnson, S. (1997). *Therapist's guide to clinical intervention: The 1-2-3s of treatment planning.* San Diego, CA: Academic Press.

Jones, C. P. (2000). Levels of racism: A theoretic framework and a gardener's tale. *American Journal of Public Health, 90*(8), 1212-16.

Jongsma, A. E., O'Leary, K. D., & Heyman, R. E. (1998). *The couples psychotherapy treatment planner.* New York: John Wiley & Sons.

Jordan, K. M., & Deluty, R. H. (1998). Coming out for lesbian women: Its relation to anxiety, positive affectivity, self-esteem, and social support. *Journal of Homosexuality, 35*(2), 41-63.

Juhnke, G. A., et al. (1999). *Assessing potentially violent students.* Greensboro, NC: ERIC Clearinghouse on Counseling and Student Services.

Kadushin, A. (1990). *Final report of updated survey: Supervisors-supervisees.* Madison: School of Social Work, University of Wisconsin.

Kadushin, A., & Harkness, D. (2002). *Supervision in social work, 4th Edition.* New York: Columbia University Press.

Kaplan, H. S. (1974). *The new sex therapy.* New York: Brunner/Mazel.

Kaplan, H. S. (1987). *The illustrated manual of sex therapy.* New York: Quadrangle/NY Times Books.

Kaplan, P. S. (2004). *Adolescence.* Boston: Houghton Mifflin.

Karls, J. M. (2002). Person-in-environment system: Its essence and applications. In A. R. Roberts & G. J. Greene (Eds.), *Social workers' desk reference.* New York: Oxford University Press.

Karls, J. M., & Wandrei, K. E. (1996). *Person-in-environment system: The PIE classification system for social functioning problems (PIE manual).* Washington, DC: NASW Press.

Katz, D., & Kahn, R. L. (1966). *The social psychology of organizations.* New York: Wiley.

Katz, P. A. (1976). The acceptance of racial attitudes in children. In P. A. Katz (Ed.), *Towards the elimination of racism* (pp. 125-154). New York: Pergamon.

Kaufmann, Y. (1979). Analytical psychotherapy. In R. J. Corsini (Ed.), *Current psychotherapies.* Itasca, IL: F. E. Peacock Publishers.

Kavanagh, D. J. (1992). Recent developments in expressed emotion and schizophrenia. *British Journal of Psychiatry, 160,* 601-620.

Kaye, W. H., et al. (2004). Comorbidity of anxiety disorders with anorexia and bulimia nervosa. *American Journal of Psychiatry, 161*(12), 2215-2221.

Kearney, C.A. (2001). *School refusal behavior in youth: A functional approach to assessment and treatment.* Washington, DC: APA.

Keith, C. (1966). Multiple transfers of psychotherapy patients. *Archives of General Psychiatry, 14,* 185-189.

Kelly, J. A. (1983). *Treating child-abusive families: Interventions based on skills training principle*s. New York: Plenum Press.

Kelman, H. C. (1961). Process of opinion change. *Public Opinion Quarterly, 25,* 57-78.

Kemper, S., & Mitzner, T. (2001). Language production and comprehension. In J. Birren & K. Schaie (Eds.), *Handbook of the psychology of aging, 5th Edition.* New York: Academic Press.

Kendler, K. S., Thornton, L. M., & Gardner, C. O. (2001). Genetic risk, number of previous depressive episodes, and stressful life events in predicting the onset of major depression. *American Journal of Psychiatry, 158,* 582-586.

Kernberg, O. (1984). *Severe personality disorders: Psychotherapeutic strategies.* New Haven, CT: Yale University Press.

Kettner, P. M., Daley, J. M., & Nichols, A. W. (1985). *Initiating change in organizations and communities.* Monterey CA: Brooks/Cole.

Khantzian, E. J. (1975). Self-selection and progression in drug dependence. *Psychiatry Digest, 10,* 19-22.

Khantzian, E. J., & Mack, J. (1983). Self-preservation and the care of self. *Psychoanalytic Child Study, 38,* 209-232.

Kim, J., & Moen, P. (2002). Retirement transitions, gender, and psychological well-being: A life-course ecological model. *Journals of Gerontology Series B: Psychological Sciences and Social Services, 57,* 212-22.

King, S. W., & Mayers, R. S. (1984). A course syllabus of developing self-help groups among minority elderly. In J. S. McNeil & S. W. King (Eds.), *Guidelines for developing mental health and minority aging curriculum with a focus on self-help groups.* NIMH Grant supported publication (#MH 15944-04).

Kirst-Ashman, K. K., & Hull Jr., G. H. (2006). *Generalist practice with organizations and communities, 3rd Edition.* Belmont, CA: Thomson/Brooks/Cole.

Kissel, S. (1965). Stress-reducing properties of social stimuli. *Journal of Personality and Social Psychology, 2,* 378-84.

Klerman, G. L., Rounsaville, B., Chevron, E., & Weissman, M. (1984). *Interpersonal psychotherapy of depression.* New York: Basic Books.

Knapp, S., & VandeCreek, L. (2003). *A guide to the 2002 revision of the American Psychological Association's Ethics Code.* Sarasota, FL: Professional Resource Press.

Knight, C. C., & Sutton, R. E. (2004). Neo-Piagetian theory and research: Enhancing pedagogical practice for education of adults. *London Review of Education, 2*(1), 47-60.

Kohlberg, L. (1966). A cognitive-developmental analysis of children's sex-role concepts and attitudes. In E. E. Maccoby (Ed.), *The development of differences.* Stanford, CA: Stanford University Press.

Kohlberg, L. (1971). From is to ought. In T. Michel (Ed.), *Cognitive development and epistemology.* New York: Academic Press.

Kolb, D. A. (1981). Learning styles and disciplinary differences. In A. A. Chickering & Associates (Eds.), *The modern American college.* San Francisco: Jossey-Bass.

Koocher, G. P., & Keith-Spiegel, P. (2008). *Ethics in psychology and the mental health professions.* New York: Oxford University Press.

Korchin, S. J. (1976). *Clinical psychology: Principles of intervention in the clinic and community.* New York: Basic Books.

Kouzes, J. M., & Mico, P. R. (1979). Domain theory: An introduction to organizational behavior in human service organizations. *Journal of Applied Behavioral Science, 15*(4), 449-469.

Krause, N. (2003). Religious meaning and subjective well-being in late life. *Journals of Gerontology, Series B: Psychological Sciences and Social Sciences, 58,* S160-70.

Kretzmann, J. P., & McKnight J. L. (1993). *Building communities from the inside out.* Evanston, IL: Northwestern University, Center for Urban Affairs and Policy Research.

Kubler-Ross, E. (1969). *On death and dying.* New York: Macmillan.

LaFromboise, T. D., Trimble, J. E., & Mohatt, G. V. (1990). Counseling interventions and American Indian tradition: An integrative approach. *The Counseling Psychologist, 18,* 628-654.

Lam, R. W., & Levitan, R. D. (2000). Pathophysiology of seasonal affective disorder: A review. *Journal of Psychiatry and Neuroscience, 25*(5), 469-480.

Lambert, M. J., Chiles, J. A., Kesler, S. R., & Vermeersch, D. A. (1998). Compendium of current psychotherapy treatment manuals. In G. P. Koocher, J. C. Norcross, & S. S. Hill (Eds.), *Psychologists' desk reference* (pp. 202-209). New York: Oxford University Press.

Landau, S. T., et al. (2007). A study of sexuality and health among older adults in the United States. *New England Journal of Medicine, 357*(8), 762-774.

Landrum, J., & Batts, V. (1985). *Helping Blacks cope with and overcome the personal effects of racism.* Paper presented at the annual meeting of the American Psychological Association Convention, Los Angeles, CA.

Landy, S., et al., (2002). *Pathways to competence: Encouraging health, social and emotional development in young children.* New York: Paul H. Brooks.

Langs, R. J. (1982). *The psychotherapeutic conspiracy.* New York: Jason Aronson.

Lauer, J. W., et al. (1979). *The role of the mental health professional in the prevention and treatment of child abuse and neglect.* DHEW Publ. No. (OHDS) 79-30194. Washington, DC: U.S. DHEW, National Center on Child Abuse and Neglect.

Lawson, G., et al. (1982). *Alcoholism and the family.* Rockville, MD: Aspen Publishing.

Lazar, I., et al. (1982). Lasting effects of early education: A report from the Consortium for Longitudinal Studies. *Monographs of the Society for Research on Child Development, 47,* (2-3, Serial No. 195).

LeCroy, C. W. (2001). Promoting social competence in youth. In H. E. Briggs & K. Corcoran (Eds.). *Social work practice: Treating common problems.* Chicago: Lyceum Books.

Lee, C. C., Oh, M., & Mountcastle, A. R. (1992). Indigenous models of helping in nonwestern countries: Implications for multicultural counseling. *Journal of Multicultural Counseling and Development, 20,* 1-10.

Lemme, B. H. (2001). *Development in adulthood.* Needham Heights, MA: Allyn & Bacon.

Leslie, R. (January 2012). HIV/AIDS and confidentiality. *Avoiding Liability Bulletin, Vol. 1.* Retrieved from http://www.cphins.com/Default.aspx?tabid=65

Levenson, J. (2017). Trauma-Informed Social Work Practice. Social Work, 62(2), 105-113.

Leventhal, A. (1994, February). *Peer conformity during adolescence: An integration of developmental, situational, and individual characteristics.* Paper presented at the meeting of the Society for Research on Adolescence, San Diego.

Lewin, K. (1931). Environmental forces in child behavior and development. In C. Murchison (Ed.), *A handbook of child psychology* (pp. 590-625). Worcester, MA: Clark University Press.

Lewin, K. (1936). *A dynamic theory of personality.* New York: McGraw-Hill.

Lewin, K. (1951). *Field theory in social science.* New York: Harper.

Lewin, K., Lippitt, R., & White, R. K. (1939). Patterns of aggressive behavior in experimentally-created social climates. *Journal of Social Psychology, 10,* 271-301.

Lewinsohn, P. M. (1974). A behavioral approach to depression. In R. Friedman & M. Katz (eds.), *The Psychology of Depression: Contemporary Theory and Research.* Washington: Winston-Wiley.

Lewinsohn, P. M., et al. (1980). Social competence and depression: The role of illusory self-perceptions. *Journal of Abnormal Psychology, 89,* 203-212.

Lewis, H. (1978). Management in the nonprofit social service organization. In S. Slavin (Ed.), *Social administration: The management of social services.* New York: CSWE.

Lewis, M. (2002). Early emotional development. In A. Slater & M. Lewis (Eds.), *Introduction to infant development.* New York: Oxford University Press.

Liberman, R. P., et al. (1980). *Handbook of marital therapy: A positive approach to helping troubled relationships.* New York: Plenum.

Lieberman, A. F. (1993). *The emotional life of a toddler.* New York: Free Press.

Linehan, M. M. (1987). Dialectical behavior therapy for borderline personality disorder. *Bulletin of the Menninger Clinic, 51*, 261-276.

Linehan, M. M., et al. (2006). Two-year randomized control trial and follow-up of Dialectical Behavior Therapy vs. therapy by experts for suicidal behaviors and borderline personality disorder. *Archives of General Psychiatry, 63*, 757-766.

Lipsky, M. (1984). Bureaucratic disentitlement in social welfare programs. *Social Service Review, 58*(1), 3-27.

Litz, B. T., et al. (2002). Early intervention for trauma: Current status and future directions. *Clinical Psychology: Science and Practice, 9*, 112-134.

Loeber, R., & Farrington, D. P. (2001). *Child delinquents: Development, intervention, and service needs.* Thousand Oaks, CA: Sage.

Lorenz, K. (1965). *Evolution and modification of behavior.* Chicago: University of Chicago Press

Lovaas, O. I. (1966). *Reinforcement therapy* (film). Philadelphia: Smith, Kline & French Laboratories.

MacCallum, F., & Golombok, S. (2008). Children raised in fatherless families from infancy: A follow-up study of children of lesbian and single heterosexual mothers at early adolescence. *Journal of Child Psychology and Psychiatry, 45*(8), 1407-1419.

Maccoby, E. E. (1980). *Social development: Psychological growth and the parent-child relationship.* San Diego: Harcourt Brace Jovanovich.

MacNair, R. H., Fowler, L., & Harris, J. (2000). The diversity functions of organizations that confront oppression: The evolution of three social movements. *Journal of Community Practice, 7*(2), 71-88.

Mahler, M. S. (1971). A study of the separation-individuation process and its possible application to borderline in the psychoanalytic situation. *Psychoanalytic Study of the Child, 26*, 403-424.

Mahoney, M. J. (2000). A changing history of efforts to understand and control change: The case of psychotherapy. In C. R. Snyder & R. E. Ingram (Eds.), *Handbook of psychological change: Psychotherapy processes and practice for the 21st century.* New York: Wiley & Sons.

Main, M., & Solomon, J. (1986). Discovery of an insecure, disorganized/disoriented attachment pattern: Procedures, findings, and implications for the classification of behavior. In M. Yogman & T. B. Brazelton (Eds.), *Affective development in infancy.* Norwood, NJ: Ablex.

Mallon, G.P. (2013). Lesbian, gay, bisexual, and transgender families and parenting. In T. Mizrahi & L. E. Davis (Eds.-in-Chief), Encyclopedia of social work (20th ed). [Electronic]. Washington, DC, and New York, NY: NASW Press and Oxford University Press. Retrieved from http://socialwork.oxfordre.com/view/10.1093/acrefore/9780199975839.001.0001/acrefore-9780199975839-e-158

Mann, C. (1994). Current issues in using anatomical dolls. *Violence Update, 4*, 1-4.

Mann, M. (1968). *New primer on alcoholism.* New York: Holt Rinehart & Winston.

March, J. G., & Simon, H. A. (1958). *Organizations.* New York: Wiley.

Marcia, J. (1987). The identity status approach to the study of ego identity development. In T. Honess & K. Yardley (Eds.), *Self and identity: Perspectives across the lifespan.* London: Routledge & Kegan Paul.

Marcus, G. (1937). *The necessity for understanding agency functions.* Unpublished manuscript, Philadelphia.

Marlatt, G. A. (Ed.) (1998). *Harm reduction: Pragmatic strategies for managing high-risk behaviors.* New York: Guilford Press.

Marlatt, G. A., & Gordon, J. R. (1985). *Relapse prevention: Maintenance strategies in the treatment of addictive behaviors.* New York: Guilford Press.

Martin, A. D., & Hetrick, E. S. (1988). The stigmatization of the gay and lesbian adolescent. *Journal of Homosexuality, 15*(1-2), 163-183.

Martin, D. (1982). Wife beating: A product of socio-sexual development. In M. Kirkpatrick (Ed.), *Woman's sexual experiences: Exploration of the dark continent.* New York: Plenum.

Martin, H. P. (1979). *Treatment for abused and neglected children.* DHEW Publ. No. (OHDS) 79-30199. Washington, DC: U.S. DHEW, National Center on Child Abuse and Neglect.

Martin, L. L. (1993). *Total quality management in human services organizations.* Newbury Park, CA: Sage.

Martin, L. L. (2000). Budgeting outcomes in state human agencies. *Administration in Social Work, 24*, 71-88.

Martin, P. Y., & O'Connor, G. G. (1989). *The social environment: Open systems applications.* New York: Longman.

Martinez, F. (1996). *Can SIDS be prevented?* Presented at Pediatric Specialty Conference, University Medical Center, Tucson, AZ.

Martinez-Brawley, E. E., & Zorita, P. M. B. (2016). Moving away from globalization and the "flattening" of Social Work: Preserving Context in International Efforts. *European Journal of Social Work, 19*(5), 650-663.

Maruish, M. E. (2002). *Essentials of treatment planning.* New York: John Wiley & Sons, Inc.

Masten, A. S. (2001). Ordinary magic: Resilience and development: Contributions from the study of children who overcome adversity. *Development and Psychopathology, 2*, 227-38.

Masten, A. S., & Coatsworth, J. (1998). The development of competence in favorable and unfavorable environments: Lessons from research on successful children. *American Psychologist, 53*, 205-20.

Masters, W. H., & Johnson, V. E. (1970) *Human sexual inadequacy.* Boston: Little, Brown.

Matsakis, A. (2003). *Rape recovery handbook.* Oakland, CA: New Harbinger Publishing.

Matza, D. (1964). *Delinquency and drift.* New York: John Wiley

Mavissakalian, M. R., Perel, J. M., & DeGroot, C. (1993). Imipramine treatment of panic disorder with agoraphobia: The second time around. *Journal of Psychiatric Research, 27*, 61-68.

Mayhall, P. D., & Norgard, K. E. (1983). *Child abuse and neglect: Sharing responsibilities.* New York: Wiley & Sons.

Mayo Clinic. (2017, August 04). Eating disorders. Retrieved September 17, 2017, from http://www.mayoclinic.org/diseases-conditions/eating-disorders/home/ovc-20182765

McCall, W. V., Reboussin, D. M., Weiner, R. D., & Sackeim, H. A. (2000). Titrated suprathreshold vs. fixed high-dose right unilateral electroconvulsive therapy: Acute antidepressant and cognitive effects. *Archives of General Psychiatry, 57*, 438-444.

McDevitt, R. M., & Ormrod, J. E. (2007). *Child development and education, 3rd Edition.* Upper Saddle River, NJ: Person Education, Inc.

McElroy, S., et al. (2001). Axis I psychiatric comorbidity and its relationship to historical illness variables in 288 patients with bipolar disorder. *American Journal of Psychiatry, 158*, 420-426.

McGregor, D. (1960). *The human side of enterprise.* New York: McGraw-Hill.

McInnis-Dittrich, K. (2005). *Social work with elders: A biopsychosocial approach to assessment and intervention, 2nd Edition.* Boston: Pearson.

McLoyd, V. C. (1998). Socioeconomic disadvantage and child development. *American Psychologist, 53*, 185-204.

McNeece, C. A., & Thyer, B. A. (2004). Evidence-based practice and social work. *Journal of evidence-based social work,* 1(1), 7-25.

McNeill T. Evidence-based practice in an age of relativism: toward a model for practice. *Social Work.* 2006;51(2):147-156.

Meadows, P. (2003). Retirement ages in the UK: A review of the literature. *Employment Relations Research Series, 18*, 50-76.

Meenaghan, T. M., & Gibbons, W. E. (2000). *Macro practice in the human services.* Chicago: Lyceum.

Meichenbaum, D. H., & Goodman, J. (1971). Training impulsive children to talk to themselves: A means of developing self-control. *Journal of Abnormal Psychology, 77*, 115-126.

Meichenbaum, D. H., & Jeremko, M. E. (1982). *Stress prevention and management: A cognitive-behavioral approach.* New York: Plenum Press.

Meiselman, K. (1990). *Resolving the trauma of incest: Reintegration therapy with survivors.* San Francisco: Jossey-Bass.

Mellon, M. W., & Houts, A. C. (2006). Nocturnal enuresis. In J. E. Fisher & W. T. O'Donohue (Ed.), *Practitioner's guide to evidence-based psychotherapy* (pp. 432-441). New York: Springer Science.

Mental Health Coordinating Council. (n.d.). Trauma-Informed Care and Practice (TICP). Retrieved August 31, 2017, from http://www.mhcc.org.au/sector-development/recovery-and-practice-approaches/trauma-informed-care-and-practice.aspx

Merton, R. K. (1952). Bureaucratic structure and personality. In R. K. Merton, A. P. Gray, B. Hockey, & H. C. Selvin (Eds.), *Reader in bureaucracy.* Glencoe, IL: Free Press.

Michels, R. (1949). *Political parties.* (E. Paul & C. Paul, Trans.). Glencoe, IL: Free Press (originally published in 1915).

Mikesell, R. H., et al. (Eds.) (1995). *Integrating family therapy.* Washington, D.C.: American Psychological Association.

Miklowitz, D. J., et al. (2007). Psychosocial treatments for bipolar depression: A 1-year randomized trial from the Systematic Treatment Enhancement Program for Bipolar Disorder. *Archives of General Psychiatry, 64,* 419-427.

Milgrom, J., Martin, P. R., & Negri, L. M. (1999). *Treating postnatal depression: A psychological approach for health care practitioners.* Chichester: Wiley.

Miller, M. (2002). *Attention-deficit hyperactivity disorder: Pharmaceutical updates.* Arlington Heights, IN: Optima Educational Solutions, Inc.

Miller, N. E. (1944). Experimental studies of conflict. In J. M. Hunt (Ed.), *Personality and the behavior disorders* (pp. 431-465). New York: The Ronald Press.

Miller, W. R., & Rollnick, S. (1991). *Motivational interviewing: Preparing people to change addictive behavior.* New York: Guilford Press.

Miller, W. R., & Rollnick, S. (2002). *Motivational interviewing: Preparing people for change.* New York: Guilford Press.

Mills, C. W. (1967). *Power, politics & people: The collected essays of C. Wright Mills.* New York: Oxford University Press.

Milner, J. S., & Chilamkurti, C. (1991). Physical child abuse perpetrator characteristics: A review of the literature. *Journal of Interpersonal Violence, 6*(3), 345-66.

Mintun, M. A., et al. (2004). Decreased hippocampal 5-HT receptor binding in major depressive disorder: In vivo measurement with [18F]altanserin positron emission tomography. *Biological Psychiatry, 55,* 217-224.

Mischel, W. (1966). A social learning view of sex differences in behaving. In E. E. Maccoby (Ed.), *The development of sex differences.* Stanford, CA: Stanford University Press.

Mitchell, J. (1993). *Pregnant, substance-using women.* Rockville, MD: Department of Health and Human Services, Substance Abuse and Mental Health Services Administration.

Mittelman, M. S., Epstein, C., & Pierzchala, A. (2003). *Counseling the Alzheimer's caregiver: A resource for health care professionals.* Chicago, IL: AMA Press.

Mittelman, M. S., Haley, W. E., Clay, O. J., & Roth, D. D. (2006). Improving caregiver well-being delays nursing-home placement of patients with Alzheimer's disease. *Neurology, 67*(9), 1592-1599.

Moffitt, T. E. (1993). Adolescence-limited and life-course-persistent antisocial behavior: A developmental taxonomy. *Psychological Review, 100*, 674-701.

Morrison, J. (1995). *The first interview.* New York: The Guilford Press.

Morse, J. J., & Lorsch, J. W. (1970). Beyond theory Y. *Harvard Business Review, 48*, 61-68.

Moses, A. E., & Hawkins, Jr., R. O. (1986). *Counseling lesbian women and gay men: A life-issues approach.* Ohio: Merrill Publishing Company.

Mowrer, O. H. (1947). On the dual nature of learning — A reinterpretation of "conditioning" and "problem-solving." *Harvard Educational Review, 17*, 102-148.

Mowrer, O. H. (1960). *Learning theory and the symbolic process.* New York: Wiley.

Mrazek, P. (1993). Maltreatment and infant development. In C. Zeaneh (Ed.), *Handbook of infant mental health.* New York: Guilford Press.

Mussen, P. et al. (1980). *Child development and personality.* New York: Harper Row.

NASW Code of Ethics. (1996; 2017). Washington, DC: NASW, Inc.

NASW Standards for Continuing Professional Education. National Association of Social Workers, Inc. Washington, D.C.

NASW Standards for the Practice of Clinical Social Work. National Association of Social Workers, Inc. Washington, D.C.

NASW Standards for the Practice of Social Work with Adolescents. National Association of Social Workers, Inc. Washington, D.C.

NASW Standards for School Social Work Services. National Association of Social Workers, Inc. Washington, D.C.

NASW Standards for Social Work Case Management. National Association of Social Workers, Inc. Washington, D.C.

NASW Standards for Social Work in Healthcare Settings. National Association of Social Workers, Inc. Washington, D.C.

NASW Standards for Social Work Mediators. National Association of Social Workers, Inc. Washington, D.C.

NASW Standards for Social Work Practice in Child Protection. National Association of Social Workers, Inc. Washington, D.C.

NASW Standards for Social Work Services in Long-term Care Facilities. National Association of Social Workers, Inc. Washington, D.C.

National Association of Social Workers, National Committee on Lesbian and Gay Issues. (1992). *Position statement: Reparative or conversion therapies for lesbians and gay men.* Washington, DC: Author.

National Association of Social Workers. (1995). *Encyclopedia of social work, 19th Edition.* Washington, DC: Author.

National Association of Social Workers. (1996). Lesbian, gay, and bisexual issues. In *Social work speaks, 4th Edition* (pp. 198–209). Washington, DC: NASW Press.

National Center on Elder Abuse. (2004). *The basics.* http://www.elderabusecenter.org.

National Center for Health Statistics. (2002). *Cohabitation, marriage, divorce, and remarriage in the United States.* Hyattsville, MD: Department of Health and Human Services.

National Eating Disorders Collaboration. (n.d.). What is body image? Retrieved September 17, 2017, from http://www.nedc.com.au/body-image

National Research Council. (1993a). *Losing generations: Adolescents in high-risk settings.* Washington, DC: National Academic Press

National Research Council. (1993b). *Understanding child abuse and neglect.* Washington, DC: National Academic Press.

NCTSN (The National Child Traumatic Stress Network). (2009). Sexual development and behavior in children. Retrieved from: http://nctsn.org/nctsn_assets/pdfs/caring/sexualdevelopmentandbehavior.pdf

Nelles, W. B., & Barlow, D. H. (1988). Do children panic? *Clinical Psychology Review, 8,* 359-372.

Netting, F. E., Kettner, P. M., & McMurtry S. L. (2004). *Social Work Macro Practice, 3rd Edition.* Boston: Pearson/Allyn & Bacon.

Neumeister, A., et al. (2004). Neural and behavioral responses to tryptophan depletion in unmedicated patients with remitted major depressive disorder and controls. *Archives of General Psychiatry, 61,* 765-773

Newacheck, P. W., & Taylor, W. R. (1992). Childhood chronic illness: Prevalence, severity, and impact. *American Journal of Public Health, 82,* 364-71.

Newman, B. M., & Newman, P. R. (2002). *Development through life: A psychosocial approach, 8th Edition.* Pacific Grove, CA: Brooks/Cole.

NICHD Early Child Care Research Network. (2006). Infant-mother attachment classification: Risk and protection in relation to changing maternal caregiving quality. *Developmental Psychology, 42*(1), 38-58.

Norton, D. G. (1978). *The dual perspective: Inclusion of ethnic minority content in the social work curriculum.* New York: CSWE.

O'Leary, K. D., Heyman, R. E., & Jongsma, A. E. (1998). *The couples psychotherapy treatment planner.* New York: John Wiley & Sons, Inc.

Oller, D. K., & Eilers, R. E. (1988). The role of audition in infant babbling. *Child Development, 59,* 441-49.

Osborn, A. F. (1957). *Applied imagination.* New York: Charles Scribner & Sons.

Osofsky, J., et al. (1993). Adolescent parenthood: Risks and opportunities for mothers and infants. In C. Zeaneh (Ed.), *Handbook of infant mental health.* New York: Guilford Press.

Paniagua, F. A. (2014). *Assessing and treating culturally diverse clients: A practical guide.* Thousand Oaks, CA: Sage.

Pantoja, A., & Perry, W. (1992). Community development and restoration: A perspective. In F. G. Rivera & J. L. Erlich (Eds.), *Community organizing in a diverse society.* Boston: Allyn & Bacon.

Passons, W. R. (1975). *Gestalt approaches in counseling.* New York: Holt, Rinehart, & Winston.

Patterson, G. R., et al. (1989). A developmental perspective on antisocial behavior. *American Psychologist, 44*(2), 329-35.

Patterson, G. R., Chamberlain, P., & Reid, J. B. (1982). A comparative evaluation of a parent-training program. *Behavior Therapy, 13*(5), 638-650.

Patterson, G. R., Reid, J., B., & Dishion, T. J. (1992). *Antisocial boys.* Eugene, OR: Castalia.

Pattoni, L. (2012, May). Strengths-based approaches for working with individuals. IRISS.

Peak, T., & Toseland, R. W. (1999). Friends don't really understand: The therapeutic benefit of social group work for caregivers of older persons. In C. W. LeCroy (Ed.), *Case studies in social work practice, 2nd Edition.* Pacific Grove, CA: Brooks/Cole.

Pearce, J. W., & Pezzot-Pearce, T. D. (1997). *Psychotherapy of abused and neglected children.* New York: Guilford Press.

Pentz, M. A., & Li, C. (2002). The gateway theory applied to prevention. In D. B. Kandel (Ed.), *Stages and pathways of drug involvement: Examining the gateway hypothesis.* Cambridge, UK: Cambridge University Press.

Perlman, H. H. (1947). Content in basic social casework. *Social Service Review, 21,* 76-84.

Perlman, H. H. (1957). *Social casework: A problem solving process.* Chicago: University of Chicago Press.

Perlman, H. H. (1971). Social casework: The problem-solving approach. In *Encyclopedia of social work (Vol. 2).* New York: NASW.

Perls, F. S. (1973). *The Gestalt approach and eyewitness to therapy.* New York: Bantam.

Perry, D. G., & Bussey, K. (1977). Self-reinforcement in high- and low-aggressive boys following acts of aggression, *Child Development, 48,* 653-657.

Perry, D. G., Perry, L. C. & Rasmussen, P. (1986). Cognitive social learning mediators of aggression. *Child Development, 57,* 700-711.

Persons, J. B., Davidson, J., & Tompkins, M. A. (2001). *Essential components of cognitive-behavior therapy for depression.* Washington, DC: American Psychological Association.

Pert, C. B., & Snyder, S. H. (1973). Opiate receptor: Demonstration in nervous tissue. *Science, 179,* 1011-1014.

Pettito, L., & Marentetto, P. F. (1991). Babbling in the manual mode: Evidence for the ontogeny of language. *Science, 251,* 1493-96.

Pfeffer, J. (1981). *Power in organizations.* Marshfield, MA: Pitman.

Piacentini, J., et al. (2010). Behavior therapy for children with Tourette disorder: A randomized controlled trial. *JAMA, 303*(19), 1929-1937.

Pike, C. K. (2002). Developing client-focused measures. In A. R. Roberts & G. J. Greene (Eds.), *Social workers' desk reference.* New York: Oxford University Press.

Pine, B. A., Warsh, R., & Maluccio, A. N. (1998). Participatory management in a public child welfare agency: A key to effective change. *Administration in Social Work, 22,* 19-32.

Pinquart, M., & Sorensen, S. (2001). Influences on loneliness in older adults: A meta-analysis. *Basic and Applied Psychology, 23*(4), 245-68.

Pollin, I. (1995). *Medical crisis counseling: Short-term treatment for long-term illness.* Evanston, IL: Norton.

Premack, D. (1965). Reinforcement theory. In D. Levine (Ed.), *Nebraska symposium on motivation.* Lincoln: University of Nebraska Press.

Prilleltensky, I. (1990). Enhancing the social ethics of psychology: Toward a psychology at the service of social change. *Canadian Psychology, 31,* 310-319.

Prochaska, J. O., & DiClemente, C. C. (1992). Stages of change in the modification of problem behaviors. In M. Hersen, et al. (Eds.), *Progress in behavior modification (Vol. 28).* Sycamore, IL: Sycamore.

Radke-Yarrow, M., & Zahn-Waxler, C. (1984). Roots, motives, and patterns in children's prosocial behavior. In J. Reykowski et al. (Eds.), *The development and maintenance of prosocial behaviors: International perspectives on positive morality* (pp. 81-99). New York: Plenum.

Ramey, C. T., & Ramey, S. L. (1990). Intensive educational intervention for children of poverty. *Intelligence, 14,* 1-9.

Ramey, C. T., & Ramey, S. L. (1998). Early intervention and early experience. *American Psychologist, 53,* 109-20.

Ramsey, P. G. (1995) Growing up with the contradictions of race and class. *Young Children, 50*(6), 18-22.

Ramseyer Winter, V., O'Neill, E. A., & Omary, A. (2017). Exploring relationships between body appreciation and self-reported physical health among young women. *Health & Social Work,* 42(2), e62-e67.

Rapoport, L. (1970). Crisis intervention as a mode of brief treatment. In R. W. Roberts & R. H. Nee (Eds.), *Theories of social casework.* Chicago: University of Chicago Press.

Rapp, C. A., & Poertner, J. (1992). *Social administration: A client-centered approach.* New York: Longman.

Rapp, C. A., Saleebey, D., & Sullivan, W. P. (2006). The future of strengths-based social work. Advances in Social Work: Special Issue on the Futures of Social Work, 6(1), 79-90.

Rapp, S. R., et al. (2003). Effects of estrogen plus progestin on global cognitive function in postmenopausal women: The Women's Health Initiative memory study: Randomized control trial. *JAMA, 286,* 2663-72.

Rehm, L. P., Kaslow, N. J., & Rabin, A. S. (1987). Cognitive and behavioral targets in a self-control therapy for depression. *Journal of Consulting and Clinical Psychology, 55*(1), 60-67.

Reisman, J. M. (1991). *A History of clinical psychology*. New York: Hemisphere Publishing Corp.

Rekers, G. A., and Lovaas, O. I. (1974). Behavioral treatment of deviant sex-role behaviors in a male child. *Journal of Applied Behavior Analysis, 7,* 173-190.

Reyes (J. A.) Associates (1979). *We can help: Leader's manual. A curriculum on child abuse and neglect.* DHEW Publ. No. (OHDS) 79-30220. Washington, DC: U.S. DHEW, National Center on Child Abuse and Neglect.

Richardson, V. (2003). A dual process model of grief counseling: Findings from the changing lives of older couples (CLOC) study. Paper presented at the First National Gerontological Social Work Conference: Atlanta, GA.

Ridley, C. R. (1984). Clinical treatment of the nondisclosing black client. *American Psychologist, 39*(11), 1234-1244.

Robinson, J. B. (1989). Clinical treatment of black families: Issues and strategies. *Social Work, 34,* 323-329.

Rogers, C. R. (1959). A theory of therapy, personality, and interpersonal relationships as developed in the client-centered framework. In S. Koch (Ed.), *Psychology: A study of science (Vol. 3)*. New York: McGraw-Hill.

Rogers, C. R. (1961). *On becoming a person.* Boston: Houghton Mifflin.

Rohrbaugh, J. B (2006). Domestic violence in same-gender relationships. *Family Court Review, 44*(2) 287–299.

Rolstad, K., Mahoney, K., & Glass, G. V. (2005). The big picture: A meta-analysis of program effectiveness research on English-language learners. *Educational Policy, 19*(4), 572-594.

Roopnarine, J. L., et al. (1994). *Children's play in diverse cultures.* Albany: State University of New York Press.

Rose, S., Bisson, J., & Wessely, S. (2001). Psychological debriefing for preventing post traumatic stress disorder (PTSD) (Cochrane Review). Retrieved from: http://www.mediscope.ch/cochrane-abstracts/ab000560.htm.

Rosenhan, D. L., & Seligman, M. E. (1984). *Abnormal psychology.* New York: W. W. Norton & Co.

Rosewater, L. B. (1988). Feminist therapy with women. In M. A. Dutton-Douglas & L. E. A. Walker (Eds.), *Feminist psychotherapies: Integration of therapeutic and feminist systems.* Norwood, NJ: Ablex Publishing Corp.

Ross, L., et al. (2003). Resiliency in family caregivers: Implications for social work practice. *Journal of Gerontological Social Work, 40*(3), 81-96.

Rothman, J. (1996). The interweaving of community intervention approaches. *Journal of Community Practice, 4,* 3/4, pp. 69-100.

Rotter, J. B. (1966). Generalized expectancies for internal vs. external control of reinforcement. *Psychological Monographs, 80,* 1-28.

Rubin, K. H., Bukowski, W., & Parker, J. G. (1998). Peer interactions, relationships, and groups. In N. Eisenberg (Ed.), *Handbook of child psychology, 5th Edition (Vol. 3)*. New York: Wiley.

Russell, S. (2006). Substance use and abuse and mental health among sexual minority youth. In A. Omoto & H. Kurtzman (Eds.), *Sexual orientation and mental health*. Washington, DC: American Psychological Association.

Rutter, M. (1985). Psychopathology and development: Links between childhood and adult life. In M. Rutter & L. Hersov (Eds.), *Child and adolescent psychiatry: Modern approaches*. Oxford: Oxford University Press.

Ryckman, R. M. (2008). *Theories of personality*. Belmont, CA: Cengage Learning/Wadsworth.

Sackett D. L., Rosenberg W. M., Muir-Gray J. A., Haynes R. B., Richardson W. S. (2000). Evidence-based medicine: How to practice and teach EBM (2nd ed.). Edinburgh, Scotland: Churchill Livingstone.

Saleeby, D. (1997). *The strengths perspective in social work practice, 2nd Edition*. New York: Longman.

Schaie, K. W., & Hertzog, C. (1986). Toward a comprehensive model of adult intellectual development: Contributions to the Seattle longitudinal study. In R. J. Sternberg (Ed.), *Advances in human intelligence (Vol. 3)*. Hillsdale, NJ: Erlbaum.

Schein, E. (1980). *Organizational psychology*. Englewood Cliffs, NJ: Prentice Hall.

Schein, E. (1990). Organizational culture. *American Psychologist, 45*(2), 109-119.

Schmidt, M. J., Riggar, T. F., Crimando, W., & Bordieri, J. E. (1992). *Staffing for success*. Newbury Park, CA: Sage.

Schneider, R. L., & Lester, L. (2001). *Social work advocacy*. Belmont, CA: Brooks/Cole.

School Social Work Association of America (SSWWA). (2001). *School social workers and confidentiality: Position statement*. Adopted March 15, 2001. Washington, DC: Author.

Schreiber, P., & Frank, F. (1983). The use of a peer supervision group by social work clinicians. *Clinical Supervisor, 1*(1), 29-36.

Schuckit, M. A. (1989). *Drug and alcohol abuse: A clinical guide to diagnosis and treatment, 3rd Edition*. New York: Plenum Press.

Schuckit, M. A. (1994). The goals of treatment. In M. Galanter & H. D. Kleber (Eds.), *Textbook of substance abuse*. Washington, DC: American Psychiatric Press.

Schuckit, M.A., & Rayses, V. (1979). Ethanol ingestion: Differences in blood acetaldehyde concentrations in relatives of alcoholics and controls. *Science, 203*, 54-55.

Schuster, C. S., & Ashburn, S. S. (1992). *The process of human development: A holistic lifespan approach, 3rd Edition*. Philadelphia: Lippincott.

Scott, W. R. (1981). *Organizations: Rational, natural, and open systems*. Englewood Cliffs, NJ: Prentice-Hill.

Sears, D. (1988). Biased indoctrination and selectivity of exposure to new information. *Sociometry, 28*, 363-76.

Sebald, H. (1986). Adolescents' shifting orientation toward parents and peers: A curvilinear trend in recent decades. *Journal of Marriage and the Family, 48*, 5-13.

Seeman, T. (1985). *Social support and angiography.* Unpublished doctoral thesis, University of California, Berkeley.

Segawa, M. (2003). Neurophysiology of Tourette syndrome: Pathophysiological considerations. *Brain Development, 25* (Supplement), 62-69.

Seidler, G. H., & Wagner, F. E. (2006). Comparing the efficacy of EMDR and trauma-focused cognitive-behavioral therapy in the treatment of PTSD: A meta-analytic study. *Psychological Medicine, 36*, 1515-1522.

Selye, H. (1956). *The stress of life.* New York: McGraw-Hill.

Selznick, P. (1949). *TVA and the grass roots.* Berkeley: University of California Press.

Shaffer, D. R. (2002). *Developmental psychology: Childhood and adolescence, 6th Edition.* Belmont, CA: Wadsworth.

Shapiro, A. K., & Shapiro, E. (1993). Neuroleptic drugs. In R. Kurlan (Ed.), *The handbook of Tourette's syndrome and related tic and behavioral disorders.* New York: Marcel Dekker.

Shapiro J. P. (2009). Integrating outcome research and clinical reasoning in psychotherapy planning. Professional Psychology: *Research and Practice*, 40, 46–53.

Shaughnessy, J. J., & Zechmeister, E. B. (1985). *Research methods in psychology.* New York: Alfred Knopf.

Shea, J. D. C. (1981). Changes in interpersonal distances and categories of play behavior in the early weeks of preschool. *Developmental Psychology, 17*, 417-25.

Sheafor, B. W., & Horejsi, C. R. (2003). *Techniques and guidelines for social work practice, 6th Edition.* Boston: Allyn & Bacon.

Shedler, J., & Block, J. (1990). Adolescent drug use and psychological health: A longitudinal inquiry. *American Psychologist, 45*, 612-630.

Sheline, Y. I., Gado, M. H., & Kraemer, H. C. (2003). Untreated depression and hippocampal volume loss. *American Journal of Psychiatry, 160*(8), 1515-1518.

Shulman, L. (1981). *Identifying, measuring, and teaching helping skills.* New York: CSWE.

Shulman, L. (1999). *The skills of helping, 4th Edition.* Itasca, IL: F. E. Peacock.

Silver, A. A., & Hagen, R. H. (1990). *Disorders of learning in childhood.* New York: John Wiley & Sons.

Sim, F., Li, D., & Chu, C. M. (2016). The moderating effect between strengths and placement on children's needs in out-of-home care: A follow-up study. *Children and Youth Services Review*, 60, 101-108.

Simkin, J. (1979). Gestalt therapy. In R. J. Corsini (Ed.), *Current psychotherapies.* Itasca, IL: F. E. Peacock.

Simon, H. A. (1957). *Administrative behavior, 2nd Edition.* New York: Macmillan.

Sit, D., Rothschild, A. J., & Wisner, K. L. (2006). A review of postpartum psychosis. *Journal of Women's Health, 15*(4), 352-368.

Skidmore, R. A. (1995). *Social work administration: Dynamic management and human relationships.* Boston: Allyn & Bacon.

Skinner, B. F. (1953). *Science and human behavior.* New York: MacMillan.

Slaikeu, K. A. (1984). *Crisis intervention: A handbook for practice and research.* Newton, MA: Allyn & Bacon, Inc.

Slavin, L. (1982). Communication of the cancer diagnosis to pediatric patients: Impact on long-term adjustment. *American Journal of Psychiatry, 139,* 179-183.

Smalley, R. (1970). The functional approach to casework practice. In R. Roberts & R. Nee (Eds.), *Theories of social casework.* Chicago: University of Chicago Press.

Smalley, R. (1971). Social casework: The functional approach. In *Encyclopedia of social work.* New York: NASW.

Smetana, J. G. (2000). Adolescents' and parents' conceptions of parental authority. *Child Development, 59,* 321-35.

Snyder, M. (1987). *Public and private realities: The psychology of self-monitoring.* New York: W. H. Freeman.

Social Work Policy Institute. (2010, June 16). Retrieved August 30, 2017, from http://www.socialworkpolicy.org/research/evidence-based-practice-2.html

Spitz, R. A. (1945). Hospitalism: An inquiry into the genesis of psychiatric conditions in early childhood. *Psychoanalytic Study of the Child, 1,* 53-74.

Spitze, G. (1988). Employment and family relations: A review. *Journal of Marriage and the Family, 50,* 595-618.

Spitze, G., & Gallant, M. (2004). "The bitter with the sweet": Older adults' strategies for handling ambivalence in the relations with their adult children. *Research on Aging, 26*(4), 387-412.

Spivack, G., Platt, J. J., & Shure, M. B. (1976). *The problem-solving approach to adjustment.* San Francisco: Jossey-Bass.

Stacey, N., et al. (1970). *Hospitals, children, and their families: The report of a pilot study.* London: Routledge & Kegan Paul.

Stampfl, T. G. (1966). Implosive therapy: The theory, the subhuman analogue, the strategy, and the technique. Part I: The theory. In S. G. Armitage (Ed.), *Behavior modification techniques in the treatment of emotional disorders.* Battle Creek, MI: Veterans Administration Hospital.

Stanovich, K. E. (1993). A model for studies of reading disability. *Developmental Review, 13*(3), 225-245.

Stein, N. (1995, June). New cognitive research making waves. *APA Monitor.*

Steinberg, L. (1995). *How your child's adolescence triggers your own crisis.* New York: Simon & Schuster.

Stevenson, M. R., & Black, K. N. (1995). *How divorce affects offspring: A research approach.* Dubuque, IA: Brown & Benchmark.

Stewart, W. (1985). *Counseling in rehabilitation.* London: Dover.

Stiegel, L., & Klem, E. (2005). Information about laws related to elder abuse. American Bar Association Commission on Law and Aging: retrieved from www.ncea.aoa.gov.

Stipek, D. J., Gralinski, J. H., & Kopp, C. B. (1990). Self-concept development in the toddler years. *Developmental Psychology, 26*(6), 972-977.

Stroebe, M., & Schut, H. (1999). The dual process model of coping with bereavement: Rationale and description. *Death Studies, 23*, 197-224.

Strube, M. J., & Barbour, L. S. (1983). The decision to leave an abusive relationship: Economic dependence and psychological commitment. *Journal of Marriage and the Family, 45*, 785-93.

Substance Abuse and Mental Health Services Administration. (2015, October 2). Risk and Protective Factors. Retrieved September 01, 2017, from https://www.samhsa.gov/capt/practicing-effective-prevention/prevention-behavioral-health/risk-protective-factors

Substance Abuse and Mental Health Services Administration. (2017, May 1). Adverse Childhood Experiences. Retrieved August 31, 2017, from https://www.samhsa.gov/capt/practicing-effective-prevention/prevention-behavioral-health/adverse-childhood-experiences

Sue, D. W. (1981). Evaluating process variables in cross-cultural counseling and psychotherapy. In A. J. Marsell & P. B. Pederson (Eds.), *Cross-cultural counseling and psychotherapy.* New York: Pergamon.

Sue, D. W., & Sue, D. (1999). *Counseling the culturally different.* New York: Wiley & Sons.

Sue, D. W., & Sue, D. (2003). *Counseling the culturally diverse: Theory and practice.* New York: Wiley & Sons.

Sue, S., & Zane, N. (1987). The role of culture and cultural techniques in psychotherapy. *American Psychologist, 42*(1), 37-43.

Sue, S., Zane, N., & Young, K. (1994). Research on psychotherapy with culturally diverse groups. In A. E. Bergin & S. L. Garfield (Eds.), *Handbook of psychotherapy and behavior change.* New York: John Wiley & Sons.

Sugar, J. A. (1989, Nov.). *Everyday experiences of forgetting in younger and older adults.* Paper presented at the meeting of the Psychonomic Society, Atlanta, GA.

Swanson, J. M., et al. (1993). Effect of stimulant medication on children with attention-deficit disorder: A "review of reviews." *Exceptional Children, 60*, 154-162.

Swim, J. K. et al. (1995). Sexism and racism: Old-fashioned and modern approaches. *Journal of Personality and Social Psychology, 68*, 199-214.

Tarasoff v. the Regents of the University of California, 551 P. 2d 345 (1976).

Tasker, F. (2005). Lesbian mothers, gay fathers, and their children: A review. *Journal of Developmental and Behavioral Pediatrics, 26*, 224-240.

Taylor, E. (1994). Syndromes of attention-deficit and overactivity. In M. Rutter, et al. (Eds.), *Child and Adolescent Psychiatry.* London: Blackwell Scientific Publ.

Taylor, F. W. (1911). *The principles of scientific management.* New York: Harper & Bros.

Taylor, M. C., & Hale, J. A. (1982). Psychological androgyny: Theories, methods, and conclusions. *Psychological Bulletin, 92*, 347-66.

Termine, N. (1988). Infants' responses to their mothers' expressions of joy and sadness. *Developmental Psychology, 24*, 223-29.

Thomas, A., & Chess, S. (1977). *Temperament and development.* New York: Bruner-Mazel.

Thomas, R. R., Jr. (1991). *Beyond race and gender: Unleashing the power of your total work force by managing diversity.* New York: AMACON.

Tönnies, F. (1887/1957). *Community and society (gemeinschaft und gesellschaft).* (C. P. Loomis, Trans., Ed.). East Lansing, MI: Michigan State University Press.

Toseland, R. W., & Rossiter, C. (1989). Group interventions to support caregivers: A review and analysis. *The Gerontologist, 29*, 438-448.

Toth, K., & King, B. H. (2010). Intellectual disability (mental retardation). In M. K. Dulcan (Ed.), *Dulcan's handbook of child and adolescent psychiatry* (pp. 151-171). Arlington, VA: American Psychiatric Publishing, Inc.

Travis, C. B. (1988). *Women and health psychology: Mental health issues.* Hillsdale, NJ: L. Erlbaum.

Trepper, T. S., & Barrett, M. J. (1986). Vulnerability to incest: A framework for assessment. In T. S. Barrett & M. J. Barrett (Eds.), *Treating incest: A multiple systems perspective.* New York: Haworth Press.

Trickett, P. K., & Susman, E. J. (1988). Parental perceptions of child-rearing practices in physically abusive and nonabusive families. *Developmental Psychology, 24*, 270-76.

Troiden, R. R. (1988). *Gay and lesbian identity: A sociological analysis.* Dix Hills, NY: General Hall, Inc.

Tuckman, B. W., & Jensen, M. A. C. (1977). Stages of small group development revisited. *Groups and Organizations Studies, 2*, 419-27.

Turiel, E. (2000). The development of morality. In W. Damon & N. Eisenberg (Eds.). *Social, emotional, and personality development, 5th Edition.* New York: Wiley & Sons.

Turner, F. (1978). *Psychosocial therapy.* New York: Free Press.

VanLaningham, J., Johnson, D. R., & Amato, P. (2001). Marital happiness, marital duration, and the U-shaped curve: Evidence from a five-wave panel study. *Social Forces, 78*(4), 1313-1341.

Vizard, E. (1991). Interviewing children suspected of being sexually-abused: A review of theory and practice. In C. R. Holin & K. Howells (Eds.), *Clinical approaches to sex offenders and their victims.* Chichester: John Wiley & Sons.

Vygotsky, L. S. (1978). *Mind in society: The development of higher psychological processes.* Cambridge: Harvard University Press.

Wagner, M. E., et al. (1985). Effects of sibling spacing on intelligence, intrafamilial relations, psychosocial characteristics, and mental and physical health. *Advances in Child Development and Behavior, 19*, 149-206.

Wald, E. (1989). Family: Stepfamilies. In *Encyclopedia of social work*. Silver Spring, MD: NASW.

Walker, L. (1981). *The battered woman syndrome study. Report to NIMH*. Washington, DC: NIMH.

Walker, L. (1984). *The battered woman syndrome*. New York: Springer.

Walker, L. (1994). *Abused women and survivor therapy: A practical guide for the psychotherapist*. Washington, DC: American Psychological Association.

Walker, R. D., & LaDue, R. (1986) An integrative approach to American Indian mental health. In C. B. Wilkinson (Ed.), *Ethnic psychiatry*. New York: Plenum.

Wallerstein, J. S. (1987). Children of divorce: Report of a ten-year follow-up of early latency children. *American Journal of Orthopsychiatry, 57*, 199-211.

Wallerstein, J. S., & Blakeslee, S. (1990). *Second chances: Men, women, and children a decade after divorce*. New York: Ticknor & Fields.

Wallerstein, J. S. (1995). *The good marriage: How and why love lasts*. Boston: Houghton Mifflin.

Wallerstein, J. S., & Kelly, J.B. (1980). *Surviving the breakup*. New York: Basic Books.

Wamsley, G. L., & Zald, M. N. (1976). *The political economy of public organizations*. Bloomington: Indiana University Press.

Ward, R. A., Sherman, S. R., & LaGory, M. (1984). Subjective network assessments and subjective well-being. *Journal of Gerontology, 59*, 93-101.

Warr, P., & Perry, G. (1982). Paid employment and women's psychological well-being. *Psychological Bulletin, 91*, 498-516.

Warren, K., Franklin, C., & Streeter, C. (1997). Chaos theory and complexity theory. In *Encyclopedia of social work, 19th Edition, Supplement 1997* (pp. 59-68). Washington, DC: NASW.

Warren, R. L. (1978). *The community in America, 3rd Edition*. Chicago: Rand McNally.

Watkins, C. C., et al. (2011). HIV/AIDS. In J. L. Levenson (Ed.), *The American Psychiatric Publishing textbook of psychosomatic medicine: Psychiatric care of the medically ill* (pp. 637-666). Arlington, VA: American Psychiatric Publishing, Inc.

Wegscheider, S. (1981). *Another chance: Hope and health for the alcoholic family*. Palo Alto: Science & Behavior Books.

Weider, H., & Kaplan, E. H. (1969). Drug use in adolescence. *Psychoanalytic Child Study, 24*, 399-431.

Weiner, I. B. (2003). The assessment process. In I. B. Weiner, J. R. Graham, & J. A. Naglieri (Eds.), *Handbook of psychology (Vol. 10), Assessment psychology*. Hoboken, NJ: John Wiley & Sons, Inc.

Weissberg, M. P. (1981). Spouse abuse. In B. S. Fauman & M. A. Fauman (Eds.), *Emergency psychiatry for the house officer*. Baltimore: Williams & Williams.

Weissman, A. (1976). Industrial social services: Linkage technology. *Social Casework, 57*, 50-54.

Werner, E. E. (1993). Children of the garden island. In M. Gauvin & M. Cole (Eds.), *Readings on the development of children.* New York: W. H. Freeman.

Werner, E. E., & Smith, R. S. (1982). *Vulnerable but invincible: A longitudinal study of resilient children.* New York: McGraw-Hill.

Wetherell, J. L., Le Roux, H., & Gatz, M. (2003). DSM-IV criteria for generalized anxiety disorder in older adults: Distinguishing the worried from the well. *Psychology and Aging, 18*(3), 622-627.

Wilhelm, S., et al. (2012). Randomized trial of behavior therapy for adults with Tourette's disorder. *Archives of General Psychiatry, 69,* 795-803.

Williamson, C. (2001). Social work practice with people with disabilities. In A. T. Morales & B. W. Sheafor (Eds.), *Social work: A profession of many faces, 9th Edition.* Boston: Allyn & Bacon.

Willis, D. J., et al. (1992). *Prevention of child maltreatment: Developmental and ecological perspectives.* New York: Wiley & Sons.

Wilson, B., & Nochajski, T. H. (2016). Evaluating the impact of trauma-informed care (TIC) perspective in social work curriculum. *Social Work Education, 35*(5), 589-602.

Winchel, R. M., Stanley, B., & Stanley, M. (1990). Biochemical aspects of suicide. In S. J. Blumenthal & D. J. Kupfer (Eds.), *Suicide over the life cycle: Risk factors, assessment, and treatment.* Washington, DC: American Psychiatric Press.

Wintgens, A., et al. (1998). Attachment, self-esteem, and psychomotor development in extremely premature children at preschool age. *Infant Mental Health Journal, 19,* 394-408.

Wolberg, L. R. (1988). *The techniques of psychotherapy.* Orlando, FL: Grune & Stratton.

Wolf, R. S. (2000). The nature and scope of elder abuse. *Generations, 24*(11) 6-12.

Wolf, S. S., Jones, D. W., Knable, M. R., Gorey, J. G., Lee, K. S., Hyde, T. M., et al. (1996). Tourette syndrome: Prediction of phenotypic variations in monozygotic twins by caudate nucleus D2 receptor. *Science, 273,* 1225-1227.

Wolitzky-Taylor, K. B., Horowitz, J. D., Powers, M. B., & Telch, M. J. (2008). Psychological approaches in the treatment of specific phobia: A meta-analysis. *Clinical Psychology Review, 28,* 1021-1037.

Wolpe, J. (1958). *Psychotherapy and reciprocal inhibition.* Stanford, CA: Stanford University Press.

Woo, S. M., & Keatinge, C. (2008). *Mental disorders across the lifespan.* Hoboken, NJ: John Wiley & Sons.

Woods, M. E., & Hollis, F. (1990). *Casework: A psychosocial therapy, 4th Edition.* New York: McGraw Hill.

Worden, J. (2002). *Grief counseling and grief therapy: A handbook for the mental health practitioner, 3rd Edition.* New York: Springer.

Worrell, J., & Remer, P. (1992). *Feminist therapies in perspective: An empowerment model for women.* Chichester: John Wiley & Sons.

Wrenn, C. G. (1985). Afterward: The culturally encapsulated counselor revisited. In. P. Pedersen (Ed.), *Handbook of cross-cultural counseling and therapy*. Westport, CT: Greenwood Press.

Yalom, I. D. (1985). *The theory and practice of group psychotherapy*. New York: Basic Books.

Yankey, J. A. (1995). Strategic planning. In *Encyclopedia of social work (Vol. 3), 19th Edition*. Washington, DC: NASW.

Yarrow, L. J., & Goodwin, M. S. (1973). The immediate impact of separation: Reactions of infants to a change in mother figures. In L. J. Stone, et al. (Eds.), *The competent infant: Research and commentary*. New York: Basic Books.

Yates, C. (2013). Evidence-based practice: The components, history, and process. *Counseling Outcome Research and Evaluation*, 4(1), 41-54.

Yeager, K. A., & Bauer-Wu, S. (2013). Cultural humility: Essential foundation for clinical researchers. *Applied Nursing Research*, 26(4), 251-256.

Young, J. E. (1982). Loneliness, depression, and cognitive therapy: Theory and application. In L. A. Peplau & D. Perlman (Eds.), *Loneliness: A sourcebook of current theory, research, and therapy*. New York: Wiley.

Zahavi, S., & Asher, S. R. (1978). The effects of verbal instruction on preschool children's aggressive behavior. *Journal of School Psychology, 16*, 146-153.

Zajonc, R. B. (1976). Family configuration and intelligence. *Science, 192*, 227-36.

Zastrow, C. H. (2003). *The practice of social work: Applications of generalist and advanced content, 7th Edition*. Pacific Grove, CA: Thomson-Brooks/Cole.

Zuckerman, E. L. (1995). *Clinician's thesaurus: The guidebook for writing psychological reports, 4th Edition*. New York: The Guilford Press.